GLOBALIZATION AND
THE ENVIRONMENT

GLOBALIZATION

Series Editors

Manfred B. Steger

*Royal Melbourne Institute of Technology
and University of Hawai'i–Mānoa*

and

Terrell Carver

University of Bristol

"Globalization" has become *the* buzzword of our time. But what does it mean? Rather than forcing a complicated social phenomenon into a single analytical framework, this series seeks to present globalization as a multidimensional process constituted by complex, often contradictory interactions of global, regional, and local aspects of social life. Since conventional disciplinary borders and lines of demarcation are losing their old rationales in a globalizing world, authors in this series apply an interdisciplinary framework to the study of globalization. In short, the main purpose and objective of this series is to support subject-specific inquiries into the dynamics and effects of contemporary globalization and its varying impacts across, between, and within societies.

Globalization and Sovereignty
John Agnew

Globalization and War
Tarak Barkawi

Globalization and Human Security
Paul Battersby and Joseph M. Siracusa

Globalization and the Environment
Peter Christoff and Robyn Eckersley

*Globalization and American
   Popular Culture, 3rd ed.*
Lane Crothers

Globalization and Militarism
Cynthia Enloe

Globalization and Law
Adam Gearey

Globalization and Feminist Activism
Mary E. Hawkesworth

Globalization and Postcolonialism
Sankaran Krishna

Globalization and Media
Jack Lule

*Globalization and Social Movements,
   2nd ed.*
Valentine Moghadam

Globalization and Terrorism, 2nd ed.
Jamal R. Nassar

Globalization and Culture, 2nd ed.
Jan Nederveen Pieterse

*Globalization and International
   Political Economy*
Mark Rupert and M. Scott Solomon

Globalization and Citizenship
Hans Schattle

Globalization and Islamism
Nevzat Soguk

Globalisms, 3rd ed.
Manfred B. Steger

Rethinking Globalism
Edited by Manfred B. Steger

Globalization and Labor
Dimitris Stevis and Terry Boswell

Globaloney 2.0
Michael Veseth

Supported by the Globalization Research Center at the University of Hawai'i, Mānoa

GLOBALIZATION AND THE ENVIRONMENT

PETER CHRISTOFF AND ROBYN ECKERSLEY

ROWMAN & LITTLEFIELD PUBLISHERS, INC.
Lanham • Boulder • New York • Toronto • Plymouth, UK

Published by Rowman & Littlefield Publishers, Inc.
A wholly owned subsidiary of The Rowman & Littlefield Publishing Group, Inc.
4501 Forbes Boulevard, Suite 200, Lanham, Maryland 20706
www.rowman.com

10 Thornbury Road, Plymouth PL6 7PP, United Kingdom

British Library Cataloguing in Publication Information Available

Library of Congress Cataloging-in-Publication Data

Library of Congress Cataloging-in-Publication Data
Christoff, Peter.
  Globalization and the environment / Peter Christoff and Robyn Eckersley.
    pages cm
  Includes bibliographical references and index.
  ISBN 978-0-7425-5658-4 (cloth : alk. paper) — ISBN 978-0-7425-5659-1 (pbk. : alk. paper) — ISBN 978-1-4422-2149-9 (electronic) 1. Global environmental change. 2. Climatic changes. 3. Environmental protection. I. Title.
  GE149.C548 2013
  363.7—dc23
                                                                    2013012112

♾™ The paper used in this publication meets the minimum requirements of American National Standard for Information Sciences—Permanence of Paper for Printed Library Materials, ANSI/NISO Z39.48-1992.

Printed in the United States of America

I dedicate this book to my co-author,
who wrote the best bits.

CONTENTS

PREFACE

We finished writing this book in the immediate aftermath of Rio+20, the much anticipated United Nations Conference on Sustainable Development held in Rio de Janeiro during June 2012. Rio+20 was supposed to put the world back on a sustainable track yet, despite the creative outpouring of ideas generated by the occasion, it will probably be remembered as Rio *minus* 20. World leaders and ministers struggled even to reaffirm global goals, principles, and strategies that had been forged twenty years earlier at the 1992 Earth Summit, held in the same city. In light of this spectacular failure of environmental multilateralism by states, perhaps it is no surprise that the People's Sustainability Manifesto, launched at Rio+20 by hundreds of civil society organizations, sought to build a global movement for localization.

While we welcome this development, and enjoy the irony of a global movement fostering localization, this book is not an anti-globalization treatise. Our primary aim is to understand the extent and manner to which globalization is implicated in both global environmental destruction *and* global environmental protection. We conclude that the contemporary form of globalization represents a further extension and intensification of a much longer process of modernization that we identify as the primary culprit of environmental destruction. This contemporary form of globalization is more environmentally destructive than any previous phase of globalization and, like a snake swallowing its own tail, is ultimately self-destructive.

In response, we suggest that a different, more reflexive form of globalization may provide a way forward, and that it is possible to redirect some of the processes of globalization and modernization along a more sustainable path. This requires, among other things, addressing the crisis of accountability between those who presently benefit from the production of ecological risks and harms, and those who suffer their consequences now and in the future. The modes of reflexive ecological modernization and globalization that we defend are grounded in a post-liberal, cosmopolitan understanding of "extended responsibility" that is more appropriate to a complex, interdependent, and globalizing world.

Many environmental problems take a long time to materialize, and so has this book. All those who know us well have smiled knowingly at the painful prospect of us writing a jointly authored book and found our reportage of the process to be entertaining, although those who live in very close proximity—particularly our daughter, Eva—would probably not describe it thus. We were supported by her tolerance and love, and we take comfort in the fact that she shares the concerns that have animated this book.

We are particularly indebted to Paul James and Boris Frankel for giving up precious time to read the manuscript and for their incisive feedback, and we are grateful to Paul James, Stephanie Trigg, and Joel Trigg for enduring many hours of discussion of this book. They fed us and were not fed up with us.

Part of the research for this book was supported by the Australian Research Council (ARC) Discovery Project funding scheme (DP0771697) awarded to Robyn Eckersley. The views expressed herein are those of the authors and not necessarily those of the ARC.

It has been a delight to work with Susan McEachern at Rowman & Littlefield and we are also grateful for her forbearance and assistance. We also extend our appreciation to the series editors, Manfred Steger and Terrell Carver, for their strong encouragement, extreme patience, and constructive feedback on the manuscript.

Melbourne, July 2012

CHAPTER 1

A WORLD FIT FOR US ALL

CRISIS? WHAT CRISIS?

We humans have long been drivers of environmental change, but for most of our evolutionary history our influence has been patchy and localized. By contrast, the 20th century stands out as the prodigal century "because of the screeching acceleration of so many processes that bring ecological change."[1] Indeed, the post–World War II period may well be remembered not for the Cold War, the moon landing, or the fall of communism but rather as the period of slow awakening to an emerging ecological crisis of planetary proportions. The world's human population took until the early 1800s to reach the one billion mark, but had climbed to three billion by 1960, doubled to six billion by the turn of the 21st century, and reached seven billion by the end of 2011. Between 1960 and 2000, world economic activity (measured as

Gross Domestic Product) rose from 1.3 to 32.2 trillion USD, reaching a peak of 61.3 trillion in 2007 just before the global financial crash.[2] It is no accident that the first "limits-to-growth" arguments emerged in the early 1970s on the back of the long post-war boom, and in the wake of accumulating evidence of resource scarcity, new sources (and rising levels) of pollution and land degradation, and the accelerated erosion of the Earth's biodiversity. It is now commonly observed that many ecological problems do not respect borders, that they represent a classic collective action problem, and that they can only be addressed by concerted international cooperation and domestic environmental regulation. Yet despite four global environmental summits (in 1972, 1992, 2002, and 2012) and a proliferation of multilateral environmental treaties and domestic environmental laws over the past forty years, the global environment has continued to deteriorate.

According to the 2005 Environmental Sustainability Index, no state in the world is on a sustainable trajectory.[3] Increasingly, we confront a narrative of planetary environmental transformation and crisis that challenges the modern vision of prosperity and human progress linked to continuous economic growth. For example, the *Millennium Ecosystem Assessment* report, commissioned by the United Nations Secretary-General and released in 2005, found that human activity has changed the Earth's ecosystems more rapidly and extensively over the past fifty years than in any previous time in human history. The report found that 60 percent of the twenty-four ecosystem services that were identified and evaluated are being degraded or used unsustainably, mostly as a result of a dramatic increase in human demand for food, timber, water, fuel, and fiber. Rates of species extinction were found to have increased by up to one thousand times the background rate of extinction. The world's poorest peoples were found to suffer the most from the degradation of ecosystem services, which has become a major cause of poverty.

The Millennium Ecosystem Assessment represents just one of a succession of major global environmental assessments that have warned that human development patterns have become unsustainable, and will increasingly undermine rather than enhance human well-being. The fifth edition of the United Nations Environment Program's *Global Environmental Outlook* (GEO-5), launched on the eve of the United Nations Conference on Sustainable Development in June 2012 ("Rio+20"), painted a grim picture of the Earth pushed to its biophysical limits.

The report assessed ninety of the most-important international environmental goals and objectives and found that significant progress had only been made in four, which are protecting the ozone layer, removing lead from fuel, increased access to improved water supplies, and boosting research to reduce pollution of the marine environment.[4] The Worldwatch Institute's regular *State of the World* reports and its analysis of environmental trends in *Vital Signs*, the successive reports of the Intergovernmental Panel on Climate Change (IPCC), the United Nations' *Human Development Reports*, and the World Wide Fund for Nature's series of *Living Planet Reports* have all made it clear that ecologically sustainable development is not a luxury but rather a fundamental necessity that we postpone at our collective peril.[5]

The looming crisis of climate change now serves as the most widely recognized character in this tragic narrative, and it has been the focus of increasing political attention since the mid-2000s. Climate scientists warn our collective political response to climate change over the next decade is critical and will largely determine the fate of the world's climate for the rest of this century and beyond. Yet even if we were to miraculously arrest and reverse global greenhouse gas emissions in the next decade, we would still be left with the "other" environmental crises—of accelerating rates of species extinction, loss of forest cover, land degradation, desertification, the accumulation of toxic chemical and nuclear waste, loss of arable land and potable water, and pollution of the terrestrial, atmospheric, and marine environment. The world's oceans are attracting increasing concern as a result of not only overfishing and coastal pollution but also rising temperatures, acidification, the bleaching and loss of coral reefs (which provide spawning grounds and nurseries for many commercial fisheries), and the expansion of ocean gyres of debris. The largest such gyre is the Great Pacific Garbage Patch—a vast floating mass of mostly toxic, non-biodegradable plastics and suspended particles of chemical sludge, around twice the size of Texas, circulating in the currents of the North Pacific Ocean. It was the buildup of toxic waste that served to catalyze the modern environment movement in the 1960s in the wake of the publication of Rachel Carson's *Silent Spring*.[6] This is a dismal testimony to more than fifty years of environmental concern and action that have been both increasingly global in their orientation and increasingly global in their organizational form.

Of course, not everyone accepts that we face a planetary ecological crisis, as distinct from merely a set of discrete ecological problems that can be managed by local, national, or international environmental regulation. A crisis suggests a critical turning point whereby action is required to prevent some kind of serious, irreversible decline or collapse. This can occur at many different levels, such as the level of the individual organism or population (arising, for example, from exposure to dangerous chemicals or radiation), the species (when, for example, a particular species becomes endangered), or larger ecological system (such as serious impairment or collapse of ecological life-support systems). Crises at any of these levels do not necessarily translate into a full-blown global ecological crisis. One example is the extreme deforestation of Easter Island by the Rapa Nui people that led to a precipitous drop in their population and the decimation of their culture. This was an entirely local ecological crisis, confined to an island community.

Similarly, acid rain, caused by sulfur-dioxide emissions from factories and coal-fired power plants, has been widely regarded as a discrete regional problem that has been successfully addressed in many parts of the world through national and regional regulation and the installation of new technologies such as sulfur dioxide scrubbers in coal-fired plants.

Even some global ecological problems that take a long time to develop, and are not quickly or easily recognized until they become serious, have been regarded as discrete and manageable. The classic case is the thinning of the stratospheric ozone layer, which has produced the so-called hole in the ozone layer over the Antarctic. The chlorofluorocarbons (CFC) that were found to be responsible for this problem were invented in the late 1920s by chemists working at General Motors. They were thought to be inert and safe and were found to have many uses—as propellant gases in spray cans, as coolants in refrigerators, as a foaming agent in plastics, and as a solvent in cleaning agents. It was not until the mid-1980s that scientists discovered that CFC gases lingered in the upper atmosphere and released chlorine, reduced the concentration of ozone, and allowed increasing amounts of ultra-violet rays from the sun to reach the Earth, causing a range of serious problems such as an increased incidence of skin cancer, cataracts, and blindness; damage to the human immune system; and reduced crop yields. The ozone problem has been addressed by the *Montreal Protocol on Substances that Deplete the Ozone Layer 1987*, and subsequent amendments, which has been widely hailed as one of the most successful multilateral environmental agreements in recent times. While halon production has increased and an illegal trade in CFCs persists, stratospheric concentrations of some of the important CFCs have leveled off or declined.

However, on closer inspection, some of these problems are not as discrete, or as manageable, as they seem. For example, it has since been discovered that the recovery of the ozone layer is being delayed by increasing greenhouse gases such as carbon dioxide and methane. Moreover, scientists observed an unexpected and unprecedented hole over the Arctic in 2011.[7] Moreover, it now appears that there are important connections—both positive and negative—between sulfur-dioxide emissions, ozone depletion, and climate change. Not only have some greenhouse gases delayed the recovery of the ozone layer, some CFCs are themselves potent greenhouse gases. It has also been found that sulfur-dioxide pollution has contributed to "global dimming" which has a cooling effect on the Earth and is partially masking the extent of global warming. Regulatory efforts to reduce acid rain and the atmospheric release of local pollutant particulates have unwittingly exacerbated global warming. Among the controversial new solar radiation management techniques that are currently mooted by those scientists and policy makers contemplating a geo-engineering response to global warming is the deliberate injection of sulfur particles into the stratosphere to reflect sunlight and slow global warming. Yet scientists have also warned that stratospheric sulfur injection may reduce the strength of the monsoonal rains in Asia and Africa, with serious consequences for water availability and agricultural production.[8]

The above examples challenge the sanguine view that local, regional, and global ecological problems should be approached as discrete concerns and managed through issue-specific environmental regulation or regimes or quick technological fixes. They also highlight the complexity, uncertainty, variability, and unpredictability of ecological problems and the limits of human understanding. While it is possible to identify some ecological problems—such as localized water pollution—that have been more or less successfully curtailed, these efforts must be set in the context of larger processes of environmental change. Indeed, it is precisely the "screeching acceleration" in the scale, rate, and severity of ecological problems around the world that suggests to us that we have moved well beyond the point of framing and managing ecological problems as isolated phenomena: these problems provide evidence of an emerging, if not yet full blown, crisis of global proportions. A major report produced for the Stockholm Resilience Centre by a group of twenty-eight internationally renowned scientists has argued that humanity must learn to understand and respect the critical "hard-wired" thresholds in the Earth's environment if it is to avoid abrupt, nonlinear, and irreversible changes that could be devastating for human civilization.[9] The report identified nine planetary boundaries—climate change, stratospheric ozone depletion, land-use change, freshwater use, biological diversity, ocean acidification, nitrogen and phosphorus inputs to the biosphere and oceans, aerosol loading, and chemical pollution—and argued that the ecological boundaries for climate change, biological diversity loss, and nitrogen input may already have been transgressed. The report also highlighted the different ways in which these planetary boundaries are strongly interconnected, such that the transgression of one or more boundaries may, through a range of different feedback mechanisms, trigger unpredictable and abrupt change.

Many Earth-systems scientists argue that our planet has drifted out of the relatively stable geological era of the Holocene into the Anthropocene, a new geological era characterized by wide-scale and accelerated human influence on the planet. Some of the more pessimistic scientists suggest that this may be the shortest geological era of all, given the increasing risk of abrupt, non-linear change that may undermine the conditions for human flourishing. Possible scenarios for such abrupt change might take the form of "an expanding cascade" (where local shocks cascade into a global crisis), "a double or triple whammy" (where two or more shocks expand into a compounding global crisis), or a "long fuse and big bang" (where there is a long and slow development of a problem that suddenly reaches a tipping point and erupts into a major crisis).[10] Although no one can predict if, when, and how different local, regional, or global ecological problems might interact to produce a series of compounding crises, the risks are real and appear to be mounting. In any event, it would be foolish to wait for more evidence of an emerging crisis before taking action. There are enough dire and irreversible ecological problems in the world today to warrant a critical inquiry into the causes, consequences, and possible solutions to global ecological change.

Is It Globalization?

Although natural scientists serve as the leading informants of ecological problems, they are not well equipped to explain a very basic puzzle. How could such a widespread set of dire ecological problems—which nobody intended and nobody wants—emerge and persist, despite a massive increase in international environmental awareness and regulation over the past forty years?

Some environmentalists have a simple answer to this puzzle: "It's globalization, stupid!" They point to the uncanny correlation between the globalization of trade, investment, production, and consumption, on the one hand, and the globalization of environmental problems, on the other. When economic globalization accelerates, they point out, so do resource depletion, deforestation, species extinction, pollution, and greenhouse gas emissions. When globalization slows as a result of a global recession, so do these rates of ecological degradation. While these critics recognize that increasing international specialization and exchange, more intense economic competition, and improvements in transportation and communication have brought many benefits, including a wider variety of cheaper goods to those in the affluent consuming centers of the world, they argue that these developments have clearly come at a considerable ecological price, particularly for those living outside the consuming centers. Globalization has enabled environmental impacts to become increasingly extended, or "stretched," over space and time. The consequences of our actions as producers and consumers can often manifest thousands of kilometers away from their source, and these impacts can occur many years after their initiating events and then linger for decades, centuries, or even millennia (in the case of the accumulation of radioactive waste or atmospheric concentrations of greenhouse gases) and sometimes last forever (in the case of species extinction). According to the environmental critics, it is globalization that has compressed the cumulative ecological impacts of human actions into an emerging global environmental crisis.

However, enthusiasts of globalization consider this response simplistic. How, they ask, can we build the technological and institutional capacity that is necessary to overcome the miseries of uneven development, or confront and overwhelm ecological problems (especially in the rapidly growing economies of the developing world) without globalization? How else can we ensure the global diffusion of the environmentally friendly technologies and environmental management skills necessary to reduce our consumption of energy and resources and to move us toward a low-carbon, sustainable future?

The aim of this book is to untangle and clarify the connections between globalization and environmental change in order to evaluate these claims and counter-claims, as well as those that fall "in-between."[11] Our task is sociological, critical, and normative. Drawing on the broad tradition of critical social theory, we seek to identify and understand to what extent, and how, the processes of globalization are implicated in ecological destruction *and* protection. We also explore to what extent, and how, these processes ought to be transformed in ways that not only avoid a looming ecological crisis but also promote environment justice.

All critical theories of economy and society recognize the important links between historical description, sociological explanation, and political prescription. All social inquiry has a purpose, whether explicit or implicit, and the purpose of critical theories is to expose social domination and promote human autonomy. Because they recognize that existing social structures—such as markets and states—are often deeply implicated in social domination, critical theories typically reject piecemeal and narrow "problem-solving" analyses and reforms that take these structures for granted.

We build upon this critical tradition—particularly neo-Gramscian political economy, the critical theory of communicative action, and sociological theories of the risk society—but bring a much more explicit ecological dimension to our inquiry by exploring the relationship between social domination and environmental degradation. It is widely accepted that globalization is an uneven process that has produced both winners and losers. It is also increasingly recognized that the global distribution of ecological risks is deeply skewed, especially in the case of climate change, where those least responsible for generating emissions are expected to suffer the harshest impacts. So while many communities, social classes, and regions have gained from globalization, many others will face a "double exposure" from the negative impacts of globalization *and* global environmental change.[12] Our concern is to understand how globalization is implicated in both the social production of ecological risks, as well as the skewed distribution of such risks through space and time. We show that the degradation of the global environment is a complex phenomenon that has been managed and mediated by impersonal social and economic structures and certain privileged social classes, professions, and forms of knowledge that have systematically brought benefits to some at the expense of others. These impersonal social and economic structures have a habit of maintaining themselves, sometimes by explicit and/or implicit coercion but mostly by perpetuating conditions of disempowerment and/or material dependency.

An analysis of power, in all its dimensions, is therefore essential if we are to fathom the puzzle that we pose. This includes material power (the power to compel, coerce, or induce via the payment of money or resource provision), rule-based power (the power of rules, which encompass both regulatory and constitutive rules), structural power (the power of social structures in constituting social roles, relationships, and capacities), and the discursive power to define what is normal and acceptable and what is unthinkable.[13] While there are plenty of examples of organized business resisting or undermining environmental regulation, a simple actor-oriented approach to power cannot recognize the way in which power also operates through social structures or discourses. Here we follow Michael Barnett and Raymond Duvall in understanding power as "the production, in and through social relations, of effects that shape the capacities of actors to determine their circumstances and fate."[14] As we shall see, it is much easier to attribute responsibility for the effects of power when it is exercised by particular agents than when it inheres in social structures, especially when those social structures have evolved over a long period, are deeply entrenched and taken for granted, and provide benefits to many, though not all.

Our central sociological argument is that intensifying contemporary globalization represents a recent phase—and needs to be understood in the context—of much longer processes of globalization and modernization. Modernization is a process that encompasses the rise of instrumental rationality, new scientific inquiry, technological development, the rise of the modern state, industrialization (in both its capitalist and communist forms), and significant changes in culture, identity, and the human relationship to the larger nonhuman world. This process had produced considerable environmental degradation well before contemporary economic globalization in its neoliberal form.

Globalization, therefore, cannot be singled out as the new or only "cause" of environmental degradation. It has many faces, but it is in summary no more than the extension of relations across world space, an extension that pre-dates the modern period, escalated during the Age of Exploration, and has since grown apace. Many of the activities that have given rise to "the most global" of ecological problems, namely climate change, were under way at the time of the Industrial Revolution, when processes of globalization tended to manifest unevenly as multiple lines of global interconnection rather than as a blanketing network of relations.

Nonetheless, we argue that many of the contemporary processes of globalization have served as very significant *intensifiers* and *accelerants* of the burning fuse of ecological degradation. These need to be linked to the way in which we produce, exchange, and manage social life rather than just to its extension across world space. Modernization, and in particular capitalist modernization with its emphasis on economic growth, is important in this respect. Indeed, what marks out the post–World War II period from earlier phases of modernization is that the environmental *effects* of the processes of modernization have accumulated to a point where they now increasingly threaten to undermine those same processes—unless they can become more reflexive in the sense of reflective or "self-critical."

Fredric Jameson once quipped that it is easier to imagine the end of the world than the end of capitalism.[15] Others may find it even harder to imagine an end to the processes of modernization. However, we are not suggesting that the unfolding of a global ecological crisis will terminate the processes of modernization, since these processes can take many different forms. Rather, we argue that the intensely globalizing phase of modernization, particularly in its neoliberal capitalist form, is producing effects that will increasingly undermine many of the social and biophysical preconditions that enabled its creation and are essential for its reproduction, along with its legitimating meta-narrative of prosperity and progress. If globalization is to produce a world that is fit for us all, then it is necessary to challenge and transform not only what Karl Marx called "the forces of production" (the technologies of production) but also what Ulrich Beck has called "the relations of definition" that shape, determine, define, assess, distribute, and manage the meaning, benefits, and risks of modernization.[16]

The tragedy, however, is that many (though not all) of the processes of globalization—in the context of the current intensely globalizing phase of modernization—are making it more difficult for human societies to critically reflect upon, and take control of, their social and environmental destinies. This arises not only because the processes of modernization are so deeply entrenched across so many domains but also because of the growing problems of displacement, distancing, and disconnection between decision makers and "environments," between producers and consumers, between perpetrators and victims, between cause and effect, and between space and place. This problem works at multiple levels and has been recognized and analyzed from a range of different disciplinary perspectives, but in markedly different languages and registers.

For example, neoclassical economists understand ecological problems as "negative ecological externalities," which are the unintended and unwanted side effects of market transactions, just as military personnel describe the damage to the environment arising from scorched-earth military tactics as just another instance of "collateral damage." However, more critical voices characterize the problem in much more colorful language. For green economist Michael Jacobs, while the allocation of resources is made possible through the "invisible hand" of the market, the allocation of ecological risks is provided by the "invisible elbow," which deals an unwelcome blow to those who are not parties to the economic transaction.[17] For sociologists of the risk society, such as Ulrich Beck, ecological risks are "the stowaways of normal production," which helps to explain why it is often so difficult to determine causation and attribute responsibility.[18] For global political ecologists such as Peter Dauvergne, the global patterns of environmental degradation arising from the global corporate, trade, and financing chains that supply consumer goods represent "the ecological shadows of consumption."[19] Words like "invisible elbow," "stowaways," and "ecological shadows" all seek to highlight and politicize a problem that has crept up behind a busily modernizing and globalizing world that has not yet been able to fully grasp the extent to which the systemic production and skewed distribution of ecological risks has become pathological. Indeed, many political economists from the South, drawing on neo-dependency theory, have argued that the international economic division of labor between the core and the peripheral regions of the world has produced not only unequal economic exchanges but also "unequal ecological exchanges" resulting in a net export of biophysical capacity from the South to the North and a net "environmental load displacement" from the North to the South.[20]

Yet the processes and problems of displacement, disconnection, and distancing extend well beyond market transactions to include systems of knowledge production and dissemination and governance. As we shall see, displacement and disconnection are especially marked between the structures and processes of economic and environmental governance. The net effect is a growing crisis of moral and political accountability between those who generate and/or benefit from ecological risks and those who suffer the consequences of such risks. This has produced a global system of "organized irresponsibility."[21] We argue that this crisis of accountability arises not from too much global integration or interconnectedness, nor from not enough global integration, but rather from the skewed kind of integration associated with disassociated economic and political global governance. Growing economic *interconnectedness* of a certain kind has produced a growing ecological *disconnectedness* and *disembeddedness* between people and places, which has inhibited the human potential for empathetic and reflexive learning about the social and ecological consequences of human actions.

However, our conclusion is not simply that environmental governance must become more global to match the global reach of markets because the goals, cultures, and processes of different social systems may still fail to mesh. We also need a different type of governance, one that recognizes, rather than denies, our biological embodiment and ecological embeddedness and the social and ecological consequences of our actions on others. In particular, we defend a normative framework of reflexive modernization and reflexive globalization that will enable all social structures, including markets, states, and other governance structures, to become routinely sensitive and (where possible) accountable to, "communities-at-risk" across space and time. This shift requires considerably higher levels of ecological literacy, social empathy, and democratic deliberation than are currently provided by existing governance structures. It also requires, among other things, effective integration of economic and environmental decision making, from the local to the global. Indeed, genuine integration at lower scales of political and cultural organization, especially the national level but also the subnational state/provincial and local levels, can serve to reduce the pressure for integration at the global level. This requires finding a new balance between the demands of functional integration (based on specialization and exchange) and spatial integration (based on the democratic demands and requirements of social and ecological communities). Only then can politics catch up with markets to ensure that they serve and protect rather than undermine social and ecological communities. Only then can we begin to address the crisis of accountability arising from the problem of distancing.

While the phenomenon of globalization is multifaceted and cannot be reduced to a single process, we argue that the contemporary dominant form of *economic* globalization (capitalism) serves as the main intensifier of environmental degradation. However, we also show how contemporary economic globalization both shapes, and is shaped by, other dimensions of globalization. The practice of increasing specialization of production and exchange, within and between countries and regions, has accelerated and intensified in recent decades with the removal of national restrictions on the flow of money, goods and services, and technological change. An increasing range of products, including both goods and services, are now "made in the World" rather than "made in China" or any other single country. Functional integration on a global scale has increasingly replaced spatial integration at more local scales, and this has enabled not only a global extension of the processes of production and sourcing of inputs but also a considerable acceleration in the volume and speed of resource exploitation, energy consumption, pollution, and emissions. This is also the process that has produced an increasing dissociation between those who generate risks, those who possess the expertise to understand them, those who suffer the consequences (now and in the future), and those who are institutionally charged to take political responsibility for them. This crisis of accountability has thwarted the human capacity for collective problem solving and reflexive learning.

REWIND, FAST FORWARD

One way of grasping this dissociation is to imagine a trend moving in exactly the opposite direction. What if the harmful ecological consequences of decisions to invest, produce, and consume were to become increasingly localized, quarantined, immediate, and well understood? Those of us living in those deteriorating locales would literally be standing amid the mounting wreckage and refuse of our consumption habits and, not liking what we see, would probably feel compelled to do something about these consequences. We could therefore expect the gravity, scale, and rate of ecological problems to diminish significantly. If we eventually reached an endpoint where all political decision makers, investors, producers, and consumers not only had to answer directly to those affected by the ecological consequences of their decisions but also suffer the same consequences themselves, then we would expect that their sensitivity to ecological signals and risks would become as routine and "natural" as sensitivity to price signals and commercial risks are in today's economic world.

Research on the management of common pool resources (i.e., those accessible to everyone, which can be degraded by overuse) has shown that socially and environmentally effective management regimes are more likely to arise in situations where the environmental problem is visible, the cause-and-effect relationships are well understood and directly traceable to human activity, the problem is reversible, and the new management regime brings clear net benefits to key constituencies.[22] Yet it is precisely because so many environmental problems lack these characteristics that the externalization of environmental risks across space and time has become so routine, and is likely to continue in the absence of a significant transformation of social structures and social relationships. Climate change provides an exemplary illustration of this problem, since it is not clearly visible or palpable to many constituencies: the cause-and-effect relationships are complex, uncertain, and not well understood by laypeople; there exists political disputation by climate deniers over whether climate change is traceable to human activity; the problem is largely irreversible across human timescales; and while the longer-term benefits of action are widely recognized, many states and key constituencies fiercely resist the short-term costs that would flow from concerted regulation.

However, if we fast forward to the end of this century and assume that states are unable to raise their level of mitigation effort beyond the voluntary, nonbinding pledges made at the Copenhagen meeting in 2009, then we can expect to see a rise in global average surface temperature by around four degrees Celsius by 2100. Under these circumstances, given that many scientists suggest even 1.5 degrees Celsius is too much and the politically agreed aspirational threshold for "dangerous warming" is two degrees Celsius, the world in 2100 will bear the brunt of a wide range of compounding crises. This will include the contraction of agricultural production and the loss of many marine fisheries; chronic food and water shortages, high food prices, and recurrent food riots; a major wave of species extinctions and the collapse of many ecosystems; natural resource scarcity and enhanced geopolitical rivalry; extreme weather events, sea-level rise, inundation of low-lying coastal areas, and the obliteration of many low-lying islands; and the biggest wave of forced migration in human history. We would also expect, under this dystopian scenario, that the international economy in 2100 would be less open than it is today, that free trade would be the exception and mercantilism, resource nationalism, and resource rivalry would be on the rise. We would also expect global inequality to be more extreme than it is today. The current "model" of globalization may yet lead to its own demise.

Now, some environmentalists might take these "rewind and fast forward" thought experiments as a vindication of localization, or the ecological virtues of small, self-sufficient communities and local economies. However, we do not take this view. While we certainly see some advantages in a greater degree of localization and regionalization to achieve a better balance between the demands of economic specialization, on the one hand, and social and environmental diversification, on the other, we see far too many disadvantages in a strategy of global delinking.[23] In any event, we humans do not fully understand the intricacies of ecosystems, so even in self-sufficient local economies the ecological consequences of human activity may not always be immediately apparent or understood by the local inhabitants in the ways presented in our artificial thought-experiment. This is not simply due to the problem of long lead times, discussed earlier. Perceptions and vernacular understandings of environmental change at the local level are not always able to grasp the multiscalar changes that can arise from the cumulative effects of the transformation of many local environments. The purpose of the exercise is to bring into relief the diminution of accountability that arises from the growing distancing between the routine economic practices of investors, producers, and consumers and their cumulative and distributional social and ecological consequences.

This distancing works at the epistemological, moral, and political levels, and suggests the need for the development of a post-liberal account of responsibility that includes yet goes beyond direct, causal, and individualistic accounts of agency, accountability, and liability. The challenge is to develop governance structures that possess the same degree of ecological sensitivity as in our localization thought-experiment but across all domains and scales of human activity. This is a tall order, but we argue that this challenge can be met by transforming and rechanneling, rather than simply reversing, the processes of globalization.

ONE PLANET, MANY GLOBALIZATIONS

To blame our ecological problems on globalization, as many environmental critics do, presupposes a common understanding about what the term means. While precision is required to retrieve the concept of globalization from being "the cliché of our times," finding precision is no easy matter.[24] There is no agreement about whether the growing cross-border connections and flows that are central to most understandings of globalization necessarily arise from a single, unified process or a disparate set of intersecting processes; what makes them "global"; whether they are new and recent or part of a longer historical process; whether they are deliberate or unintended; and whether they should be enthusiastically welcomed, resisted, or redirected. Indeed, there is deep disagreement in globalization studies over not only the issue of characterization but also periodization, causation, explanation, impacts, and evaluation. Not surprisingly, academic and political protagonists in the globalization debate often talk past one another. Moreover, defining the term too broadly can render it meaningless or indistinguishable from closely related processes such as liberalization, Westernization, or modernization.[25] Conversely, defining the term too narrowly can render it irrelevant.

Nonetheless, we will start with a general characterization of globalization, critically unbundle it into manageable components, and then reassemble them in ways that we hope will shed light on global environmental change. As a first and very general characterization, globalization may be understood as the extension of social and ecological relations across world space. It is a set of processes that is producing certain kinds of global interconnectedness and interdependence between individuals (humans and other species), communities, and countries, while at the same time contributing to a heightened social reflexivity about the local.

As sociologist Roland Robertson points out, globalization is not only producing a growing consciousness of the world as a whole but also an intensified emphasis on the local.[26] The contradictory or ambiguous effects of globalization can be seen in relation to political borders. While global capital flows relatively freely, state borders have been hardened to the movement of certain kinds of people—in particular, migrants, temporary workers, and asylum seekers. In this respect, globalization has contributed fundamentally to the increasing vulnerability of individuals, communities, and ecosystems to systemic risks. These processes involve cross-border interactions and flows of various kinds—including money, people, goods, diseases, pollution, ideas, and communications systems in general—that are transforming environments, societies, and social identities.

Although globalization is typically discussed as if it were a singular or unified phenomenon, and is often reduced by some to an ideology of neoliberalism or process of Westernization, on closer inspection it emerges as a complex, uneven, and often contradictory set of processes operating in a range of different intersecting domains, producing not only homogenization and heterogenization but also hybridization. Identifying these different domains, the different logics by which they operate, and how they interact and shape each other is a necessary first step in disentangling the relationship between globalization and ecological change. We identify four domains of the social: economic, scientific/technological, cultural, and political.

ECONOMIC GLOBALIZATION

The economic domain is associated with the production, use, exchange, management, and valuing of resources. Economic globalization in its current dominant form refers to the spatial expansion and deeper integration of capitalist markets, facilitated by the removal of border restrictions on the movement of money, materials, and goods (financial and trade liberalization). It encompasses the expanding and accelerating transborder flows of goods, services, investment, and financial transactions; the "unbundling" of the production process into global supply chains to take advantage of economies of scale and efficiencies in different locations; the rise of globalizing corporations with operations in many different localities; and the extension and intensification of commodification and mass consumerism. For many observers, and particularly the hyper-critics and hyper-enthusiasts, this is the "pointy end" of globalization. It has attracted the most intense political debate and, for understandable reasons, it is the primary target of environmental critics. We therefore devote much of the next chapter to exploring the histories of economic globalization and environmental change and examining their relation-ship, in order to evaluate these claims and counter-claims. However, we also seek to keep in view the deep and intricate relationships between economic globalization, other domains of globalization, and the broader processes of modernization.

SCIENTIFIC AND TECHNOLOGICAL GLOBALIZATION

Scientific and technological globalization refers to the global spread of scientific knowledge and new technologies. The spread of new tech-nologies is often regarded simply as a facet of economic globalization. For example, the rapid development of new technologies of transport, such as jet engines and containerization in international shipping, and the revolution in information and communication technologies have made it possible to speed up and extend geographically international economic coordination and exchange. However, these technological developments are the fruits of a broader and much longer process of scientific inquiry that has its own dynamic and transnational (now global) character. Scientists band together, exchange, and test ideas in global networks or "epistemic communities." The scientific method of inquiry transcends the nationality of its practitioners, and many of the objects of scientific inquiry (most notably, geology, chemistry, and climatology) are genuinely global in scope or planetary in concern. Scientific discourses have also played a crucial role in the detection of ecological problems (which are not readily discernible to laypeople) and in agenda setting and monitoring in environmental policy and ma-jor environmental regimes.

CULTURAL GLOBALIZATION

Cultural globalization covers the growing reach and intensification of symbolic exchanges between societies arising from the increasing movement of people (via such processes as migration and mass tourism), goods and services, and—especially—the spread of modern communication technologies. This has included the increasing dominance of particular languages (most notably English) and the spread of both high and popular culture, ranging from Western classical music, pop, and rock, to fashion and films (from Hollywood and Bollywood). These developments have increased general awareness of cultural diversity while also facilitating new forms of cultural homogenization and hybridization and prompting reactive processes of retraditionalization against the forces of cultural homogenization. At the same time, cultural globalization has facilitated the spread of human rights norms and a cosmopolitan ethic and social identity—according to which "we" are all citizens of the world, of equal moral worth, irrespective of nationality, religion, and race. This has also been accompanied by the development of a "planetary consciousness" or "Earth imaginary," including an awareness of the diversity and richness of the Earth's biodiversity, the complexity of its ecosystems and atmosphere, and the stresses to which it is now subjected from human activities. From the comfort of their living rooms, watching wildlife documentaries such as the *Living Planet*, through to using travel guides such as the *Lonely Planet* to navigate the discomforts of exploring new places, more and more people are learning that exotic cultures, ecosystems, and species are increasingly under threat.

POLITICAL GLOBALIZATION

The globalization of politics encompasses the political actors, networks, and governance structures that have actively fashioned, facilitated, and promoted globalization as well as the political and regulatory responses to this process. This domain also includes global political movements and global political ideologies (including the anti-globalization movement and its nemesis, the ideology of neoliberalism or globalism) and the global extension and convergence of modes of regulation, including the creation and extension of international governance institutions. We also include in this domain the development of sophisticated military technologies (such as global surveillance systems and intercontinental ballistic missiles) and the emergence of one superpower with global influence and global military reach in the post–World War II period.

While much of the political debate about globalization has been preoccupied with the question of whether the autonomy and steering systems of nation-states are in decline, and what forms of governance are on the rise, it is now increasingly acknowledged that the nation-state form—as a structure of exclusive territorial rule with the monopoly of legitimate violence within the territory and a defined relationship to its "people"—had itself become thoroughly globalized by the latter half of the 20th century following the end of the decolonization period. The globalization of a system of sovereign states began in Europe more than four hundred years ago, symbolized by the Treaty of Westphalia of 1648. It has culminated in the spread of sovereign states over the entire land mass of the Earth, save for the Antarctic (which is nonetheless controlled by states under the Antarctic Treaty System). Of course this structure of rule is now supplemented with a range of transnational governance rules and networks, including private and nongovernment regulation and certification organizations, as well as a range of new hybrid (state/nonstate) governance structures. The state system still remains the primary governance structure, and states remain the primary gatekeepers and linchpins between the subnational, on the one hand, and the regional, international, and global, on the other. Needless to say, this global system of sovereign states (particularly the military and economic rivalry that are often by-products of the anarchic structure of the state system) is not especially conducive to the enlightened management of common or transboundary ecological problems.

Although each of these four domains of globalization has different material and ideational dimensions and follows different logics and temporal pathways, they are mutually constitutive rather than externally related and autonomous. Each domain both shapes and is shaped by the other domains, but not necessarily always in the same way, to the same degree, or at the same time. The drivers of change in each of these domains operate with different intensities at different times. There can be no assumption that the historical or spatial pattern of globalization within each of these domains is identical or even comparable. This means that the processes of globalization—and the patterns of development that are shaped by these processes—are invariably uneven, as are the distributive impacts of both benefits and burdens. The resulting hot spots, cold spots, and channels and flows, nodes and troughs of activity, including *between* and *within* regions and nations, are thus marked by inequalities and unevenness in each of the domains noted above.

All this makes it impossible to reduce the combined processes of globalization to a single cause, and equally impossible to separate cause and effect. Nonetheless, breaking down globalization into different domains helps us to understand the larger process of interaction and mutual constitution, while acknowledging that there are many different ways of analytically carving up the process.

ENVIRONMENTAL AND "ECOLOGICAL" IMPLICATIONS

So how do these domains of globalization—the economic, scientific/ technological, cultural, and political—relate to the planet's biophysical environments?

We humans are constituted by the biophysical environment that, simultaneously, we are also increasingly refashioning. Our focus in this book is on how different domains of globalization both enable and constrain particular understandings and material practices vis-à-vis the biophysical environment, how they produce environmental effects, and how they respond to these effects. In other words, the four domains of globalization are each shaped and constrained by the biophysical contexts in which they operate and upon which they draw. Each domain is materially embedded in, and dependent on, a biophysical environment for resources and sustenance and the release of wastes. This includes the immediate local environment as well as more distant environments insofar as biocapacity is "imported" from elsewhere. At the same time, activities in each domain work to materially transform as well as socially "produce" the biophysical environment. The processes of social interaction in each domain simultaneously produce different social constructions and understandings of—or ecological discourses about— particular environments.

While the biophysical environment provides the substratum of all human societies, we do not single it out as a separate domain of globalization because our focus here is on the *socially* produced environmental flows and transformations, scientific and cultural understandings of those processes and effects, and political responses. All these social domains intersect in complex ways. So, for instance, the globalization of environmental awareness is a feature of cultural and political globalization, while the emergence of global environmental ideologies and global environmental governance structures forms part of the globalization of politics and governance. Global environmental change is the phenomenon we seek to explain, and our concern is to understand to what extent different domains of globalization are implicated in producing, interpreting, and responding to change.

Our social constructivist approach to the environment seeks to avoid the pitfalls of both naïve realist and hyper-constructivist understandings of the environment. The former does not acknowledge the ways in which human understandings of nature are always and already unavoidably filtered through different cultural, disciplinary, and institutional frames. The latter denies any agency or alternative "life-worlds" in the nonhuman world by reducing the planet's natural environment to nothing more than a human construction, to passive material awaiting the investment of human meaning. We acknowledge that the environment is much *more* than what humans construct it to be, that it encompasses a rich variety of species and ecological relationships and processes, but we also acknowledge that we have no collective interpretive access to it other than through human sensory perception and human language. Scientific discourses provide a particularly powerful understanding of the natural world based on a systematic method of inquiry that requires theories and hypotheses to be made public and rigorously tested; such discourses are continuously evolving, are often fallible and incomplete (and, for all we know, may never be complete). Nonetheless, scientific discourses provide our primary means of detecting, mapping, and understanding human-induced environmental changes on a *global* scale. Vernacular environmental discourses, based on daily interactions, close-range observations, or lived experience by local people (such as farmers and fishers, bird-watchers, hikers, amateur field-naturalists, indigenous peoples), contribute valuable sources of information and fine-grained insights on local/particular environments but they cannot comprehend interactions at a global scale. Other discourses—including economic, literary, and political/ ideological discourses—play an important role in interpreting the social and ethical significance of the environmental information provided by both scientists and others.

For example, recognition of the *problem* of extinction—our concern about the complete disappearance of a species from the planet—is a thoroughly modern affair, which requires the ability to differentiate one species from all other similar species, a thoroughly modern sense of geological time, a global grasp of the species' range and habitat, and the capacity for surveillance that can confirm its disappearance. However, a popular awareness of the need for species protection did not arise until the 19th century and the first laws for conservation that move beyond regulating the taking of certain species did not occur until the latter part of that century: the first international treaty (restricting the hunting of fur seals) was formulated in the early 20th century while whaling in the global marine commons was not regulated until after 1945, although the loss of individual whale species was already noted in the mid-1800s, including by Herman Melville in *Moby Dick*.

The processes of scientific and cultural globalization have enabled the spread of new understandings of the "natural" world as a source of wonder, curiosity, and intrinsic value, a silo of genetic diversity for new drugs and medicines, or a place of spiritual renewal and recreation. Wild nature, in particular, has become more valuable the more it has become endangered. Widely circulating, popular interpretations of science have delivered messages of a planet in peril, from the eerie silence of Spring to the "end of nature." For example, Bill McKibben's best-selling book, *The End of Nature*—the first popular book on the problem of climate change—laments the end not of physical nature but of the *idea* of nature as an autonomous force displaced and replaced by a world overlaid and transformed by human actions, both deliberate and accidental. For McKibben, the human destruction and/or remaking of nature is a monstrous and momentous occasion because "Nature's independence *is* its meaning; without it there is nothing but us."[27] Yet the idea of "wilderness" or "wild nature" has also been criticized as a romantic, peculiarly "Western" idea that denies the myriad ways in which humans have co-evolved with their environments.

In economic discourses, nonhuman species and the biophysical environment are constructed as "natural resources," "raw materials" for the manufacturing process, or as "sinks" for pollution and wastes. In military discourses, "the environment" provides a form of "cover" and the backdrop for camouflage (army fatigues are green and brown!). In different domains of environmental policy, the environment is constructed as providing services (often in the economic language of "natural capital" or "ecosystem services"), as "scenery" for eco-tourists, or sometimes as a precious asset to be preserved and protected. Discourses of indigenous people can reveal the environment as "home" and the source of creation.

The different constructions of the environment within any given domain of globalization are shaped by, and sometimes only made possible by, material and ideational developments in other domains. One small example suffices to illustrate these entangled processes of mutual constitution. "The Blue Marble"—the title of the famous picture of Planet Earth taken on December 7, 1972, by the crew of the Apollo 17 en route to the Moon—is one of the most reproduced photographs of all time. It has served as a unifying symbol of our fragile planet and of our mutual dependence on a "spaceship earth" that travels alone in an indifferent black sea of infinite space. Yet the photograph was a product of the Cold War—the ideological and technological, economic, and military struggle for global dominance between the two superpowers, the United States and Soviet Russia. The Moon mission was the United States' symbolic and practical response to the Soviet challenge—a space race that began with Sputnik, the first satellite to circle the Earth in 1957, and was then accentuated by the first manned orbit of the Earth in space, by the Russian Gagarin in 1961.

Apollo 17 rode aloft on a rocket derived from a design used for intercontinental ballistic missiles—the nuclear arsenal lying primed beneath the plains of America's Midwest—produced by the scientist Werner von Braun, who had designed V2 rockets for the Nazis during World War II. A global network of radio-telescope communications had made it possible to track the mission's progress and had enabled some six hundred million people—one-sixth of the Earth's entire population at this time—to see the first lunar landing three years prior. The globalized print media soon published and reproduced the photograph worldwide. The image is now clichéd.

In all, a complex network of mutually constitutive domains of globalization—economic, scientific/technological, cultural, and political—underpin and overwrite this mobilizing icon in the global environmental narrative. The links between globalization, environmental transformation, and environmental awareness and understanding are therefore anything but straightforward. They suggest that—as Barry Commoner once offered as a law of ecology—everything is connected to everything, but not in the same way or at the same time.

THE GLOBAL DIMENSIONS OF
ENVIRONMENTAL CHANGE

So far, we have been using the terms *environment* and *global environmental change* rather loosely. In many ways, the word *environment* is a rather limited word to refer to the "more than human world," which is made up of rich variety of nonhuman species, ecological communities, and complex biophysical processes. The verb *environ* means to encircle or surround, and the noun *environment* literally means that which surrounds the organism, which suggests that the environment is merely a static and passive backdrop, with no agency. The word "ecology" provides a richer understanding of the biological and physical world since it refers to the relationships between organisms and their environments. It also allows for a more dynamic understanding of the processes of mutual constitution by different organisms, including humans, and their many different environments. Nonetheless, we continue to use the term *environment* in this inquiry not only because it is commonly used to describe the so-called natural world but also because our focus is on the role of humans as agents of global environmental change.

The phrase *global environmental change* is widely used by both scientists and policy makers to refer to environmental transformations on a global scale. It emerged with the rise to prominence of major global environmental problems in the late 1980s (namely, the depletion of the ozone layer and global warming) and has endured because it has proved to be more widely palatable than the more controversial language of global "limits to growth" or "global environmental crisis."[28] While it may be seen largely as a euphemism for environmental change that is mostly negative rather than positive for the well-being of both humans and nonhuman communities, we nonetheless find it useful since we do not assume that *all* processes of globalization are bad. Nor do we assume that globalization is the only driver of global environmental change.

Stephen Yearley observed, in reflecting on the global character of environmental problems, that the early wave of globalization scholarship in the 1980s and 1990s tended to overlook the environment, yet "the Earth and its environment can make some claim to utter, physical global-ness."[29] The period in which globalization studies emerged is also the period that is typically taken as marking the rise of genuinely global environmental problems, such as the thinning of the ozone layer and climate change, and a corresponding growing awareness of the global dimensions of the ecological crisis. However, it is important not to conflate the obvious physical "globalness" of Planet Earth with global environmental change, or assume that the only genuinely global environmental problems are those that operate on a global scale—such as ocean acidification, climate change, and the thinning of the ozone layer. Nor should the simultaneous emergence of these global-scale environmental problems with the rise of globalization studies be taken to mean that there was no global environmental change prior to this period, and therefore globalization must be the only culprit. The limits-to-growth debate, based on the first systematic studies of global trends in population, resource consumption, species extinction, and pollution, emerged in the early 1970s, before the emergence of the neoliberal phase of globalization and systematic scholarship on globalization in the 1980s and beyond.

So what kinds of environmental effects or changes warrant the label "global," which is a spatial metaphor for something that is worldwide, spanning the entire globe or the Earth as a whole? Our framework for understanding global environmental change seeks to capture broad-scale systemic changes as well as changes at small spatial scales that produce cumulative global effects.[30] The former involve changes to the Earth's biosphere, such as ozone depletion and global warming already noted. The latter refer to the global effects of cumulative local changes that are replicated around the world, such as local habitat destruction that contributes to the overall loss of planetary biodiversity. Indeed, this latter type has two global dimensions: the global ubiquity of similar local practices and local environmental effects, as well as the global cumulative effects of those practices.

These two global dimensions of environmental change—the systemic and cumulative—also help us to distinguish between the proximate causes and the broader driving forces of global environmental change. Proximate sources refer to the final or near-final human activities—such as driving a car or cutting down a forest—that produce local effects that contribute to global environmental change, while the broader driving forces refer to the four domains of globalization, which represent phases of a much longer process of modernization.

The global dimensions of environmental change identified above do not readily map onto the way in which the "the global" has been used to describe the processes of globalization by some globalization scholars. For example, David Held has defined a process or set of interactions as "global" if it spans or connects regions or continents; that is, it must be more than transboundary but need not cover all aspects of the globe.[31] Yet cross-border interactions that are spatially confined to a region may nonetheless produce more global environmental impacts than interactions that are more spatially extensive. For example, cross-border flows of people, goods, money, and wastes within regions like the European Union or North America (between the United States, Canada, and Mexico) would not qualify as "global" on Held's understanding, even though they may be more intensive, faster, and have more momentous global environmental impacts than transcontinental flows of trade between, say, Australia—an island continent—and states on the African continent.

Of course, those who study globalization are interested not only in geography—in *spatial* changes—but also the global effects of, and responses to, changes in the *intensity* (volume and speed) of cross-border interactions, as is made clear in David Held and Anthony McGrew's definition of globalization as "the expanding scale, growing magnitude, speeding up and deepening impact of interregional flows and patterns of social interaction."[32] If rapid local changes can produce cumulative global environmental effects, then they too must form part of our study. Table 1.1 seeks to draw together the various global dimensions of environmental change, which includes yet goes beyond the biophysical global effects discussed above to include global social systems, new forms of global environmental awareness, and global responses.

OUR CORE PROPOSITIONS

To recapitulate, then, our sociological task in this book is to understand how, and to what extent, the four domains of globalization that we identify may have caused or contributed to systemic and/or cumulative global environmental change, which includes both environmental degradation and environmental protection. This necessarily requires us to explore processes other than globalization that may also have

Table 1.1. The Global Dimensions of Global Environmental Change

Global systems (producing both effects and responses)
Economic
- the global capitalist system

Scientific and Technological
- the techno-scientific system of epistemic communities
- systems of global monitoring and surveillance

Political
- the globalized state system of exclusive territorial rule
- the globalized networks of nongovernmental and international actors and organizations

Cultural
- global communication systems and popular networks (e.g., e-mail and Twitter) and media organizations with global reach

Global knowledge/awareness
- global discourses of global environmental change, including through global epistemic communities (scientific/technical, theoretical, and applied), but also through political and cultural debate
- global cultural production and associated popular awareness of the environment through the dissemination of books, maps, images, films, songs, websites, blogs, conversations, etc.

Global effects
- systemic environmental changes such as global warming, ocean acidification, and ozone depletion, which involve changes to the planetary biosphere
- the global environmental effects of cumulative local and/or regional practices, many of which form links in the chain of globally extensive processes of production and consumption, technological diffusion, trade and exchange, communication, and pollution

Global political responses
- the emergence of transnational and international environmental movements, nongovernment organizations (NGOs), policy think tanks, and international organizations seeking policy and regulatory changes
- the development of international environmental treaties, strategies, and action plans and the creation of international organizations, such as the United Nations Environment Program
- the emergence of green parties in many different countries around the world with common global values and ideas in their political platform
- the global diffusion and convergence of many environmental policies, regulations, principles, and standards, such as "sustainable development strategies," the polluter pays principle, the precautionary principle, and ISO14000 environmental management standards
- the global development of hybrid transnational environmental regulatory responses involving public/private partnerships and stakeholders
- the emergence of global and transnational private and "civic" forms of environmental regulation, such as corporate environmental responsibility, new environmental certification standards, and voluntary eco-labeling

contributed to global environmental change, so we can identify the particular contribution that globalization has made relative to the broader processes of modernization.

Our critical task is to expose the various forms of power—material (including coercion and bribery), rule-based, structural, and discursive—that perpetuate and normalize environmental degradation. And our normative task is to explore how and to what extent the processes of modernization and globalization need to be transformed in ways that promote environmental protection and environmental justice.

To help orient the reader, we draw together our ten core propositions that provide the overall shape of our argument, which is developed and illustrated in the remainder of this book.

1. Globalization may be understood as the extension of social and ecological relations across world space. It is a process or set of processes producing greater global interconnectedness and interdependence between individuals (humans and other species), communities, and countries in ways that are increasing the vulnerability of communities and ecosystems to systemic risks.

2. Processes of globalization have extended modernizing practices across world space, and a new global phase of modernization is increasing the spatial reach and intensity (speed, volume) of interactions in ways that are producing more global effects, including accelerated global environmental change.

3. Global environmental change encompasses both systemic global changes to the Earth's biosphere as well as the global reproduction of changes at more local scales that then produce globally cumulative environmental effects.

4. The first popular recognition of the *global* dimension of environmental change emerged well before the most recent phase of neoliberal economic globalization, which began in the late 1970s/1980s and has wrongly been singled out as the primary culprit of the modern environmental crisis by many environmental critics of globalization.

5. Contemporary globalization, understood as the global phase of modernization, is therefore not the primary or only cause of global environmental change, although it has certainly intensified such

change to the point where we are moving toward an environmental crisis of planetary proportions.

6. The continuation and intensification of global environmental change threaten to undermine the ecological, economic, political, and cultural conditions that enabled the emergence and development of globalization. However, the processes of globalization have also generated a variety of different political and governance responses to global environmental change, some of which critically challenge the processes of unreflexive globalization.

7. The tragedy is that many of the processes of globalization that are exacerbating global environmental problems are also making critical reflexivity more difficult because of the problems of displacement, distancing, and disconnection between decision makers and "environments," between producers and consumers, between perpetrators and victims, between cause and effect, and between space and place. The intensification of global environmental change therefore represents a crisis of accountability.

8. The solution to the ecological problems created by modernization is not anti-modernization but rather reflexive (self-aware and self-limiting) modernization. Likewise, the solution to the global environmental changes that are intensified by globalization is reflexive globalization, not anti-globalization.

9. "Simple" modernization encompasses the ongoing application of instrumental reason (including technological fixes and the application of technocratic/bureaucratic rationality to environmental problems), the perpetuation of the state system, neoliberal capitalism (which has now largely superseded communism), and individualism.

10. Reflexive modernization (and reflexive globalization) entails critically confronting and transforming the processes of knowledge generation and dissemination, the forces of production, the relations of production, and the relations of definition (who defines and manages ecological risks) in ways that are more risk-averse and more accountable to those who may potentially suffer the consequence of unelected risks. This includes the development of greater levels of ecological literacy, social solidarity, and democratic deliberation in all the key social structures to overcome the problem of distancing and to ensure that all

political and economic decisions are accountable, in substance or in effect, to social and ecological "communities at risk" in both space and time.

The following chapter looks much more closely at the mutually entwined histories of the four domains of globalization we have identified in order to draw out and explain how each has shaped, and been shaped by, the biophysical environments in which they operate and upon which they draw. We focus in particular on the mutually constitutive processes of economic and cultural modernization and how they have produced new understandings, new social identities, and new environments. This includes an examination of shifts in processes of production and trade, consumption and consumerism, as well as cultural and political responses to the environmental effects of these processes. We also explore in more detail the discourses and practices of ecological modernization and defend our own interpretation of reflexive modernization and reflexive globalization.

Since we cannot do justice to the wide range of ecological problems that feed into global environmental change, we have chosen to focus on two quintessential examples of global environmental change that are both serious and irreversible, and that provide illustrations of systemic and cumulative environmental change respectively: climate change and biodiversity loss. In chapters 3 and 4, we track the complex ways in which our different domains of globalization (and their precursors) have combined to create looming climate and biodiversity crises and identify the wide-ranging transformations that are required to stem these crises.

In the last chapter, we turn to the vexed question of governance and take stock of the political and governance responses to global environmental change identified in table 1.1. Here we focus on the lack of integration between the environmental treaty system and the key structures of global economic governance, as well as the lack of integration between economic and environmental policy at the national level. We show how integration failure is closely linked to the more general crisis of accountability for ecological problems, which is exacerbated by the globalization of both capitalism and the territorial structure of rule of the state system. Finally, we explore how these global systems might be transformed in ways that promote both sustainability and environmental justice.

CHAPTER 2

A Short History of Globalization and the Environment

We travel together, passengers in a little spaceship, dependent upon its vulnerable reserves of air and soil, committed for our safety to its security and peace, preserved from annihilation only by the care, the work and, I will say, the love we give our fragile craft.

—Adlai Stevenson, Geneva, July 1965

INTRODUCTION

In chapter 1, we singled out economic globalization as representing the "pointy end" of globalization and the primary target of environmental critics. In this chapter, we track the history of economic globalization, with a special focus on expanding global production and consumption made possible by increasing international specialization and exchange.

We show how the economic domain of globalization remains inextricably interwoven with our three other domains of globalization (scientific/technological, cultural, and political) in ways that have routinized and normalized the ongoing production of ecological impacts and risks.

To set the scene for this history, we begin with the transformational moment—from the early 1960s to the early 1970s—that marks a fundamental break with previous understandings of the relationship between humans and the planet: the emergence of the idea of ecological limits to human progress.

To account for this moment, we then double back and trace the rise of industrialism in the context of the "long history" of modernization and its global extension. Next we show how this long, slow-burning fuse to environmental crisis burned faster and became shorter with the intensification of industrialization and globalization over the past half century. In reviewing these long and short histories we track changes in material practices as well as ideas and discourses, including the new environmental discourses that have emerged in response to both local and global environmental change. Finally, we look more closely at two key elements of this "short fuse" by exploring the rise of consumerism and its implications for social identities in the life-world and society and by critically examining the trade and environment debate.

DISCOVERING LIMITS

Rachel Carson's *Silent Spring* (1962) is commonly regarded as the catalyst for widespread public awareness of the environmental impacts of industrialization and for the birth of the "modern" environmental movement.[1] Although *Silent Spring* had been preceded in the 1950s by a wave of air and water pollution legislation in the United Kingdom, Australia, and elsewhere, Carson's work was, in some senses, the public culmination of scientific studies in the 1950s and 1960s that were *ecological* in orientation, as opposed to focused narrowly on human amenity. Published in the United States in 1962, translated into twenty-two languages, and thereafter an international phenomenon, *Silent Spring* focused attention on the range of unintended ecological risks of the chemical revolution that had occurred since the 1940s. Carson offered a powerful and elegiac commentary on the unforeseen impacts of the versatile and popular pesticide DDT (and other similar biocides) on nontarget species. DDT was persistent and bio-accumulative and played havoc with the stability of ecosystems, including by undermining the reproductive capacities of certain bird species. DDT was also shown to be widely dispersed, found even in the tissue of whales, seals, and polar bears, far from the original sites of application. More generally, Carson exposed the unintended consequences of a narrow application of instrumental reason to the environment and galvanized a popular awareness of the complex and intricate interrelationships and processes of the Earth's ecosystems. She also helped to generate a dialogue about the global extension of environmental consequences.

Carson was not alone in heralding the problems of globalized environmental risk. Simultaneously, the Campaign for Nuclear Disarmament (CND)—formed in 1958 in the United Kingdom—was raising concerns about the dangers of civilian nuclear power and the catastrophic consequences of nuclear war, which came close to materializing during the Cuban missile crisis in 1962. A series of major accidents—such as the *Torrey Canyon* disaster, caused when a laden oil tanker foundered off the coast of Cornwall in 1967—further amplified public concern in the West about poorly regulated industrial practices and pollution. And a group of enlightened industrialists called the Club of Rome began to consider what the longer-term impacts of unrestrained economic growth might mean for the planet's systems. While *Silent Spring* fired up a generation of environmental activists to protest against the use of toxic chemicals, it was the Club of Rome that offered a much more potent political provocation by calling for a halt to "the screeching acceleration of so many processes that bring ecological change."

At the end of World War II, growth in economic output was considered by all governments as central to political stability and prosperity in the postwar world. The Soviet Union and its new satellite states drove down the path of centrally planned industrial development while the new capitalist economic order was led by the United States, based on its model of market expansion, liberalism, rapid industrialization, enhanced trade, and increased material consumption. The ideological foundation of this new order was captured in Walter Rostow's aspirational narrative of historical progress with its five stages of economic development echoing the language and enthusiasm of the "space race," beginning with benighted primitive traditional societies and, after a series of stages including "pre-take-off" and "take-off" during which traditional societies disintegrate and heavy industrialization occurs, culminating in a "period of mass consumption"—with affluent, American-style society as its apogee.[2] A range of international institutions were established in a collective attempt to create global stability and foster development following the devastation of Europe, the final collapse of the old imperial order, and an emerging postcolonial world containing many new states. These included institutions to enhance international cooperation (the United Nations, in 1945), promote development (the International Bank for Reconstruction and Development and the International Development Association, both parts of the World Bank, in 1944), promote international trade and financial stability (the World Bank and the International Monetary Fund, in 1944), and improve health and welfare in developing countries (the World Health Organisation, 1948).

Yet not everyone was overawed by the vista of such a limitless Promethean transformation of the natural world. Two reports published in the early 1970s—the Club of Rome's *The Limits to Growth* and *The Ecologist* magazine's *A Blueprint for Survival*—foreshadowed the coming of a growing scepticism about the universal and enduring benefits of untrammelled industrialization.[3] Although they did not use the term *globalization*, they were written from a global perspective. Aurelio Peccei, then Vice President of Fiat and Olivetti, had in the 1960s become concerned about the prospect of unbridled economic growth and global population growth. In 1968, he and Alexander King gathered together a small group of like-minded academics, bureaucrats, diplomats, and industrialists concerned with "the predicament of mankind." They first met in Rome and therefore became known as the "Club of Rome," which sponsored the report *The Limits to Growth*. Published in 1972, *Limits to Growth* quickly sold twelve million copies in more than thirty translations and, like *Silent Spring* a decade before, initiated an international debate—but one that amplified and went beyond the anxiety about the spatial extension of environmental impacts already publicized by Carson. Building on the idea of a finite planet "captured" in the Blue Marble photos, *Limits to Growth* modelled the consequences of exponential growth in five key global variables—population growth, industrial production, agricultural production, the consumption of nonrenewable natural resources, and pollution from 1900 to 2100. The computer model—called World3—ran three different scenarios and showed that even with optimistic assumptions regarding advances in technology, the world would encounter planetary limits in the 21st century, leading to the collapse of world population and economic systems.

Limits to Growth was the most prominent among a barrage of publications in the late 1960s and early 1970s that warned of imminent ecological overshoot and collapse. Their authors became known, disparagingly, as the neo-Malthusians.[4] The idea of limits—whether of human reason and understanding, human technological ingenuity, or population growth or economic growth—ran against the grain of the conventional developmental narrative that had been predominant for the past two centuries. Indeed, the idea of limits remains so heretical that even the environmental movement remains divided over whether it is a necessary or desirable feature of the case for a sustainable society. This is notwithstanding the fact that the limits-to-growth discourse of the early 1970s helped to launch the modern environmental movement by drawing attention to the planetary implications of exponential growth in population, resource and energy consumption, and pollution. It is no small irony that it was a group of industrialists that helped to catalyse a radical environmental movement that would campaign against the Promethean ideology of industrialism in both its capitalist and communist forms.

The initial process for developing the *Limits to Growth* report itself highlights the inextricable connections between scientific and technological change, on the one hand, and global environmental change, on the other. Professor Carroll Wilson of MIT, a member of the Club of Rome, suggested that Jay Forrester be involved in its development. Forrester, then a professor at the Alfred P. Sloan School of Management at MIT and the author of *Industrial Dynamics* (1962) and *Urban Dynamics* (1969), had developed a method of interrogating complex systems—"systems dynamics"—through his work on mathematical programs to deal with weapons systems in World War II. His efforts had attracted the attention of those interested in solving intricate problems of urban planning. The advent of the computer in the 1950s and 1960s substantially enhanced related computational capacities.

Forrester developed a global systems dynamic model (published in 1971 as *World Dynamics*) that was then adopted for use in the "Project on the Predicament of Mankind." Guided by Dennis Meadows, this model evolved into the World3 computer program used to simulate global patterns of development, based on projections of then current behavior, which became the basis for *The Limits to Growth* report. Many criticisms were leveled against World3, including its inflexibility, high level of aggregation, data weaknesses, lack of reflexivity (capacity to learn), and lack of a capacity to backcast.[5] Yet what is of interest for present purposes is that here, for the first time, was an attempt to consider an aggregated and manipulated *global* picture of the planet, human development, and its impacts, based on accumulating national data on economic activity, demographic changes, and resource use, that nation-states and the United Nations were now systematically harvesting to guide economic planning, welfare activity, and social control.

The *Limits to Growth* report, along with its recommendations for fundamental policy changes, was immediately attacked as alarmist, the product of "the computer that cried wolf." Yet its authors never defended their arguments as predictions; they had merely offered projections based on different scenarios. In any event, the ultimate and very simple message of *Limits to Growth*, that Planet Earth has finite ecological capacities and limits, has since been repeatedly vindicated in a steady succession of reports, including updates by the Club of Rome and regular global reports by the United Nations Environment Program and the World Watch Institute.[6] A recent study by Graham M. Turner that ran the *Limits to Growth* model on the basis of observed historical data for the period 1970–2000 confirms the robustness of *Limits to Growth*'s projections across all of its key parameters.[7]

Across the Atlantic, *Limits to Growth*'s concerns were affirmed sharply in *A Blueprint for Survival*. Published by the British *Ecologist* magazine just before the first United Nations Conference on the Human Environment in Stockholm in 1972, *Blueprint for Survival* was in such high demand that it was republished by Penguin Books later in the same year.[8] A product and reflection of the ferment of the radical 1960s, *Blueprint for Survival* provided a more direct confrontation with industrial society, economic growth, and the centralized modern state. It too offered a systemic rather than symptomatic analysis and, while its projections were not based on computer modeling, like *Limits to Growth* it also predicted the irreversible degradation and possible breakdown of ecosystems and societies.

Blueprint for Survival claimed that economic growth was produced by a confluence of unreflexive institutions and dynamics. The profit motive driving capitalist enterprises required the production of surpluses to ensure survival and create capacity for future investment, thereby producing an in-built dynamic for growth. The environmental destruction wrought by industrial technologies prompted the development of "technological fixes" that often produced further ecological problems (e.g., pesticides and fertilizers created the need for more pesticides and fertilizers). Governments were dependent on economic growth to secure taxation revenue and to avoid economic crises, maintain business and consumer confidence, overcome unemployment, and manage inequality through welfare expenditures. The fate of governments in liberal-democratic societies depended on their ability to generate economic growth without which, it was assumed, social unrest would increase and crisis result. Industrial growth, particularly in its early phases, also propelled population growth.

Blueprint for Survival contrasted these features with those of a system based on a steady-state (no-growth) economy that involved minimum disruption of ecosystems, zero population growth (that therefore constrained demand), and a social system based on security and equity (thus eliminating the need for economic growth to mask the inability of the welfare state to redistribute wealth and generate social equality). Here, in broad outline, were the key elements of a new and radical political ideology that prompted the formation in 1973 of the world's first green parties in the Australian island state of Tasmania, in New Zealand, and in the United Kingdom.[9]

The emerging concern over the global environmental effects of industrialization was given a simple mathematical expression by Paul Ehrlich in his influential equation I = PAT, where "I" represents environmental impact, "P" represents population, "A" represents affluence, measured as rising consumption, and "T" represents technology.[10] In short, environmental impact would increase with rising population, increasing consumption, and/or the increasing use of environmentally destructive technologies. While the formula underscored the unsustainable trajectory of the post–World War II world, it could not explain the intricacies of social systems, such as the role of class, power, ideas, culture, and technological innovation, or the interactions between these variables. In a much publicized debate with Paul Ehrlich, Barry Commoner argued that technological innovation and social development would reduce environmental impacts to sustainable levels and avoid the need for coercive measures such as population control, favored by Erhlich's Zero Population movement.[11] This exchange foreshadowed the broad contours of an ongoing debate about the meaning, scope, and possibility of sustainable development.

At its heart, the debate prompted by *Limits to Growth, Blueprint for Survival*, and the neo-Malthusians focused on two new and difficult questions. What might be the planetary capacities for sustainable human activity? And could economic growth and technological progress indeed overcome physical planetary limits? Before we address these questions, it is necessary to understand the developments that gave rise to the novel idea of limits.

REMAKING THE PLANET— THE LONG FUSE OF MODERNIZATION

The limits-to-growth discourse was a response to the pace and effects of postwar industrialization (and militarization) that were, in turn, a consequence of a long-evolving process of modernization that had hitherto appeared to be unrestrained by environmental considerations. Modernization is a dynamic, multifaceted process that had its most intense early expressions in the West and has, at one level, transformed traditional or "pre-modern" societies (beginning with medieval Europe) into what are said to be "modern" societies. As we saw in chapter 1, it encompasses scientific change along with new rationalities, social relations, identities, and human relationships with nature.

At its most general level, modernization has reordered social and environmental relations in ways that increasingly separate space and time into realms that are detached from immediate, face-to-face, embodied experience, producing more abstract social and ecological relations and institutions. Local place is increasingly overlaid by abstract space; local time, based on the local seasons and rhythms of nature, is increasingly overlaid with abstract time differentiated into global time zones.[12] Knowledge and expertise, and the tasks associated with the daily production of goods and services, become increasingly specialized and globally dispersed. Likewise, the biophysical world is increasingly exploited, disassembled, reassembled, transported, and consumed in different parts of the world.

These processes have produced enormous benefits, such as increased human life expectancy through improved nutrition and medical treatment, advancements in human knowledge and education, social welfare systems, and a dizzying array of new technologies, products, and services that have enriched human well-being. Yet the same processes have also led to new diseases of affluence (obesity, cancer) alongside abject poverty and malnutrition in many parts of the world. They have also produced nuclear weapons, denuded ecosystems, and drastically reduced global biodiversity, and they now threaten to alter the Earth's climate in irreversible and potentially catastrophic ways.

In contemporary debates, economic globalization—underpinned by the driving forces of market expansion and capital accumulation—is typically identified as the predominant driver of global environmental change. However, to understand recent patterns of global environmental change, it is necessary to adopt a longer historical view of the modernization process, one that encompasses both material practices and the ideas and discourses that legitimated them. We focus first on the material practices of production, beginning with the Age of Empires that saw the global extension of increasingly destructive forms of resource exploitation and the development of globally extensive and intensive modes of trade in resources, commodities, and wastes. We then turn to ideas and discourses, focusing on the legacy of the Enlightenment, including ideas of progress and development, the global extension of Western scientific discovery and technological transformation, and the new environmental thinking that emerged in reaction to the transformation of the biophysical environment.

FROM THE AGE OF EMPIRES TO THE AGE OF GLOBAL PRODUCTION

By the late 19th century, the process of European imperial expansion and colonization that had begun in the 1500s was largely completed. The world had been divided into a number of colonial blocs, of which the British Empire was the most extensive, but which had initially included the Spanish, Portuguese, and Dutch, and then Belgian, French, and German empires in Latin America, Africa, Asia, and the Pacific. Within each empire, colonies were dominated by and exploited in similar ways to the benefit of their metropolitan masters. In this sense, the Age of Empires saw the "global" extension of new relations of exploitation involving profound cultural, political, economic, and ecological changes. The indigenous practices and forms of knowledge that preceded colonization were on the whole, if not always sustainable, often ecologically restrained and had successfully managed productive landscapes, sometimes for millennia. These peoples, cultures, and landscapes were disrupted and most often destroyed by new, harshly exploitative colonial resource regimes that were usually insensitive to the environments on which they were imposed.

What followed were processes that intensified the conquest of subjugated peoples and environments. Social transformations set in motion by this expansionist phase of European colonization continued to accelerate not only in the colonies but also in the metropolitan nations that benefited from the plunder drawn from distant outposts. In the colonies, pastoral, plantation, and mining cultures and workforces sprang up, with a small elite to dominate and ensure stability of resource extraction. New cities and ports were developed for trade with European centers of manufacture. The response in Europe included population growth (from 82 million in 1500 to approximately 163 million by 1750 and 408 million by 1900) and the processes of wealth accumulation, mercantilism, and, eventually, industrialization. These processes increased the demand for natural resources from the colonies.[13] The growth of major ports, towns, and cities in Europe also encouraged the movement of populations from the rural hinterland to urban centers.

As chapter 4 will elaborate, the Age of Empires, an early phase of globalization, not only saw the colonization of peoples but also of ecosystems—a process that Alfred Crosby has called "ecological imperialism."[14] This process intensified as the material demands, and therefore the pressures for resource extraction, of the industrializing metropoles (the capitals of Europe) grew. It was characterized by the creation of pasture and croplands out of native grass and woodlands, the transglobalization of alien species, and the use of invasive technologies—the axe, the shovel, the gun, and the plow—to subdue the ecological "frontier." In most places the rapidity of these ecological changes was profound. For instance, as Geoffrey Bolton writes,

At the beginning of 1788 no hoof had ever been imprinted on Australian soil. By 1860 the continent was carrying twenty million sheep and four million cattle, mostly in its south eastern quarter. By 1890, there were over a hundred million sheep and nearly eight million cattle pastured in nearly every quarter of the country except the desert interior. Their spread was accomplished in 100 years and in that time the original bush gave way to a landscape created very largely in the interests of the flocks of sheep, the herds of cattle and the men and women [and overseas interests] whose economy depended on them.[15]

The Age of Empires saw the rise of Europe as the heartland of manufacturing and consumption.[16] Between 1750 and 1880, Europe's share of world manufacturing grew from less than 20 percent to more than 65 percent.[17] Global trade expanded in volume and value, with the latter increasing tenfold between 1850 and 1913.[18] Raw materials, food, and fiber—nitrates and copper from Chile; timber, meat, and wool from Australia; cotton from the United States (until the Civil War); sugar cane from the West Indies; spices from the East Indies; tea from India—fueled the Industrial Revolution in the United Kingdom as well as Germany, France, and Belgium. These metropolitan centers produced the manufactured goods—textiles and clothes, furniture and foods—that were consumed in increasing quantities as Europe's wealth and population grew and that were exported to foreign markets. London in the 19th century served as the "headquarters of a new global economy."[19] Yet, as Eric Hobsbawm observes, "obviously the entire world could not be turned into a planetary system circling around the economic sun of Britain, if only because Britain was not the only already developed or industrializing economy," albeit the world's most extensive one.[20] Indeed this pattern of relations between the center and periphery of capitalism began to change during the second half of the 19th century with changes in trade relations, terms of trade, patterns of mass migration, and the emergence of new sites of technological innovation, increasing productivity, and/or cheap labor both inside and beyond Europe.[21]

DEVELOPMENT AND THE AGE OF ENLIGHTENMENT

The period from the 17th century through to the start of the 20th century saw the emergence, geographic projection, and consolidation of a set of inextricably entwined beliefs about economic development and social progress that shaped and in part directed these imperial projects and legitimated the subjugation of non-European peoples and the exploitation of their environments. Economic development as a belief and practice was an essential component of the project of state building. "Opening up the continent for development" served as the catchcry of governing elites in New World regions such as North America and Australia and persisted after the process of decolonization was largely completed.

Economic development had been a central preoccupation of the 19th-century European political economists, such as Adam Smith, David Ricardo, and Karl Marx. Liberals and Marxists alike fully absorbed the Enlightenment idea of progress and assumed that economic development, technological progress, and the exploitation of the natural world would provide plenty for all. For instance, for the German political economist and philosopher Karl Marx, economic development had primacy over and dictated forms of political, cultural, and scientific-technological change. Capitalism was but one stage in a long and linear process of historical evolution and progress. Rural life was considered backward and labor-saving technologies were seen as liberating forces. In the words of his colleague Friedrich Engels, such technologies would assist in "the ascent of man from the kingdom of necessity to the kingdom of freedom."[22] Despite their many differences, both liberalism and socialism—the two most influential political ideologies that shaped the modern world—shared cornucopian assumptions of a limitless Earth and a linear, goal-oriented process of human improvement. The world was regarded as potentially (and soon to be) knowable and rationally controllable.

Yet the notion of "development" was never confined to the realm of the economic. Intimately linked to the concepts of "progress," "civilization," "modernity," and "evolution," "development" gained cultural—ideological—force and a predominant place among the terms used to describe and mobilize change. Fomented in Europe as it engaged with the rest of the world, the spread of the modern notion of "development" was a top-down process. Hobsbawm writes,

> The dynamics of the greater part of the world's history [in the 20th and 21st centuries] are derived, not original. They consist essentially of the attempts by the elites of non-bourgeois societies to imitate the

model pioneered in the West, which was essentially seen as that of societies generating progress, the form of wealth, power and culture, by
economic and techno-scientific 'development' in a capitalist or socialist
variant. There was no operational model other than 'westernisation'
or 'modernisation' or whatever one chose to call it. Conversely, only
political euphemism separates the various synonyms of 'backwardness'
. . . which international diplomacy has scattered around a decolonized
world ('under-developed', 'developing', etc).[23]

This description may be overly Eurocentric, but, bearing in mind
this qualification, it describes the globalizing dominance of the modern
in a compelling way. Here we single out five interrelated components
in the discourse of development that underpinned the Europe-centered
phase of modernization that reached its zenith during the Age of
Empires.[24] The first and overarching idea, already noted, was that of
historical progress. History was seen as evolutionary, linear, secular, te-
leological. New scientific developments in biology and geology brought
into being an understanding of "long" or geological time and linked
human development to speciation and evolution in the natural world
and to the evolution of the physical environment.

The second was the idea of *scientific and technological superiority*. The
ships, compasses and charts, and guns, beads, and blankets that made imperial conquest possible had proved their superiority. "However strong
and sincere the belief that magic would turn machine-gun bullets aside,
it rarely worked to make much difference. Telephone and telegraph were
better means of communication than the holy man's telepathy."[25]

The third was the belief in the *moral superiority* of the modern,
derived from a self-serving distinction between a "conquering" culture
and its dominant religion—Christianity—and the "inferior" faiths and
cultures of "other" subjugated peoples.

This was closely allied to a fourth conceit, that of *racial superiority*, which legitimated the conquest and colonization of non-European
peoples and nonwhite races. Just as the sun never set over the British
Empire, the 19th century world was the White Man's Paradise and just
inheritance, and half a century later, Europe was meant to be rightfully
dominated by the Aryan race.

Finally, the idea of human progress was premised on an *anthropocentric worldview* that licensed the domination and subjugation of the

nonhuman world. Even the Copernican and Darwinian revolutions did little to dislodge the dominant belief that humans were the center of the universe, and that they stood apart from, and above, the rest of nature, which was made by God for their use and benefit. In a controversial essay on the historical roots of the ecological crisis, Lyn White Jr. argued that Christianity was the most anthropocentric religion in the world. As he put it, under Christianity "no item in the physical creation had any purpose save to serve man's purposes. And, although man's body is made of clay, he is not simply part of nature: he is made in God's image."[26] This view of humanity's pivotal place in the world has also been traced to the Christian idea of a Great Chain of Being (and before that, to the writings of Aristotle), which positioned animals and then plants on the lower rungs of creation. Women (who were believed to be less rational) and indigenous peoples (who were regarded as uncivilized) were also positioned closer to animals.[27]

The European creation of an experimental scientific method liberated from the constraints of religious prejudice—perhaps the major achievement of the Enlightenment—brought into being an understanding of the features and processes of physical nature that made it more malleable to human desires. The new picture of the world delivered by the so-called fathers of modern science, such as Isaac Newton, was best captured in the metaphor of a gigantic clock that could be disassembled into its component parts, examined, and manipulated. For the German sociologist Max Weber, the rise of scientific rationality led to the "disenchantment of the world," in the sense that everything became, in principle, knowable through rational explanation: metaphysical, animistic, and nonscientific understandings of the universe would fall by the wayside.[28] In their place, the new science unleashed a torrent of intellectual and technological innovations that then literally "powered" European economic, cultural, and political transformation. Robert Hughes in *The Shock of the New* captures the astonishing energy of one of the world-transforming waves of innovation, based on the power of science and technology for creation and destruction, that ran through the last quarter of the 19th century and into the start of the 20th century.[29] To paraphrase him: in 1887 Thomas Alva Edison invented the phonograph, the most radical extension of cultural memory since the photograph. Two years later, Edison and J. W. Swan, independently, developed the first incandescent filament light bulb. There followed the recoil-operated machine gun (1882); the first synthetic fiber (1883); the Parsons steam turbine (1884); coated photographic paper (1885); the Tesla electric motor, the Kodak box camera, and the Dunlop pneumatic tire (1888); cordite (1889); the diesel engine (1892); the Ford car (1893); the cinematograph and the gramophone disc (1894); X-rays, radio, the movie camera, and the principles of rocket drive (1895); the first airplane (1903); and the theory of relativity (1905).[30]

However, the European belief in progress via development was not without its critics, both within and beyond Europe. Indeed, every element of this phase of modernization has been challenged, albeit with varying degrees of success. The German philosopher Johann Gottfried Herder, in his unfinished *Ideas on the Philosophy of the History of Mankind* (1784–1791), was unimpressed by *Kultur* (meaning the evidence of human development) and argued that "nothing is more indeterminate than this word, and nothing more deceptive than its application to all nations and periods."[31] He also questioned the idea of the historical self-development of humanity as a unilinear process and what he called the European domination of the planet. As he put it, "Men of all the quarters of the globe, who have perished over the ages, you have not lived solely to manure the earth with your ashes, so that at the end of time your posterity should be made happy by European culture. The very thought of a superior European culture is a blatant insult to the Majesty of Nature."[32]

Herder was a leading voice in the Romantic movement, which emerged in the 18th century as a reaction against instrumental rationality and a rapidly industrializing Europe and North America. Industrialization was seen as a destructive force that severed "man" from a soul-nurturing, cleansing nature. The movement celebrated the aesthetic of a wild and sublime nature and was a major influence on the early wilderness preservation movements in New World regions such as North America, Australia, and New Zealand. The discourse of preservation was sharply juxtaposed to the discourse of resource conservationism or the "wise use" of natural resources that guided the emerging land-, forest-, and water-management bureaucracies in these regions. Whereas resource conservationism adopted a thoroughly instrumental view of the biophysical environment as a natural "resource" that should be rationally managed *for* development rather than recklessly exploited, preservationism argued that "wild nature" should be preserved *from* development, "saved" in national parks and reserves. These contrasting views were epitomized in the clash in the late 1890s between Gifford Pinchot, the first chief of the U.S. Forestry Service, and John Muir, the founder of the Sierra Club.

Yet the historical roots of modern environmental discourses are many and varied and can be found at both the center and periphery of empire. Indeed, Richard Grove, in his book *Green Imperialism*, argues that European environmental consciousness is not a new invention but that its wellsprings emerged in the context of imperial expansion between 1660 and 1860. He shows that

> this new kind of consciousness can be observed to have arisen virtually simultaneously with the trade and territorial expansion of the Venetian, Dutch, English, and French maritime powers. This new consciousness was characterized by a connected and coherent intellectual evolution of ideas and concepts which had complex yet identifiable roots in an Edenic and Orientalist search and in the encounters of a whole variety of innovative thinkers with the drastic ecological consequences of colonial rule and capitalist penetration.[33]

Complex and contradictory impulses governed this newfound environmental knowledge. Alongside new systems and technologies to capture, catalog, and interpret new species and systems—as Gascoigne terms it, "science in the service of Empire"—there also emerged an Edenic or paradisal view of the islands colonized, exploited, and then ecologically destroyed by these invading and trading cultures.[34] Lush tropical forests of islands such as Mauritius, St. Helena, and the Canary and Caribbean islands were soon flattened—and their indigenous peoples destroyed—to create plantations producing resources for their imperial masters. It was the rapidity of the transformation of these ecosystems that led to the emergence of a globalizing scientific discourse about the environmental impacts of colonization and to attempts by ecologically enlightened colonial administrations from the 18th century onward to conserve natural resources and protect endangered wildlife.

Some of the knowledge about ecological management of the crisis-ridden colonial plantations was derived from—and appropriated from—subjugated indigenous cultures. In British India, for example, Grove emphasizes the importance of adopted Indian views on the relationship between trees and plantation maintenance and climate change for the emergence of Western scientific understanding and administration of the colonized environments. Grove's view of the sources of European colonial environmental discourse is a deliberate antidote to the American academic perspective that the Yankees invented resource conservation.

What is most noteworthy about this early European phase of modernization is that it not only facilitated and legitimated environmental destruction but also generated diverse reactions against this destruction. As Donald Worster has shown, while the word *ecology* (the study of the interrelationship between living organisms and the inorganic world) was only coined in 1866 by the German biologist Haeckel, the underlying idea had a long history before it had a name.[35] This embryonic science evolved in a variety of different forms and sensibilities, which Worster has divided into an Imperial and Arcadian tradition. The former, exemplified in the work of the Swedish botanist and zoologist Carl Linnaeus, who introduced the modern taxonomy of classifying species, sought to establish "Man's dominion over nature" through the application of scientific reason. The latter, illustrated in the figure of the amateur field naturalist and the writings of Henry David Thoreau, was more romantic and sought to restore a peaceful coexistence between humans and other organisms. Imperial ecology was pressed into the service of the modernization process (e.g., resource conservationism) while Arcadian ecology reacted against it (e.g., preservationism).

Yet while Worster's highly schematic and oversimplified approach maps nicely onto the modernization versus anti-modernization binary, it struggles to shed light on the differences between "simple" versus "reflexive" modernization. As Peter Hay points out, Romantics were more interested in the inner self than the outer world or the social distribution of environmental goods and bads, and Romanticism is only one, perhaps minor, current in the broad stream of contemporary Western environmentalism.[36]

Two noteworthy points emerge from this long history. First, imperial conquests with global reach and subsequent industrial development led to the rise—well before the 20th century—of an international "environmental knowledge community" of administrators and scientists seeking to promote the rational management of natural resources and in some cases the protection of wildlife and environmental assets.

Second, these environmental ideas were variously absorbed by states through the creation of new administrative and regulatory systems to govern the management of natural resources and the environment, from forests and farmlands to energy sources and wastes. Yet the state's newfound environmental purpose was to stand in tension with its more fundamental role in promoting development, and this contradiction has not yet been resolved.

THE SHORT FUSE— GLOBALIZATION IN THE 20TH CENTURY

If the early European phase of modernization lit a long and slow-burning fuse leading toward global environmental change, the latter half of the 20th century saw the fuse burn much faster and brighter. Here we focus on the accelerated phase of economic globalization facilitated by the expansion and global integration of capitalist markets. Together with a rapidly growing world population, this new phase of global modernization has enabled a massive expansion in the spatial scope and volume of global production and consumption that has generated both systemic global environmental changes as well as a range of globally ubiquitous local environmental effects. The expansion and global integration of capitalist markets has many elements, including the growth of international trade, the transnationalization or "deterritorialization" of production, the growth in foreign direct investment (FDI), and the globalization of finance. However, we focus primarily on trade and the expansion, changing form, and shifting location of production and consumption, since they involve intended and unintended transfers of parts of the biophysical environment across national borders, and the accelerated exploitation of and impacts on local and global environments.

We have already commented on the emergence of Europe as the global center for manufacturing in the 19th century. However, in the late 19th century, the United States began its rise to international dominance as the center for industrial production—a position it retained throughout the 20th century. The development of Fordist methods of industrial production in the 1920s in the United States (and soon adopted elsewhere) saw the intensification of functional specialization with more finely orchestrated assembly lines, a more minute division of labor, and the standardization of production processes, components, and products that lowered the unit costs of production and therefore the price of products. As this model of production spread in the United States, Europe, Japan, and elsewhere, so too did productivity, exports, real wages, and mass consumption.

After 1950, increasing competition in the international market for manufactured goods also inaugurated a reorganization of production processes toward a post-Fordist model of flexible specialization. The squeeze on profits from more intensified competition saw the reorganization of production across different sites and in more flexible modules. This "unbundling" of the production process into global supply chains—to take advantage of cheaper land, infrastructure facilities, labor, and natural resources in different jurisdictions—increasingly drew developing countries into global production networks. Developments in information technology enabled the development of virtual production networks, a partial shift away from standardized production, and a rise in small-batch, niche manufacturing for niche markets.

In the 1960s, Japan, then other Asian economies—South Korea, Singapore, Hong Kong, and Taiwan, and later Thailand and Malaysia—emerged as major alternative locations for capitalist manufacturing (and consumption). During the interwar period, Europe and the United States shared 75 percent of world manufacturing production, but this fell to 50 percent by the start of the 21st century as other sites emerged.[37] By 2011, China had replaced the United States as the world's largest national source of manufacturing output (accounting for 19.8 percent, with the United States at 19.4 percent).[38] Other rising centers now include India, Indonesia, South Africa, Vietnam, Mexico, and Brazil.

These changes were accompanied and propelled by a spectacular growth in international trade. Between 1950 and 2008, the volume of international trade expanded by a factor of thirty-two and most of this growth has occurred in the past two decades.[39] Between 1992 and 2009, the value of internationally traded products had tripled, and international trade's share of global gross domestic product (GDP) had increased from 39 percent in 1992 to nearly 60 percent just before the 2008 global financial crisis.[40] World trade has also consistently grown faster than world economic output, which means that "each year a little bit more of the world's total economic production is produced in one country and consumed in another."[41] The growth in transnational commodity or "value chains" has been accompanied by a rise in intra-firm trade between the subsidiaries of multinational corporations, which accounted for around one-third of world trade by the end of the 20th century. By 2006, trade in intermediate inputs amounted to 56 percent of trade in goods and 73 percent of trade in services.[42]

In all, in the decades following World War II, we have seen a spectacular growth in mass production and consumption, facilitated by major shifts in the organization of production and trade, and an associated increase in the use of material resources. For instance, in the period from 1950 to roughly the present, annual global oil production increased from 10.4 million barrels a day to 80 million barrels a day.[43] Annual steel production grew from 200 million tonnes to 1,414 million tonnes, and car production increased from 8 million cars to 49 million each year.[44] Cement production rose from 133 million tonnes per annum to 3,600 million tonnes, wood production from 2,516 million cubic meters to 3,291 million cubic meters, and the yearly production of plastics from 1.3 million tonnes to 230 million tonnes.[45] In 1965, annual global coal consumption was 1,427.5 million tonnes oil equivalent (Mtoe). By 2010, this had risen to 3,555.8 Mtoe.[46]

There is no single driver propelling this growth in global economic activity, specialization, and exchange. The ceaseless quest for profits by firms (including banks and other financial institutions) carries its own in-built motivation for expansion and the exploitation of new markets, but the globalization of capitalist markets would not have been possible without technological, cultural, political, and especially regulatory change.

The rapid development of new forms of transport, such as jets and containerization in international shipping, and the information and communication revolution have made it possible to speed up global economic coordination, exchange, and travel. Cheaper mass transport, a growing global middle class, and the intensifying commodification of "exotic" cultures and places have helped to drive an expansion in tourism.

The removal of restrictions in trade in goods and services through new trade agreements and the deregulation of service industries such as banking have increased flows of foreign direct investment (FDI) and facilitated increased specialization and exchange. Alongside the expansion in the number and range of new multilateral trade agreements managed under the World Trade Organization, there has been a significant growth in preferential trade agreements (PTAs) in the post–Cold

War period that have facilitated the deeper economic integration and regulatory harmonization required for cross-border production networks, particularly between developed and developing countries. Over the past two decades, the number of PTAs has increased fourfold while the Doha round of multilateral negotiations has stagnated.[47]

Geopolitical developments have accelerated the expansion of international trade and global production and consumption. The collapse of the Soviet Union and economic reforms in China have integrated more producers and consumers around the world into capitalist markets and seen the emergence of "Factory Asia."[48] China's accession to the World Trade Organization (WTO) in 2001 further opened China's huge domestic market to exporters and foreign investors and paved the way for Chinese investment and exports to the rest of the world. A further expansion in trade can be expected following Russia's accession to the WTO in 2011 after an eighteen-year negotiation process.

The rise of the ideology of neoliberalism in the 1980s is also central to the story of accelerated economic globalization. The dominant consensus in the developed countries of the West in the immediate post–World War II period was to promote a more liberal, multilateral economic order in the aftermath of the Great Depression and World War II. John Ruggie described this consensus as "embedded liberalism" because it was contained and constrained by social norms that made it acceptable for governments to continue to intervene in their domestic economies to buffer them from external shocks and protect employment.[49] Embedded liberalism represented a compromise between the economic nationalism of the 1930s and a more open liberal economic order based on no, or minimal, restrictions on the international movement of capital, goods, services, and labor. However, the embedded liberal order broke down in the wake of the U.S. repudiation of the gold standard, the rise of stagflation, and the fiscal crisis of the state in the 1970s. Neoliberalism, spearheaded by the Reagan administration in the United States and the Thatcher government in the United Kingdom in the 1980s, became the new orthodoxy. As Robert Cox explained, this was to transform "states from being protective buffers between external economic forces and the domestic economy into agencies for adapting domestic economies to the exigencies of the global economy."[50] The neoliberal orthodoxy extolled the efficiency of private enterprise and sought to reduce the role of the state and public sector in all its forms. The effect of this radical economic reform agenda was to produce what Philip Cerny has called "the competition state," the primary task of which was to make economic activities located within the territory of the state more competitive in global terms.[51] Public policies were therefore increasingly judged in the context of comparative international competitiveness and the state's "traditional" welfare services and its "emergent" environmental services were seen to be brakes on economic growth.

The 1980s also saw the most ambitious round of trade negotiations since the establishment of the GATT in 1948. Launched in 1986, the Uruguay round of trade negotiations sought to reduce trade restrictions on agriculture products and textiles and extend the trading system into new areas such as services (e.g., education, insurance, and banking), intellectual property, and investment. The Uruguay round concluded with a raft of new agreements, managed under the umbrella of the newly created World Trade Organization.

The neoliberal phase of economic globalization has certainly intensified global environmental change, and we address these effects below. However, it was the Long Boom of industrialization during the 1950s and 1960s that had already produced all the signs of an emerging ecological crisis of global proportions. As we have seen, the pivotal turning point in our story is the late 1960s and early 1970s, which saw the simultaneous emergence of the idea of ecological limits to growth; the dawning of a global environmental consciousness; the appearance of global environmental actors, movements, green parties, and organizations; and the more systematic development of global and national environmental governance. We have also shown that these developments were the culmination of the much longer process of modernization.

This timing raises an interesting political question. Widespread ecological problems and the idea of ecological limits surfaced *before* the neoliberal phase of globalization. Why then did a more intensified phase of global environmental degradation follow?

Governments certainly had the collective capability to stop the shortening of the fuse toward a full-scale global ecological crisis, but in the 1970s the idea of ecological limits to growth was new, unconventional, challenging, and marginal. While it helped to set in motion a new global environmental research and regulatory agenda, galvanize a modern environmental movement, and prompt the formation of new green parties, it was generally anathema to both business and governments because it challenged one of the core activities of the modern state—the promotion of conventional (materials-based) economic growth. The tragedy is that the neoliberal phase of economic globalization, with its ideological opposition to and practical diminution of the capacities of the state, has made it more difficult for governments to enact the kind of comprehensive environmental regulation that would stop the burning fuse.

Both *Limits to Growth* and *Blueprint for Survival* had suggested that economic growth and environmental protection stood in a simple, zero-sum relationship: more growth meant more environmental degradation, so the solution to environmental degradation, they suggested, was to put a brake on growth. However, since the publication of *Our Common Future* (or the Brundtland Report), which catapulted the concept of sustainable development to the center of global environment and development debates, this simple zero-sum relationship has been fundamentally challenged.[52] Since Brundtland, the common consensus is that there is room for the development of virtuous synergies between capitalist economic development and environmental protection. However, whether this is so and how much room for compromise remains are matters of real and ongoing contention, as we discuss in following chapters.

Our Common Future defined sustainable development as "development that meets the needs of the present generation without sacrificing the needs of future generations."[53] The report also rejected the idea of absolute limits in favor of relative limits, which were a function of the state of technology and social organization, not just the ability of the biosphere to assimilate human activity. Sustainable development therefore could be achieved, it was argued, by integrating development and environmental considerations through the pursuit of greener rather than indiscriminate growth, which meant using less materials and energy and producing less waste per unit of GDP through constant technological innovation in production methods and product design. The Brundtland Report also confronted the increasing disparities in wealth and income between the developed and developing world and identified poverty eradication as a key prerequisite for sustainable development. It recommended more economic growth and trade, with faster growth rates in the global South to build capacity and catch up with the global North.

The Brundtland Report's sustainable development discourse was clearly much more comforting than the limits-to-growth discourse and was enthusiastically welcomed by governments (in the North and the South), business, and environmentalists. It provided the organizing principle for the United Nations Conference on Environment and Development (the "Earth Summit") held at Rio de Janeiro in 1992 and it continues to serve as the dominant "meta-environmental discourse" of the international community. It underpins the 1992 Rio Declaration on Environment and Development and a host of multilateral environmental treaties, including the United Nations Framework Convention on Climate Change (1992). Steven Bernstein has characterized the decisions and agreements made at the Earth Summit, including the endorsement of market-based environmental policy instruments, as "the compromise of liberal environmentalism." In effect, sustainable development was selected because it maintained that environmental protection was compatible with a liberal international economic order.[54]

Yet two problematic assumptions lie at the heart of the Brundtland Report's recommendations. The first is that *more* economic growth is necessary to achieve the wealth and capacity to pursue sustainable development and satisfy the needs of rich and poor globally. The second is that *green* economic growth in a capitalist-style global market economy will lead to an absolute decoupling of that international economy from the increasing material resource use and environmental degradation that would inevitably follow from continued conventional economic growth. There is no evidence to suggest that these two assumptions hold, especially in the context of the additional pressures associated with continuing population growth.

While the early limits-to-growth discourse overemphasized the tensions between capitalist economic growth and environmental protection, the dominant discourse of sustainable development has grossly underestimated them. Indeed, this discourse has increasingly speciated into a narrower and technologically focused discourse of "weak" ecological modernization that has reduced the sustainability quest to the pursuit of eco-efficiency (greater resource and energy efficiency, less waste output) as a means of enhancing national economic competitiveness and promoting economic growth.[55] It is no small irony that this "win-win" approach was endorsed by the "new report to the Club of Rome," called *Factor 4*, which maintained that wealth will likely double if resource use can be halved.[56] Although we show in chapter 5 that there are stronger and more critical accounts of ecological modernization, this technologically optimistic version gained strongest political and commercial support.

The core problem is that improvements in the *relative* eco-efficiency of firms, households, and national economies cannot translate into an *absolute* decrease in global environmental degradation in the absence of comprehensive and ambitious overarching sustainability limits supported at multiple levels of governance (local, national, and global). Yet if regulating production (the "supply" side of the equation) through the application of limits has so far proved to be a struggle, then addressing the forces that generate consumption (the "demand" side of the equation) has proved to be even more challenging. And so it is to the problem of consumption that we now turn.

CONSUMING THE PLANET

In the middle of the Pacific Ocean, far from any shore, a vast gyre of waste the area of Spain swirls slowly. Meanwhile at a supermarket in Alice Springs, a town in the central Australian desert, tourists from the United States, China, Germany, and Sweden buy prawns from Thailand, oranges from California, and garlic from Mexico, without concern for seasonal constraints or the processes by which these foods have been produced. Both are outcomes and instances of consumerism, the deeply embedded and now globally dispersed culture of endless demand, production, and hyperconsumption, which is propelling economic globalization and global environmental change. As Peter Dauvergne has demonstrated in mapping the ecological shadows of consumption across a range of case studies, from cars to beef and from refrigerators to fur coats, rising consumption is inflicting irreparable damage on the earth's ecosystems and atmosphere.[57]

Thomas Princen defines overconsumption as "that level or quality of consumption that undermines a species' own life-support system and for which individuals and collectivities have choices in their consuming patterns. Overconsumption is an aggregate level concept."[58] Here we show how the culture of globalized consumerism encourages overconsumption while rendering the ecological consequences of choices invisible to individual consumers.

FROM CONSUMPTION TO CONSUMERISM

We all engage in what may be termed "basic consumption," consuming parts of the environment to meet our basic needs. Securing sufficient food, clothing, and shelter remains the primary and dominant—even desperate—concern for people in many parts of the planet. Yet consumption is rarely reducible to the satisfaction of basic needs (the meaning of which vary through the ages and among different cultures), since humans also consume for other purposes, such as social status, the fulfillment of desire, and the need for belonging.

For example, there is a long history of ostentatious consumption that runs from ancient Egypt and the Roman Empire through the Renaissance to the present, through which natural resources were transformed into displays of wealth and statements of power. Fine clothes and jewelry, furniture, and other refinements came to define the status of some to the exclusion of others. From the 19th century onward, this hitherto exclusive realm of "luxury" consumption became increasingly economically accessible to a rising bourgeoisie, and the rise of mass production in the 20th century increased the range and affordability of consumer items for those on lower incomes. During the second half of the 20th century, an increasing number of consumers in developed and then developing countries expanded their consumption from the satisfaction of relatively basic needs to non-basic needs, from relatively durable goods to disposable goods, and from a relatively limited to a constantly expanding range of goods and services. Many of what were formally known as consumer durables (such as televisions, washing machines, refrigerators, printers) are now cheaper to replace than to repair and are discarded alongside paper tissues, paper cups, wooden chopsticks, and last season's fashions in our increasingly disposable world. This shift in the style, content, and pace of consumption signals the rise of consumerism as a new ideology and ephemeral practice for immediate gratification.

Zygmunt Bauman has characterized consumerism as "a type of social arrangement that results from recycling mundane, permanent and so to speak 'regime-neutral' human wants, desires and longing into the *principal propelling and operating force* of society that coordinates systemic reproduction, social integration, social stratification and the formation of human individuals."[59] Others, in more prosaic language, suggest that consumerism dupes consumers into "using money they don't have to buy things they don't need to impress people they don't like." Although Bauman considers consumerism now to be the underlying driver of key forms of production and consumption, accumulation, and environmental destruction, this powerful claim is lopsided. Consumption, production, and capital accumulation are mutually dependent, and the so-called sovereign consumer whose atomistic decisions are supposed to drive investment and production decisions in the competitive markets of neoclassical economic textbooks turns out to be a much more complicated and socially ensnared beast.[60] Here we return to Ehrlich's I=PAT formula, with a special focus on rising affluence.

Affluence is typically associated with a higher income and therefore a higher volume and quality of consumption relative to others. However, increasing or changing consumption is not simply a function of greater wealth but also changes in social structures and cultural context. Five changes—some long-standing, others recent—are constitutive of consumerism in this latest phase of modernity: secularization, the evolution of new forms of social abstraction and commodification, capitalism's imperative to create new markets, the underlying ideological drivers of progress and economic growth, and the transformations of identity.

Increasing *secularization* has created a space (or an absence) to be filled with new experiences and objects. The "absence of God" and the loss of heaven and the rewards of the afterlife have created a space for earthly indulgence without moral penalty and—simultaneously—a space of psychic despair to be plugged with things and experiences that might hold off the realization of mortality. Gone are the governing puritanical demands for austerity, modesty, endurance, the steady accumulation of wealth, and deferred gratification, and gone is the avoidance of the "sins" of pride, gluttony, greed, and envy that were associated with excessive or ostentatious consumption.

New forms of *abstraction and commodification* have enabled the exchange of commodities over extended time and space. The invention of charge cards, such as Diners Club in 1950 and American Express in 1958, and credit cards, beginning with BankAmericard in 1958, has enabled immediate rather than deferred gratification and accelerated consumer spending (along with consumer debt). The development of increasingly abstract systems for recording credit in its multiple and perilous forms has enabled investment and trade in resources and goods both for production and consumption over time (e.g., through long-term investments bearing interest or reward, through to futures markets speculating on potential economic behavior) and distance (electronic transfers of currency to initiate or pay for goods and services). Physical places for acquisition and consumption—shops, department stores, arcades, shopping centers, and stock markets—are now being displaced by abstract (cyber) spaces in which globally linked commodity markets can work nonstop and consumers can buy or play online from anywhere and anytime.

Third is *capitalism's drive to create new markets*, which has seen Western-style consumerism colonizing the planet, including its most populous countries—China and India—at the same time as "Factory Asia" has flooded Western economies with cheap consumer goods. The evolution of large internal markets within China and India is now at the point where, even if the associated resource-hungry and polluting regimes of production and "American-style" levels of consumption were confined to one of these countries alone, these would—in their current forms—produce a global environmental catastrophe.

Alongside the geographic expansion of capitalist markets is the increasing commodification of hitherto untouched life worlds. "Exotic" cultures and crafts are marketed for "home consumption" *ex situ*, or *en situ* through the rise of mass tourism. Valueless wild nature has been turned into a valuable commodity through nature documentaries and eco-tourism. Teenagers and children are swelling the ranks of global consumers. The transformation of the private sphere has also created new spaces, needs, and desires for consumable objects and new labor-saving technologies and services. Domestic lives, reshaped by the demands of work, are increasingly open to colonization by new forms of consumption aimed both to "save" time and effort and to meet new demands for leisure. Cars, refrigerators, vacuum cleaners, and microwaves liberate "domestic labor"—including to do the paid work required to provide the income necessary to buy these items or at least keep the credit card at bay. According to Bauman, the net effect of these developments is "the annexation and colonisation by consumer markets of the space stretching between human individuals."[61]

Like the rise of "developmentalism," the rise of consumerism is both infused with and legitimated by "simple" modernity's *ideologies of progress and of limitless economic growth*. The modern notion of progress through material improvement—*citius altius fortius* (faster, higher, stronger)—propels the invention of technologies, products, and processes designed to make life easier, more efficient, more productive. Gene technology searches for breeds of "super plants" while medical "advances" are now edging toward producing a new breed of post-humans whose physical and intellectual capabilities and longevity radically exceed those of ordinary humans, with their many imperfections and foibles. Intimately linked to this ideology of progress is the ideology of limitless economic growth, where the idea of an unbounded transformation of nature (including at its genetic core) is central to the achievement of human development, social welfare, and social harmony. Together, these dominant ideologies drive patterns of consumption in the developed world and those emerging in the developing world.

Finally, modern advertising has played a major role in *refashioning desire and identity* in ways that encourage unbridled consumption. Social critics such as Vance Packard (1957) and Stuart Ewen (1977), and more recently the popular television series *Mad Men*, have shed light on the role of the "hidden persuaders" of the advertising industry that, since the 1950s, has changed dramatically in its style of engagement with consumers. Advertisements in the 1950s became less "informational" and more about teaching us "how to consume," breaking taboos about meeting novel "wants" that related to "modern" styles of being.[62] The advertised product would contribute a sense of modern immediacy, sexual attractiveness, power, and style. Fashions in the form of "new season" clothes, "new models" of cars, radios, cigarettes, phones, and so on, were deliberately manufactured as transient markers of class and status ("affluence") and addictive generators of anxieties about social exclusion ("old-fashionedness"). This fashionable transience—along with the deliberately limited durability of many commodities—was intended to ramp up levels of consumption. New fashions, new products, and new markets depended on the creation of ideal and desirable images. From the perfect fruit to perfect lifestyles and perfect faces and bodies, this process has even led to the commodification and consumption of self-image (ranging from "self-perfecting" cosmetic surgery to carefully crafted ideal "identity representations" on Facebook and social networking sites).

A "SOCIETY OF CONSUMERS"

By the 21st century, in "modern, developed" societies and among the middle classes of the rapidly growing economies of the developing world, these cultural drivers of consumerism have led to the creation of what Zygmunt Bauman has called "a society of consumers" based on reconfigured relations and dependencies between restless human subjects whose identities increasingly are constructed by the new practices of consumption.[63] The mobilization of desire has produced a form of identity unknown before the latter part of the 20th century. Insatiability is now an essential part of consumerism's anxious subject; the markers of identity have become increasingly externalized and signaled through frenetic consumerist behavior, as for most acts of consumption, gratification is at best fleeting, making shopping an endless exercise in searching for the next new experience of "capture" and fulfillment. Compared to the traditional farmer or villager or even an early 20th-century city dweller, these new subject-consumers are almost another species.

To satisfy this new insatiability, not only raw materials and goods but also people are increasingly on the move globally. International tourism delivers seasonal consumers like a plague of invading locusts, swelling local populations. Some 935 million people—a number that increased despite the global financial crisis and is equivalent to almost one-seventh of the planet's population—traveled as tourists in 2010.[64] The world's most visited tourism destination that year was France, which, with an estimated total population of 65.3 million, hosted an additional 76.8 million tourists while the United States, with a population of 312 million, was visited by almost 60 million tourists.

Problematically, even modest efforts to restrict consumption—think of the struggles to enact laws to ban smoking—are not only seen as an assault on corporate activity but also as fundamental infringements of liberty and identity in the consumerist society, since freedom is increasingly equated with the practice of consumption, not just citizenship.

Of course, the environmental impact of overconsumption is inextricably linked to changes in population and technology in Erhlich's I=PAT equation. A growing global population, *ceteris paribus*, increases aggregate global consumption and even more so if an increasing number of that growing population are joining the consumer society. Likewise, new technological developments, such as more efficient forms of natural resource extraction and products that are designed to quickly become obsolete, increase energy use and the exploitation of natural resources along the commodity chain. However, technologies are best understood not as abstract tools but rather as socially embedded practices associated with particular forms of consumption and production. We therefore revisit the pointy end of the globalization debate and ask whether increasing global economic specialization and exchange (trade), which has enabled a massive expansion in production and consumption, is necessarily incompatible with ecological sustainability.

TRADING OFF THE PLANET

The intensification of international specialization and exchange in the latter half of the 20th century has provided consumers worldwide with a wider choice of products at lower prices. According to standard trade theory, this is as it should be. Overall economic output is increased if each country specializes in producing and trading in those goods and services in which it has a comparative advantage. This is also the guiding philosophy of the World Trade Organization: increasing international specialization and exchange delivers economic growth, absolute gains for all trading parties, and enhanced global welfare.

However, increasing international specialization and exchange has also generated a growing range of environmental impacts. Many of these impacts are experienced locally, at the point of extraction (e.g., deforestation and loss of biodiversity caused by land clearing for agriculture or mining), at the various sites of manufacturing along global commodity chains (e.g., production-related pollution of land, air, and water), and at the point of consumption (increasing energy use and emissions from the growing use of appliances) and final disposal (e.g., growing mountains of consumption-related pollution and waste, some of which is exported).

The lengthening in global supply chains has also increased the use of fossil fuels for transport, resulting in increased emissions from international shipping and aviation and especially nationally networked road transport.[65] The growing volume of international shipping has also increased coastal and marine pollution, including through the growing incidence of ocean dumping.[66] Alongside the trade in goods, there is also a growing trade in "environmental bads," such as the illegal trade in toxic wastes, endangered species (or parts thereof, such as tusks and horns), and timber from illegal logging operations. As we will see in chapter 4, trade also carries with it unwanted "stowaways" such as "alien invasive species" that are concealed, for example, in wooden packaging or the bilge water of ships. These species subsequently take root in new ecosystems, drive out indigenous species, and accelerate the overall loss of biodiversity.[67]

Global specialization and exchange also produces uneven development, along with an uneven geographical distribution of environmental impacts and risks. Developed countries tend to be "upstream" in global supply chains and have a relatively larger share of imported content in their exports, having "outsourced" the "dirty" (resource and energy intensive) production stages to "emerging" economies.[68] This has enabled certain countries in the global North to improve the quality of their biophysical environment at the expense of the global South in ways that blur responsibility for environmental problems.[69] The failure to account for the full but displaced costs of production and consumption creates the local illusion of progress toward ecological sustainability while maintaining high-consumption lifestyles through the purchase of cheap imports. It helps to explain why emissions from some developed countries declined over the period 1990 to 2008 while emissions from developing countries grew rapidly.

In effect, what appears on the surface to be balanced and reciprocal economic exchanges between firms and their subsidiaries in different countries turns out to be very unbalanced in ecological terms.[70] The problem of "unequal ecological exchange" is one variation of the more general problem of the "race to the bottom," which has been a stock-in-trade argument of environmental critics of economic globalization. Empirical research has highlighted the complexity of both push and pull factors influencing a firm's decision to relocate all or part of its production processes to other jurisdictions. Labor and resource costs, access and security of supply, the availability and quality of infrastructural support, and regulatory stability are among the many factors that participate in often highly expensive decisions to transfer production. Empirical evidence shows that relocation in response to environmental regulation becomes much more likely when environmental compliance costs form a relatively large share of the costs of production, and where such compliance costs are significantly lower in other jurisdictions, other things being equal.[71]

In all, there is strong evidence to link expanding global trade to increasing environmental degradation, including global environmental change. There is also strong evidence showing how trade facilitates an unequal appropriation of ecological space between richer and poorer countries, along with a skewed distribution of negative environmental impacts. Yet there is a vigorous debate between environmental critics of economic globalization, on the one hand, and trade economists and advocates of economic liberalization, on the other, over whether it is accurate to "blame" expanding trade and global economic integration for increasing global environmental degradation.

TRADE VERSUS THE ENVIRONMENT?

As we saw in chapter 1, many environmentalists have argued that it is economic globalization—particularly the expanding volume of international trade—that is driving global environmental degradation and they have targeted trade liberalization as aiding and abetting this degradation. However, these views are considerably at odds with the dominant consensus among political elites, including governments, economic advisors, the World Bank, IMF, and the director-general of the World Trade Organization.[72] According to this consensus, these arguments are misplaced, that neither economic globalization in general, nor trade liberalization in particular, is necessarily incompatible with environmental protection and that, on balance, liberalization is more likely to assist than hinder the quest for global environmental protection.

Proponents of trade liberalization typically argue that economic growth, facilitated by expanding international trade, is a necessary step toward sustainable development. As we have seen, the compromise of liberal environmentalism that underpinned the 1992 Earth Summit assumed that sustainable development was consistent with a liberal international economic order. This discourse claims that specialization and exchange not only enables the most efficient allocation of resources but also builds environmental capacity and increases wealth and income, which leads to a rising environmental demand and stronger environmental regulation. This argument is often represented in the inverted U-shape of the Environmental Kuznets Curve, which posits that in the early stages of development, when incomes rise from a relatively low base, environmental degradation will increase but eventually start to decrease as incomes continue to rise. To the extent that trade allows a net appropriation of biophysical capacity from South to North, such "unequal ecological exchange" would not be considered an unfair exchange but rather a necessary step in the development and capacity-building process that is preferable to no trade.

Some promoters of trade liberalization often accuse environmentalists (especially in the North) of practicing a form of eco-imperialism by seeking to impose their own environmental and ethical standards on the South, suggesting that differences in environmental standards are perfectly natural due to different cultural values and development priorities. According to this view, while it is legitimate to ensure that traded goods are safe and do not cause harm to consumers in importing countries, it is illegitimate for environmentalists in developed countries to dictate the processes and methods of production in developing countries.[73]

Proponents of trade liberalization argue that protectionism is not only inefficient but also bad for the environment, particularly environmentally perverse subsidies that distort prices and encourage the overexploitation of natural resources such as fisheries and forests or fossil fuels. At the turn of the century, perverse subsidies have been estimated to total around $2 trillion worldwide.[74] Conversely, the removal of restrictions on trade enables the global diffusion of environmental goods and services, such as wind turbines and solar panels. Finally, they argue that the environmental exemptions in the WTO rules allow national regulators to impose trade restrictions for environmental purposes if they are not a disguised form of protection.

These arguments underscore the uneven and sometimes contradictory environmental implications of international trade and point to the naïveté of a simple condemnation of increasing international specialization and exchange. Whether international trade produces net environmental damage or environmental benefits depends on a host of different economic factors, including the physical scale of trade (the *scale effect*), the types of technologies used in production and transport (the *technology effect*), the composition of a country's economy (the *composition effect*), the types of goods that are traded (the *product effect*), and the national and international *regulatory* context as well as underlying environmental factors.[75] These different factors can pull in different directions. However, the *net* environmental effects of shifts in all of the factors in the most recent phase of economic globalization are overwhelmingly negative, primarily due to the scale effect, and this has shortened the fuse leading to a full-blown global ecological crisis.

For example, in a major review of the relationship between trade liberalization and greenhouse gas emissions jointly conducted by the WTO and UNEP it was found that the scale effect overwhelmed the technology and composition effects.[76] This was found to be more pronounced in non-OECD countries than in OECD countries.[77] Indeed, the review of the empirical research found that more open trade will likely *increase* greenhouse gas emissions, in part because of the global nature of the externality. It was also found that the Environmental Kuznets Curve did not exist for greenhouse gas emissions.[78]

More general empirical research on the Environmental Kuznets Curve hypothesis has produced inconsistent results. While there is some evidence for the curve in OECD countries in relation to local pollutants, such as sulphur dioxide emissions, there is little evidence in non-OECD countries or in countries with considerable income inequality. Indeed, the "collapsing, compression and telescoping" of past development patterns and trajectories, particularly in large cities in the developing countries, has meant that environmental degradation is now experienced at lower levels of income in developing countries than developed countries.[79] At the same time, rising average incomes have not seen a corresponding improvement in environmental regulation or environmental quality in many developing countries.

We argue that the relationship between international trade and global environmental change is best understood through a critical political economy and political ecology lens rather than a neoclassical economic framework. The regulations that shape international trading and investment are not simply shaped by differences in the supply and demand of the "factors of production." They are also shaped by vast disparities in wealth, income, and bargaining power of different states, corporations, and consumers that have prevented the full internalization of the environmental costs of production, transport, consumption, and disposal along global supply chains. In effect, those with higher incomes and wealth have been able to appropriate and consume more biophysical space at the expense of those whose lives are curtailed by poverty, as well as future generations and nonhuman species, and they have not been held fully to account for the environmental load displacement and externalities generated from this appropriation.

However, this is not an argument against trade, or globalization in general. Rather, it is an argument for a different kind of regulation and a different kind of globalization that promotes sustainable production, consumption, and trade.

CONCLUSION—THE RETURN OF LIMITS

Ultimately, it is not trade or global economic integration *per se* but rather indiscriminate economic growth (i.e., economic growth that fails to account for the ecological costs of production and consumption) that is driving global environmental change. This indiscriminate growth has been accelerated with the global extension of capitalist markets, which have no in-built mechanism to ensure that the scale of national, regional, or global economic activity is compatible with the carrying capacity of ecosystems or biodiversity protection. This is an accountability failure of markets and states, consumers and citizens. Unsustainable trade continues because national environmental regulations are too weak or too weakly enforced or are not yet in place, and because the trading rules do nothing to promote sustainable production and consumption on an active and systematic basis.

Ecological economists have argued that, in theory at least, it is possible to decouple economic growth from environmental degradation. Herman Daly, for example, has argued that it is possible to have economic development under capitalist markets without increasing the physical scale of material-energy throughput in the economy, provided such markets are subjected to sustainability limits. Such a steady state economy would still be a very dynamic economy that would continue to "develop" but without growing in a physical sense in terms of the depletion of biophysical resources or production of wastes, just like planet Earth.[80] Under this model, the economy would take its proper place as "a wholly owned subsidiary of the environment, and not the other way around," to borrow former U.S. Senator Gaylord Nelson's famous quip.[81] This suggests that there is nothing necessarily unsustainable about either international or intranational economic exchanges if appropriate environmental regulatory systems (including cultural ones, based around self-regulation) are in place to discipline economic activity in ways that respect the capacities and limits of local ecosystems and the planetary boundaries discussed in chapter 1. In other words, an enhanced regulatory effect has the potential to enhance the technology effect, cancel out the scale effect, ensure environmentally safe products, and allow the principles of comparative advantage to be put to work on the bases of prices that account for the full ecological costs of production. However, as we show in chapter 5, this also requires a shift from simple to reflexive globalization—a shift that requires much more accountable markets, states, and governance systems in general.

CHAPTER 3

AN OVERHEATED PLANET

INTRODUCTION

In October 2009, just before the ill-fated United Nations climate conference in Copenhagen, the then President of the Maldives, Mohamed Nasheed, convened an underwater Cabinet meeting in the Indian Ocean. Dressed in scuba gear, seated around a table, and using hand signals and slates, the participants sent out an "SOS" message to the world to emphasize the perilous future of poor, low-lying nation-states if global greenhouse gas emissions continue on their upward trajectory. The Maldives Islands lie in the Indian Ocean some 430 miles from India and form the planet's lowest-lying country, with the lowest natural high point—some 2.3 meters or 7.5 feet above sea level. The population of 395,000 people live on 200 of the Maldives' 1,200 islands, most of which are no more than 3 feet above the waves. The Maldives are in the front line among the many low-lying island and coastal nations threatened with inundation by sea level rise due to global warming.[1]

Mohamed Nasheed's effort to publicize the potential obliteration of his nation highlights the central injustice of global warming: those least responsible for generating the emissions that produce global warming are likely to suffer its worst direct and indirect impacts. As we shall see, pinning down moral, political, and legal responsibility for human-induced climate change is no easy matter because it is the cumulative effect of a wide range of activities that began well before the problem was recognized and understood—and well before the acceleration of globalization in the late 20th century.

Since 1750, land clearing, farming, and burning fossil fuels for energy have made a discernible contribution to global warming. These activities have produced sufficient emissions to affect the planet's climate by increasing atmospheric concentrations of heat-trapping or "greenhouse" gases—in particular, carbon dioxide (CO_2) and methane. The atmospheric concentration of CO_2, the most important of the greenhouse gases, has increased from approximately 280 parts per million (ppm) pre-1750 to 400 ppm in June 2013.[2] Looked at from the point of view of Earth's CO_2 cycle, CO_2 (and other greenhouse emissions) have been entering the atmosphere at a rate beyond the planet's capacity to absorb them in its vegetation, soils, and oceans. Exceeding this "carbon budget" is, at its heart, the main cause of recent global warming.

There is no consensus about the level of global warming that constitutes "dangerous anthropogenic interference" in the Earth's climate. The critical value-laden questions we must ask are: How dangerous? Dangerous for whom? Or what? And when? Even 1.5 degrees Celsius average warming will, over time, cause seas to submerge low-lying regions and islands like the Maldives and will generate severe social and ecological impacts. Even lower levels of warming are already having considerable impacts and there are reasons to believe that current estimates of what are "safe" levels of emissions are too high.[3] Nevertheless, we have seen an international political consensus form around keeping the planet's average temperature increase to below 2 degrees Celsius above pre-industrial levels, to avoid the worst impacts of climate change. This requires keeping atmospheric concentrations of CO_2-e to below 450 ppm (CO_2-e includes CO_2 plus other greenhouse gases converted to an equivalent CO_2 metric in terms of radiative forcing).

It is estimated that the 2 degrees Celsius threshold will be reached when a further approximately 1 trillion tonnes of CO_2 are added to the Earth's atmosphere. Since 2000, we have already used almost half that quota. The atmosphere has already accumulated some 420 ± 50 giga-tonnes—a gigatonne is 1,000 million or a billion tonnes—of CO_2 since 2000, from human activities including deforestation.[4] Conservatively, only another 500 gigatonnes of CO_2 can be added if we are to have even a 75 percent chance of staying below this temperature threshold and thereby avoid causing "dangerous climate change."[5] Yet despite twenty years of international negotiations on climate change, and growing public and scientific concern, the rate and volume of greenhouse gases accumulating in the atmosphere continues to increase. At current rates of emissions, our planetary carbon budget is likely to be exhausted within the next two decades.

CURRENT CONDITIONS, FUTURE PROSPECTS

Although global warming is expressed in terms of a gradual increase in global average surface temperatures, this can translate into non-linear changes and significant regional and local variation in temperatures, with the rate of warming much faster in polar regions than in equatorial regions. Rising temperatures are also accompanied by increases in extreme or "wild weather," such as changes in the frequency, intensity, duration, and timing of droughts and wildfires, hurricanes and wind storms, precipitation (rain, hail, and snow) and floods, and extremities of both high and low temperatures—as well as gradual changes to sea levels and in the temperature and chemical composition of oceans.[6] In combination, these slow and abrupt changes will undermine human security—particularly in terms of food production, shelter, and economic stability—and will also accelerate rates of extinction in other species. Ultimately, the impact of climate change depends on the severity of the change and the capacity of a community or a species to adapt to that change.

In 2003, Sir John Houghton, former Head of the UK Meteorological Office and co-chair of scientific assessment for the UN Intergovernmental Panel on Climate Change (IPCC), warned that "the impacts of global warming are such that I have no hesitation in describing it as a 'weapon of mass destruction.' Like terrorism, this weapon knows no boundaries. It can strike anywhere, in any form—a heat wave in one place, a drought or a flood or a storm surge in another. Nor is this just a problem for the future."[7]

Impacts of this kind are already evident. Global average temperature has risen by almost 0.8 degrees Celsius since 1850. This may not seem much but the consequences have been increasingly dramatic. For instance, the twelve years of the 21st century (2001–2012 inclusive) rank among the fourteen warmest years in the 133-year period of record keeping.[8] Moreover, since the 1970s, each decade has been hotter than the one that preceded it. Seven countries—Armenia, China, Iran, Iraq, Kuwait, Republic of the Congo, and Zambia—set all-time temperature highs in 2011. For the continental United States, 2012 was the warmest calendar year on record, with 362 record highs and no record lows, according to the National Climatic Data Center.[9] These temperatures contributed to the ferocity of the major fires that swept across Oklahoma and of Hurricane Sandy, the second most costly hurricane in the United States after Hurricane Katrina in 2005. The Northern Hemisphere summer of 2012 also produced a record melting and shrinking of Arctic sea ice.[10] Scientists warn that if this rate of melting continues, the Arctic summer could be ice-free in a decade, triggering more extreme weather, the accelerated disintegration of the Greenland ice sheet, more rapid sea level rise, and the release of carbon dioxide and methane previously locked in the once frozen but now thawing permafrost in the Arctic and sub-Arctic lowlands.

In the southern hemisphere, the Australian summer of 2012–2013 was the hottest on record in terms of both maximum and mean temperatures.[11] The previous year, 2011, was Australia's second wettest year (over land) on record, producing a flood that covered an area the size of France and Germany combined, which cost the country between $AUD 15 and $AUD 30 billion in damages and lost production. 2011 also brought Thailand its most expensive disaster ever recorded: flooding submerged around one-third of its provinces and caused $US 45 billion damage (equal to 14 percent of Thailand's gross domestic product).[12]

The year before that—2010—was the equal warmest year on global historical record (equal with 2005, for global surface temperatures) and also the wettest. In 2010 Russia suffered its hottest summer since records began some 130 years earlier, including a nation-wide temperature record of 44 degrees Celsius (111 degrees Fahrenheit at Yashkul).

The month-long heat wave caused hundreds of wildfires that cost the economy some US$15 billion, an estimated 56,000 heat-related deaths, the declaration of a national state of emergency, and states of emergency relating to crop losses in twenty-eight provinces. Crop losses were such that the government suspended grain exports in order to limit price increases for consumers and associated political unrest.

If the volume of greenhouse emissions continues to grow at its present rate of global increase over the next two decades, our planet will experience average warming of at least 4 degrees Celsius (+7 degrees F) above preindustrial levels by the end of this century.[13] This increase is likely to have catastrophic consequences for food security, since farm output will be drastically curtailed with the increasing number and severity of droughts, floods, and storms causing crop failures. Such warming will lead to the permanent loss of summer sea ice in the North Pole (further accelerating warming); to a contraction or loss of glaciers in Asia and Latin America, causing dramatic water shortages for large, dependent populations; and to the eventual loss of land ice on Greenland and parts of the Antarctic. Warming of 4 degrees Celsius (+7 degrees Fahrenheit) is expected to lead to sea level rise of over seven meters over the next two centuries and seventy meters over the long term, causing the displacement of millions of people living in coastal settlements and low-lying islands. It is also expected to thaw frozen soils in the tundra/taiga regions, releasing methane (a highly active greenhouse gas) and causing a feedback loop that will further accelerate warming. Elevated levels of atmospheric CO_2 are also causing ocean acidification. Altered temperature, precipitation, wildfire, and storm patterns are expected to threaten or hasten the extinction of a significant percentage of the planet's terrestrial and marine species. Moreover, these various impacts and transformations are expected to continue to intensify and persist well beyond the 22nd century. It is highly likely—given the evidence of the past—that these global changes would cause significant social crises and conflict, including conflict over diminishing food and other resources.[14]

We focus on climate change as our first major case study for two reasons. First, as we noted in chapter 1, climate change represents the quintessential example of global environmental change, incorporating every one of the global dimensions we identified in table 1.1. It is *the* overarching ecological problem of our epoch since most other ecological problems are invariably made worse by climate change and are therefore lost causes in the longer term if we fail to deal with this overarching threat. Climate change also offers a powerful illustration of the links between different forms of globalization and global environmental change. The core task of this chapter is to track how this environmental change has unfolded through the prism of our four domains of globalization, including their various precursors.

Second, climate change presents an almost unparalleled challenge for global governance, from the planetary to the local. The Earth's atmosphere is a global space that is owned by no one. Although it provides common benefits and, like the oceans, is often included in the list of "global commons," it has not been effectively governed for the common good.

Over the past half century, the atmospheric commons have been affected by nuclear fallout from atmospheric testing, ozone-depleting chemicals, and climate-altering emissions. Although treaties have been developed to govern and limit each of these unintended outcomes of human activities, they have so far had little success for the last and most significant global problem. Instead, we see an unfolding "tragedy of the commons" of global proportions and uneven and unjust localized impacts, as the Presidents of the Maldives and Palau have sought to highlight. Two decades of international climate negotiations and national climate policy development have produced diminishing returns, and the window for an effective response is rapidly closing. We assess the state of climate governance in the final section of this chapter.

Climate change is widely understood to be a global problem that requires global action for its resolution. But while many of the current and projected impacts on the atmospheric and marine commons—caused by changes in atmospheric concentrations of various gases and in ocean chemistry—are themselves truly planetary in their extension, they mainly arise from the incremental local actions such as driving cars, felling forests, producing goods, or using household appliances. Many climate-related impacts are also ultimately local, with very substantial variations from place to place—as the Maldives government sought to highlight. These complicated global and local linkages present a tough challenge for global climate governance, with the intertwined issues of accountability and justice at its core.

Following the structure of the previous chapter, we begin by looking at climate change in relation to the long fuse of modernization, followed by the short fuse of recent globalization. In looking at the complex interactions between the changing biophysical environment and the various domains of globalization that are producing and responding to global warming, we find that the histories in each domain fit together in surprising ways.

THE LONG HISTORY OF GLOBAL WARMING

The history of human-induced climate change involves an intertwining of two complicated stories about globalization. One is a narrative about the development and global diffusion of technological innovations and processes of industrialization, both of which are key dimensions of the broader process of modernization. The other is a tale about the long, isolated gestation of scientific ideas about the planet. The two stories only unite during the recent postwar period of hyperindustrialization and accelerated globalization.

We begin with industrialization, focusing on the activities, technologies, and fuels that have manufactured a warming planet. We then follow the parallel rise of a global scientific community that has created the highly abstract science of climate change and that now serves as the "chief informant" enabling us to understand the overarching environmental problem of our age. These two histories, and the contest between scientific awareness and the deeply embedded use of fossil fuels in economies around the world, are among the most important elements in the current struggle over climate change governance, to which this chapter will finally turn.

MANUFACTURING GLOBAL WARMING

When, in 1848, the German political philosopher Karl Marx wrote, "All that is solid melts into air," he was reflecting on how the forces of modernization, associated with the social and economic forces of capitalism, were leading to the transformative breakup of the old certainties and restraints of traditional societies.[15] Little did he realize that the burning of coal—which was fueling the rise of industrial capitalism—was producing a gaseous residue that literally "melted into air," with unintended, unforeseen, long-term, and revolutionary transformative consequences for the global atmosphere and the Earth's species and ecosystems.

Successive energy revolutions involving the use of fossil fuels—first coal, then oil and gas—have, in combination with growth in population and energy demand, been the main contributors to human-induced climate change. However, these energy revolutions cannot be understood in isolation from the broader processes of industrialization, urbanization, and modernization that have both produced, and been propelled by, technological change. By the time science enabled us to understand the problems associated with fossil fuel use, these processes had joined forces with a globalized capitalism in ways that have made it especially hard for politics and governance to respond to the science.

THE AGE OF COAL

Coal was first used for domestic heating and smelting in Europe, and specifically England, in the 13th century. Decried as a foul substance that "infected and corrupted" the air, it remained out of favor in England until the 16th and 17th centuries, when demand for it grew in response to two new pressures. First, the overharvesting of forests for ship building caused wood shortages and increased its cost as a fuel, making coal more economically competitive at a time when urbanization was accelerating. Then Europe entered the Little Ice Age—a period extending from around 1550 to 1850—and the demand for heating grew accordingly. By 1700, coal production in Britain was perhaps ten times what it was in 1550, and around five times more coal was mined there than in the rest of the world combined.[16]

Once easily accessible alluvial coal deposits were exhausted, deeper mines became a necessity. But as mines passed below the water table, drainage and dewatering—pumping out underground water—became critical practical and technological problems, especially in nations such as Britain, which were increasingly dependent on coal. At first, horse-powered, wind-powered, and occasionally water-powered pumps were used for dewatering, but none proved sufficient to the challenge and so, while demand increased, mine output began to fall. Then, in the first decade of the 18th century, Thomas Newcomen transformed the newly invented piston steam engine to enable it to pump water. By the

1760s, hundreds of coal-powered Newcomen engines were pumping water from coal mines all over England and Scotland. James Watt then further improved this invention: his first two coal-fired steam pumps were employed in 1776 to pump water from a coal mine and to blow the bellows in an iron foundry.

Linking coal to the steam engine underpinned the Industrial Revolution by greatly increasing machine power and productive capacity. Two further refinements then completed the industrial foundations of what we can recognize as the "Modern Age." The first was the adaptation of Watt's steam engine to transport coal, followed by people and all manner of produce. In 1825, George Stephenson's locomotive first hauled coal along a twenty-six-mile railway between Darlington and Stockton and, in 1830, commercial passengers on the Liverpool and Manchester railway. As Stephenson pushed the engine to a record thirty-five miles an hour, passengers were able to transcend the limitations of animal-power with a force and speed that compressed space and time and signaled a step forward in the seeming "conquest" of nature. This invention truly "marked a moment of acceleration in the speed of industrialization, and it fed the growing myth that technological progress was unstoppable."[17] Coal-fired trains and steamships soon linked continents, increasing the speed and volume of traffic in people and goods.

The second refinement was the invention of the turbine, which harnessed coal-fired energy to the generation of electricity. Coal gas was already widely used for lighting in industrialized cities in the latter part of the 19th century, but the development of the highly efficient steam turbine for electricity generation by the start of the 20th century ensured the place of coal as a major source of energy for industrial power and urban light, and as the basis for the boom in 20th-century production and consumption.

In all, the Age of Coal and the Industrial Revolution are inextricably linked. By the 1780s, coal was used to make coke to fuel furnaces producing cast iron, and Britain became the world's most efficient and largest manufacturer of iron. The British coal industry expanded tenfold between 1700 and 1830 (when it produced 80 percent of the world's coal), and coal production thereafter doubled between 1830 and 1854.[18] By 1848, the year of failed revolutions, Britain produced more iron than the rest of the world in total and had become the workshop of the world. While timber was plentiful in the United States, its use there as an industrial fuel was also quickly replaced by coal, which produced greater energy per unit of mass. In the United States, coal consumption doubled each decade between 1850 and 1890, and in the late 1890s, the United States became the world's largest coal producer—ahead of the United Kingdom and Germany in third place. By 1900, coal provided 71 percent of the United States' energy—while wood provided 21 percent and oil, natural gas, and hydropower less than 3 percent each.[19]

The technological, economic, and social transformations accompanying the Age of Coal were rapid and far-reaching. Barbara Freese describes life in mid-19th century Manchester, then perhaps the world's largest manufacturing center, thus:

> Coal made the iron that built the machines the workers operated as well as the factories they worked in, and then it provided the power that made the machines and factories run. Coal gas provided the lights the workers toiled under, letting their workday start before dawn and end after dusk. When they left the factory doors, they would walk through a city made of coal-fired bricks, now stained black with the same coal soot that was soiling their skin and clothes. Looking up, they would see a sky darkened by coal smoke; looking down, a ground blackened by coal dust. When they went home, they would eat food cooked over a coal-fire and often tainted with a coal flavour, and with each breath, they would inhale some of the densest coal smoke in the planet.[20]

Now, in the second decade of the 21st century, the same description can be applied with equal force to life in over a dozen Chinese cities. Globally, coal is the major source for stationary energy in most major industrialized and industrializing countries, supplying around 70 percent of total energy requirements.[21]

THE AGE OF OIL

The other major fossil fuel contributing to global warming has been oil (and, more recently, gas), as an energy source for power, lighting, transport, and to a lesser extent, heating. In ancient times oil, in the forms of bitumen and tar, was taken from seepages or hand-dug pits and used to caulk vessels and as medicine. Only in the mid-1800s was it sought and used in greater quantity, when a small crude oil industry developed in Eastern Europe, where it was refined into kerosene and used for lighting with special glass lamps designed for this purpose. When an American, George Bissell, innovatively employed a drilling technology developed by the Chinese several thousand years earlier to bore for subterranean salt deposits, oil could be recovered in large quantities. The combination of Eastern European lamps, Chinese drilling technology, and growing demand for an alternative fuel caused by the declining availability of sperm whale oil led to the world's first successful oil well being sunk in Pennsylvania in 1859.

By 1862 American annual production—at that time also global annual production—had risen to 3 million barrels, climbing to 3.6 million barrels by 1866. But it was not until the problems of refining oil in bulk to make kerosene, and transporting it by pipeline, rail, and sea, were solved that oil became a cheap alternative to other fuels for lighting. In 1861, the first shipment of oil was sent to Europe by sea, beginning a long upward curve in international trade to meet demand for the fuel, which was soon to become a geopolitical resource and a key dimension of U.S. energy and foreign policy.

As demand increased, alternative sources were found. In Russia, drilling began in the early 1870s. Russian oil production reached some 10.8 million barrels a year in the mid-1880s and 23 million barrels by 1888, while American production climbed to around 30 million barrels. The development of oil tankers and the opening of the Suez Canal to oil traffic in 1892 further expanded the opportunities for sea trade. Growth in demand and increased opportunities for profit encouraged exploration and speculation. Oil boomed in Texas in 1901; oil fields were discovered in Indonesia in the 1880s, in Latin America in the 1900s, and the Middle East in the 1930s. Substantial oil supplies seemed to secure a passport to national economic development—either directly through the new forms of industrialization or via wealth derived from export (although it later proved to be a curse for many developing countries).

The demand for kerosene collapsed at the end of the 19th century as urban centers initially adopted gas for artificial lighting and cooking, and then coal-fired electricity. However, the invention and refinement of petrol- and diesel-fueled internal combustion engines, and the automobile or "horseless carriage," created an alternative source of demand for oil that was rapidly internationalized.

As we saw in chapter 2, mass production made cars affordable, advertising made them desirable (not only for the leisure-oriented middle class but also the working class), and the modification and auto-dependent suburbanization of cities made car use easier and, in some cities, virtually essential. The manufacture and use of the multiplicity of commodities associated with automotive transport rapidly became a central social and economic feature of all large developed nations in the 20th century. For instance, in 1900 there were around 8,000 cars in the United States, which would become the 20th century's center of car culture. By 1950, that number had grown to 43 million, and to 248.5 million in 2009.[22] In 2010 alone, 78 million cars and light vehicles were produced for sale around the globe, including 18.3 million in China, 9.6 million in Japan, 7.8 million in the United States, and 5.9 million in Germany.[23] Globally, transport—including cheap mass air transport—now produces some 13 percent of all greenhouse emissions.

The Age of Oil overlaid and amplified the modernizing effects of the Age of Coal. The unearthing and harnessing of massive amounts of fossilized prehistoric solar energy have dramatically reconfigured the pace and intensity of production and consumption and transformed urban and rural life. Instead of a team of men or horses, diesel-powered engines with hundreds and thousands of "horsepower" or "manpower" now extract ores, haul earth, plow fields, lift loads, transform raw materials, and transport humans and goods. These oil-powered engines speed minerals, timber, grain, and manufactured goods in bulk to distant markets via road, rail, sea, and air. These same engines create skyscrapers illuminated day and night by thousands of fossil-fuel fired lightbulbs or fluorescent tubes. Oil has also made new, lethal, rapid forms of mechanized warfare possible. Troops are deployed by trains and trucks; machine guns are oiled; warships, trucks and tanks, fighter planes, and bombers are fueled and sent into battle. In all, oil and coal now power, lubricate, and light most aspects of everyday life in the developed world. Social, economic, and military dependency on oil evolved quickly in the 20th century and just as quickly became deeply embedded in the transnational commodity chains that underpin contemporary patterns of production and consumption.

It is important to recognize that this new dependency has not been driven by some authorless force called globalization. Rather, it has been driven by a wide variety of different social agents including governments, the military, oil companies and oil cartels such as the Organization of Petroleum Exporting Countries (OPEC), car companies, property developers, and, above all, by the responses of eager consumers. All were initially unwitting generators, in some cases literally, of the problem of global warming. However, now that the problem has been revealed, many states, corporations, and communities are still prepared to defend their entrenched interests and resist efforts to work toward a low-carbon economy and society. Access to oil still remains a major strategic and security issue, just as access to cheap coal is seen as a source of economic strength, despite the emergence and growth of the "leave it in the ground" movement in many countries.[24]

Despite the rapid global growth in use of renewable energy (such as wind and solar power), consumption of fossil fuels continues to soar. Global production of oil was 3 million barrels in 1862. By contrast, in 2012—150 years later—the IEA forecasts global oil demand to climb to 89.9 million barrels *per day*, or 32 billion barrels per annum—a new peak, signaling a rapid rebound from the recession-driven declines of 2008–2009.[25]

Deposits of coal and oil are found on every continent and the dispersed location of fossil fuels facilitated their global use once technologies for transporting and using them became commercially accessible. Unlike coal, however, significant oil and gas fields are far more geographically concentrated and no longer found in sufficient quantities in the United States and China to meet the needs of the planet's two biggest oil users. Both now are the world's first and second largest oil importers, respectively, and dependent on external supplies.

By contrast China, the world's largest coal user, produces over three billion tonnes per annum and is virtually self-sufficient, although its growing demand is making it increasingly reliant on imports, while the United States, the second largest user of coal, is self-sufficient and a net exporter.[26]

Cheap and abundant oil has been central "to the vigor and growth of the American economy and to the preservation of a distinctly *American* way of life," including a car culture that equates private automobiles with personal freedom.[27] During the Cold War, oil was used by the United States as a strategic resource in pursuing its strategy of containment and in the overall management of its Western leadership.[28] Access to crude oil remains a major strategic concern, particularly for the

United States. Oil provides nearly 40 percent of its total energy needs (including 94 percent in transportation and 40 percent in industry). The United States became a net importer in late 1940s, and its dependence on oil and other liquid fuels reached a peak of 60 percent of net imports in 2005, although by 2012 this had fallen to around 41 percent mainly due to the growth in U.S. oil and gas production.[29] China became a net importer of crude oil in 1996.[30] As global oil supplies appear to have peaked in the first decade of the 21st century, competition for this resource will intensify and oil prices increase unless significant improvements occur in global energy efficiency and energy conservation, unconventional oil sources become viable, demand falls, or a transition to non-fossil fuel energy sources occurs.

From the outset of attempts to mitigate climate change in 1992, the struggle over emissions targets and controls has been intimately tied to the "power" struggle over energy sources, and global military and economic influence, particularly between the United States, Russia, and now China. The oil fields of the Middle East in particular, and the shipping lanes and pipelines leading from them, have become objects of high and increasing strategic focus, national security, international contest, and sometimes warfare. Those countries without domestic (fossil) energy resources have had to import them in order to develop according to the energy model that now prevails globally.

Despite twenty years of climate negotiations, the price of fossil fuels remains relatively cheap compared to renewable energy sources, not only because the longer-term social and ecological impacts of their use are not factored into their price but also because they are heavily subsidized. According to the IEA's estimates, subsidies for fossil fuel consumption rose from $300 billion in 2009 to $409 billion in 2010 despite a commitment by the G20 in 2009 to phase out these environmentally perverse subsidies.[31] The relatively low price of fossil fuels has facilitated the continuing growth in their international trade and use over the past century.

The foregoing brief history should make it clear that fossil fuels have been central to the Industrial Revolution and to the rise of great powers. While Britain initiated and led this revolution, by the late 19th century the United States had overtaken it as the world's most significant industrial power before becoming the world's only superpower at the end of the Cold War. China, India, and other developing countries are showing no signs of forsaking fossil fuels in their development plans, despite investment in renewables, as they also seek to achieve or consolidate economic prosperity and Great Power status in the 21st century.

This brief history gives a sense of the extent to which fossil fuels have become structurally embedded in the material practices—and also the aspirations—of developed and developing economies and their inhabitants, of the interlocking relationships between those economies, and therefore of the structural and manifest political power of the interests associated with the use of fossil fuels. It also points to one of the greatest sources of dispute between developed and developing countries, relating to the historical responsibility for global warming and the benefits accrued over those earlier centuries. A central argument of China and the G77 has been that the nations of the "developed world" amassed their wealth through industrial development fueled by coal and oil. In doing so, they inadvertently (and more recently, knowingly) overused their share of the global atmospheric commons and have left the planet an unintended global legacy of climate change for which they are disproportionally responsible (figure 3.1).

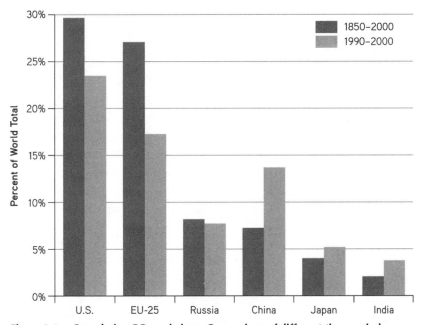

Figure 3.1. Cumulative CO_2 emissions: Comparison of different time periods
Source: Kevin A. Baumert, Timothy Herzog, Jonathan Pershing. 2005. "Navigating the numbers." World Resources Institute, p.33

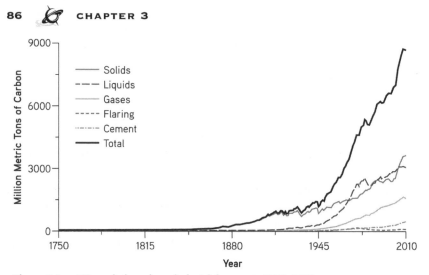

Figure 3.2. CO_2 emissions from industrial sources 1750–2010

Source: Boden, T.A., G. Marland, and R.J. Andres. 2012. "Global, Regional, and National Fossil-Fuel CO_2 Emissions." Carbon Dioxide Information Analysis Center, Oak Ridge National Laboratory, U.S. Department of Energy, Oak Ridge, Tenn., U.S.A. doi 10.3334/CDIAC/00001_V2012

Tom Boden and his co-researchers report that, since 1751, approximately 356 billion tons of carbon have been released to the atmosphere from the consumption of fossil fuels and cement production (figure 3.2). Half of these emissions have occurred since the mid-1970s.[32] Developing countries argue that countries with a historical responsibility for emissions and therefore climate change have a greater burden of responsibility for combating climate change and for assisting the development of those countries that will be denied the opportunity to enjoy the same access to the global atmospheric commons. These claims have been variously contested and reframed by certain developed countries. As we shall see, the United States, in particular, has rejected all charges of historical responsibility and focused its climate diplomacy on the future growth in emissions and on brokering a deal based on legal symmetry of commitment and shared prospective responsibility for mitigation.

Finally, mention must be made of the contribution made by agriculture and land clearing to climate change. It is estimated that between 1850 and 1990 some 124 billion tonnes of carbon were added to the atmosphere through changes in land use (predominantly the clearing of vegetation), about half that released by the burning of fossil fuels. About 108 billion tonnes came from the clearing of forests. Of this, approximately two-thirds came from tropical forests and the remainder from temperate zone and boreal forests. Another 16 billion tonnes was released from nonforested lands, mainly through cultivation of grassland soils.[33] Agriculture is also a significant source of the highly potent greenhouse gas methane.

The IPCC's Fourth Assessment Report noted that "in 2004, energy supply accounted for about 26% of greenhouse gas emissions (GHGs), industry 19%, gases released from land-use change and forestry 17%, agriculture 14%, transport 13%, residential, commercial and service sectors 8% and waste 3%."[34] Moreover, reflecting the influences of both global economic expansion and the growth in material demand accompanying population growth, "emissions of the [six major] GHGs . . . increased by about 70% (from 28.7 to. 49.0 $GtCO_2$-e) from 1970–2004 . . . with CO_2 being the largest source, having grown by about 80%. The largest growth in CO_2 emissions has come from power generation and road transport. Methane (CH4) emissions rose by about 40% from 1970, with an 85% increase from the combustion and use of fossil fuels. Agriculture, however, is the largest source of CH4 emissions."[35]

UNDERSTANDING CLIMATE CHANGE

We have argued that the material practices that have produced global warming emerged in the 18th century, were refined in the 19th century, and were widely and rapidly adopted around the world in the 20th century. However, their climatic consequences were not recognized until an intellectual framework was created for understanding the relationship between emissions-generating activity, changing concentrations of atmospheric GHGs, global warming, and climatic impacts.

We live with weather from day to day. Asked about longer-term changes in weather, we draw on anecdotal evidence or our patchy memories of our experience of hot days, wet days, storms, droughts, or floods. In some cultures, we also call on written records of variable accuracy, which transmit traces of events that occurred in time beyond living memory.

By contrast, "climate" or "climate change" refers to long-term weather patterns and changes. Whereas changes in the weather are experienced on a day-to-day basis in particular places, "climate" and "climate change" are abstract constructs for comprehending patterns of change over different territorial scales, based on theories that organize and interpret an accumulation of longer-term observations, including primary data drawn from weather monitoring systems, and physical evidence about Earth's systems. "Climate change" in this sense is thus a thoroughly modern construction that is increasingly global in its span. Indeed, it is the abstract nature of climate science that makes it vulnerable to climate change deniers who exploit the disconnect between the immediate localized, "lived" experience of weather and the abstract historical reconstructions or future projections of climate change offered by sophisticated global climate models. They are able to draw on local experience to dispute and undermine abstract scientific claims that are, by their nature, beyond individual human experience.[36]

The capacity even to puzzle about such issues itself depended on the new spirit of questioning and empirical inquiry unleashed by the Enlightenment, and the concomitant invention of instruments to survey, record, and manipulate data about the physical environment to support the formulation and testing of more abstract theories. The development of a scientific understanding of climate change developed out of intersecting transnational scientific lines of inquiry about weather and climate, about the chemical and physical properties of air and heat, and about the Earth's geological history (including its Ice Ages) well *before* evidence of *human-induced* climate change arose.[37]

The emergence of a scientific interest in weather and climate was predicated on, and encouraged by, the broader ambitions of the Enlightenment. Considerable attention was paid to both matters in the context of emerging and competing explanations of the apparent success of certain races, cultures, and then nations, over others. At the start of the 1700s, intellectual concern about weather and climate was infused by the desire to answer the question: why was it that European (white) races seemed to be culturally and materially superior to those from elsewhere? Initially, leading Enlightenment thinkers such as Montesquieu and Hume took opposing positions—either attributing European development, deterministically, to the invigorating effects of a temperate and cold climate, or in the latter case, denying climate such influence.[38]

Concern about climate and weather was also associated with the historically new "nation-building" project. For instance, British weather and the "national climate" were regarded as more conducive to the progress of British civilization and the growth of its economic power.[39] However, this concern also extended to more practical considerations. Knowledge about weather was sought in order to better understand the influence of, to predict, and to adapt to weather's impacts on agriculture and transport (especially at sea). Starting with the Italians in 1654, and then the English, French, Germans, Russians, and Americans, "gentlemen scientists" and their emerging scientific societies began systematically to gather meteorological data and publish their interpretations of rainfall, temperature, and weather patterns more generally, in the hope of producing a rational, scientific picture of weather and climate—and to justify their hopes for national success.

By the mid-19th century, meteorological records, rather than memories and "ancient authorities," provided the basis among scientists for conjecture about climate. As James Fleming notes, "The establishment of national weather services and applied climate networks [by the 1850s] was also fundamental to the emergence of effective international cooperation in meteorology and climatology. . . . International cooperation and an international bulletin of weather observations began in the 1870s."[40] The first international meteorological conference occurred in Brussels in 1853, and congresses in Vienna and Rome led to the establishment of the International Meteorological Organization (IMO) in 1873.

The creation of such an empirically oriented, transcontinental scientific endeavor and weather-observational network depended on and contributed to the development of internationally standardized scientific instruments, concepts, and empirical approaches for considering climate and weather. The development of instruments with which to measure temperature and rainfall—the thermometer and the barometer were invented in the 1600s and standardized in the 1700s—enabled the collective project of weather mapping to develop.

Already in the 19th century, scientific thinkers such as American geophysicist William Ferrel were beginning to consider atmospheric and marine processes on a planetary scale. These 19th-century scientists set in motion the evolution of a global climate-scientific epistemic community—a planet-wide body of scientists with their associated monitoring and analytical systems—that enabled the development of a more abstract understanding of changes in the Earth's climate.

A second, independent line of scientific inquiry critical to the climate change narrative also emerged in the 19th century through the work of two scientists whose efforts focused on temperature and atmospheric chemistry and physics. In 1824, the Frenchman Joseph Fourier provided the first rudimentary observation of the "greenhouse effect," in which the sun played a major role in determining terrestrial temperatures. This understanding was further developed by John Tyndale who, in 1859, investigated the different radiative properties of various gases—their ability to absorb or transmit heat. He determined that water vapor and CO_2 absorbed thermal radiation and therefore recognized that both were crucial in the role of atmosphere in regulating diurnal and global temperatures.

A third line of inquiry also contributed to the articulation of the puzzle of climate change. Ever since Charles Lyell had established that geological forces (rather than the hand of God) had transformed the face of the planet over "deep time," scientists had puzzled about the source of these forces. Specifically, they puzzled over the processes that drove the advance and retreat of glaciers that were recognized to have shaped many European landscapes. Clearly climates *did* change over "deep" or geological time, so what caused these changes? And was the planet stable, or warming or cooling (and therefore threatened by a new Ice Age)? In 1865 Lyell even approached Tyndale for his opinion about the possible influence of changes in the Earth's orbit on the advent of ice ages in one hemisphere or other.

In 1895, Svante Arrhenius—while puzzling over the problem of the causes of glaciation—used Tyndale's work to estimate the consequences of changes in atmospheric concentrations of CO_2 on global temperatures, and concluded that a change of about 40 percent in the atmospheric concentration of CO_2 might be responsible for initiating glacial advance and retreat.[41] He eventually calculated that "any doubling of the percentage of CO_2 in the air would raise the temperature of the earth's surface by 4 degrees [Celsius]; and if the CO_2 were increased fourfold, the temperature would rise by 8 degrees."[42] Nils Eckholm in 1899, and later Thomas Chamberlin, also nominated atmospheric CO_2—and emissions from fossil fuels—as a possible future source of climate change.

For the first four decades of the 20th century, climate science remained speculative, unsettled, and contested internationally, with a range of competing theories proposing influences for long-term climate change and for Earth's intermittent Ice Ages. For instance, in 1920, Milutin Milanković proposed long cyclical changes corresponding to changes in the aspect of the Earth's orbit as the prime cause of these Ice Ages. Koppen and Wegener nominated continental drift. Others—with little or no evidence to support them—proposed volcanic dust, cosmic dust, and changes in solar activity (especially sunspots). Chamberlin proposed changes in ocean circulation.

The turn toward a scientific narrative emphasizing the importance of fossil fuels for climate change began with Guy Callendar's work during the 1930s. In a particular paper he read to the Royal Meteorological Society in 1938, he proposed that the burning of fossil fuels over the past half century had generated around 150 gigatonnes of CO_2, three-quarters of which had remained in the atmosphere—an increase of 6 percent in atmospheric CO_2 since 1900. Callendar suggested that the radiative properties of this additional CO_2 had caused a measurable increase in global temperature of about a quarter of a degree Celsius over the same period.[43] He later estimated a 10 percent rise in atmospheric CO_2 of 30 parts per million (from 290 ppm to 320 ppm) had occurred from the pre-1900 period to 1935, and predicted the rate of increase would accelerate due to accelerating fossil fuel use.[44] Callendar's arguments gained in authority in the immediate postwar period, during the evolving debate about the contributions of industrialization to the climatic impacts of human activity.

WARMING TO THE TOPIC

Scientific attention to climate change intensified in the period immediately following World War II. This was propelled by the consolidation of scientific opinion around the importance of CO_2 as a greenhouse gas, and assisted by the formation of global institutions better able to focus and synthesize scientific discussion and the emergence of a handful of scientists prepared to project their growing concerns about their findings into the political and policy realm. Additional scientific work in the 1940s and 1950s on the radiative properties of CO_2, other gases, and water vapor, and on radiative transfer between the atmosphere and oceans, led scientists like the physicist Gilbert Plass to suggest that atmospheric accumulation of CO_2 might be a greater problem than initially believed, with a rate of increase of around 30 percent a century, and the doubling of atmospheric CO_2 leading to an average temperature increase of 3.6 degrees Celsius in the absence of other influences.[45]

Like Callendar, Plass in 1956 warned that "the accumulation of CO_2 in the atmosphere from continually expanding industrial activity may be a real problem in several generations. If at the end of this century, measurements show that the CO_2 content of the atmosphere has risen appreciably and at the same time the temperature has continued to rise throughout the world, it will be firmly established that CO_2 is an important factor in causing climatic change."[46]

Plass's warning was echoed by oceanographers Revelle and Suess, who in 1957 wrote that "human beings are now carrying out a large scale geophysical experiment of a kind that could not have happened in the past nor be reproduced in the future. Within a few centuries we are returning to the atmosphere and oceans the concentrated organic carbon stored in sedimentary rocks over hundreds of millions of years."[47]

It was on the strength of such scientific concern that David Keeling began the first rigorous monitoring of atmospheric concentrations of CO_2 in 1958 at Mauna Loa in Hawaii. By the early 1960s Keeling's work had provided conclusive empirical proof that the concentration of atmospheric CO_2 was increasing steadily and that scientific concerns about global warming were well-founded.[48]

What began as individual, curiosity-driven research by scientists such as Fourier and Tyndale about the composition of the atmosphere and its influence on climate evolved, through the work of Arrhenius, Callendar, Plass, Keeling, and others, into a global scientific monitoring and research program that provided a new vantage point for the consideration of humanity's planet-transforming activities. Yet while the long fuse of modernization produced an emerging scientific consensus around the causes of global warming, the short fuse of globalization has made it harder to respond to this discovery.

TURNING UP THE HEAT, SOUNDING THE ALARM

INTERNATIONAL SCIENTIFIC INSTITUTIONAL RESPONSES

As we saw in chapters 1 and 2, the global economy expanded rapidly in the second half of the 20th century, dependent upon and reflecting consumption of fossil fuels. David Keeling's rigorous monitoring of atmospheric concentrations of CO_2 registered the resultant environmental change and injected a new note of urgency and alarm in what had hitherto been languid and detached scientific consideration of climate change as an intellectual problem. Over the ensuing decades, the growing anxieties of climate scientists became institutionalized and then disseminated into popular culture. From that point, the issue quickly became politicized and led to the construction of a new multilayered regime of climate governance, which emerged first at the national level among leading scientific nations and then was extended locally and internationally. However, this regime has been driven and riven by tensions between local, national, and international interests and has faltered in response to political movements and industry lobbies that have refused to accept the findings of climate science or the broader policy implications of those findings.

It is no small irony that the United States, as the world's largest historical emitter and a laggard in climate policy at the national level, has played a significant leadership role in fostering climate change research. The United States led in the formation of "nationally institutionalized" climate science. In 1965, the Environmental Pollution Panel of the President's Science Advisory Committee reported to President Johnson that "carbon dioxide is being added to the earth's atmosphere by the burning of coal, oil, and natural gas at the rate of 6 billion tons a year. By the year 2000 there will be about 25 percent more carbon dioxide in our atmosphere than at present."[49]

As a consequence, the U.S. National Academy of Science (NAS) took up the baton. A second warning about global warming came in 1966 from its Panel on Weather and Climate Modification, headed by geophysicist Gordon MacDonald, who later served on President Nixon's Council on Environmental Quality.[50] Less than a decade later, the NAS undertook an assessment of current knowledge about human-induced climate change and advocated for increased research funding and effort in this area.[51] In 1979, an Ad Hoc Study Group of the NAS reported that the most probable warming associated with a doubling of atmospheric CO_2 would be 3 degrees Celsius plus or minus 1.5 degrees Celsius.[52] In 1981, the Council on Environmental Quality—part of the Executive Office of the President—recommended that

> in responding to the global nature of the CO_2 problem, the United States should consider its responsibility to demonstrate a commitment to reducing the risks of inadvertent global climate modification. Because it is the largest single consumer of energy in the world, it is

appropriate for the United States to exercise leadership in addressing the CO_2 problem.[53]

The development of national scientific institutions concentrating on, or significantly involved in, developing climate science and advising related policy has been paralleled in most other industrialized and now major industrializing countries. This is particularly so for those states which have been major contributors to the evolution of atmospheric science (such as Britain, through the Meteorological Office, and Germany) and increasingly now among significant recent contributors to the problem of global warming, such as China, which need to be able to participate autonomously in international climate dialogue.

Scientific debate on climate change was also fostered by the postwar growth of international scientific forums and research institutions. The World Meteorological Convention in 1947 restored confidence to an international scientific community disrupted by World War II. The professional International Meteorological Organization (IMO), founded in 1873, was superseded in 1953 by the World Meteorological Organization (WMO), an agency of the United Nations that assisted in the coordination and standardization of global weather data systems and institutional mechanisms. The International Geophysical Year in 1957 provided a transnational platform, somewhat removed from increasingly tense Cold War geopolitics, for communication about scientific climate knowledge and concerns, driven by contributions from the national behemoths for such research—the United States, Britain, and Russia.

By the 1970s, a convergence of (predominantly) scientific institutions and interests began to generate increasing political pressure for a global response to the "climate problem." Three contributions stand out: those of the WMO, the Brundtland Report, and the IPCC.

In the late 1970s and 1980s the WMO established a critically important series of climate conferences. The first World Climate Conference, held in Geneva in 1979, led to the creation of the World Climate Program, the World Climate Research Program and, ultimately, the establishment of the IPCC in 1988. Separately, through the 1980s, atmospheric scientists under the auspices of the WMO held a series of meetings in Villach, Austria. The most significant of these occurred in 1985, at which scientists considered the role of carbon dioxide and other greenhouse gases in producing climate variations and associated impacts. The conference formally concluded that, "as a result of the increasing concentrations of greenhouse gases, it is now believed that in the first half of the next century a rise of global mean temperature could occur that is greater than any in man's history."[54] The conference recommended that governments take this assessment into account in their policies and that public information campaigns on climate change and sea level rise should be increased.

The Second World Climate Conference, in November 1990, was even more important. The conference considered the IPCC's first report, and its response led directly to UN General Assembly Resolution 45/212 in the same year. This resolution established the Intergovernmental Negotiating Committee on a Framework Convention on Climate Change (INC) under the auspices of the General Assembly and with a mandate to develop a climate treaty or convention, if possible by the Earth Summit in Rio in June 1992.

A second contribution came from the United Nations' Brundtland Report, *Our Common Future*. Published in 1987, the report warned that key among environmental pressures is "the burning of fossil fuels [which] puts into the atmosphere carbon dioxide, which is causing gradual global warming. This 'greenhouse effect' may by next century have increased global temperature enough to shift agricultural production, raise sea levels, flood coastal cities, and disrupt national economies." *Our Common Future* catapulted climate change onto the global political stage, prompted debate in the UN General Assembly, and developed momentum for an international climate treaty. In Bolin's words, "The scientific community had brought the climate change issue to the political agenda with support from the two UN organizations UNEP and WMO."[55]

However, of the various international institutions established in recent times to provide scientific advice about global warming, the IPCC is the most important. Created in 1988 by the WMO and the United Nations Environment Programme (UNEP), the IPCC was established to provide periodic assessments "on a comprehensive, objective, open and transparent basis, [of] the scientific, technical and socio-economic information relevant to understanding the scientific basis of risk of human-induced climate change, its potential impacts and options for adaptation and mitigation."[56]

The IPCC's assessment reports are accepted as the most authoritative summary of the various dimensions of international climate science, based on comparisons, reviews, and summaries of climate models, data sets, and peer-reviewed published research. The lengthy process for producing each report, which requires line-by-line agreement by governments, has tended to produce especially cautious findings that are somewhat dated by their time of release. Nonetheless, the basic conclusions of the IPCC's major reports remain sound, have been widely reported, and have been highly influential in serving as a bridge between scientific climate discourse and popular climate discourse, as well as in shaping the opinions of national policy makers and negotiators. The co-authors of the IPCC's Fourth Assessment Report (2007) were joint recipients of the Nobel Peace Prize.

CONTESTED CLIMATE DISCOURSES

Until the late 1980s, the problem of climate change remained predominantly a discussion between climatologists and meteorologists. However, by the end of the 1980s climate change, along with the "hole in the ozone layer," had been picked up by the media as an international environmental cause célèbre and become a matter of high public concern and political salience.[57]

In 1988, physicist James Hansen, head of the NASA Goddard Institute for Space Studies, appeared before the U.S. Congress and provided a powerful testimony on climate change that soon attracted global media attention. The New York Times reported Hansen as declaring that "the earth has been warmer in the first five months of this year than in any comparable period since measurements began 130 years ago, and the higher temperatures can now be attributed to a long-expected global warming trend linked to pollution." He also argued that "it was 99 percent certain that the warming trend was not a natural variation but was caused by a buildup of carbon dioxide and other artificial gases in the atmosphere."[58]

From this point onward, the rarefied and complex scientific discourse about climate change was joined by a growing cacophony of ethical, political, and economic climate discourses that have offered a variety of different characterizations of the problem and the solution. Following James Hansen's much publicized statement in 1988, global warming became a new rallying point and campaign issue for most of the major national and international environmental NGOs and networks, including Greenpeace, WWF, and Friends of the Earth, and, later, major development NGOs such as Oxfam. Growing concern over climate change also prompted the formation of a range of new NGOs and networks exclusively focused on combating climate change. The largest of these is Climate Action Network (CAN), a global network of more than seven hundred NGOs from more than ninety countries, with national and regional branches, dedicated to protecting the atmosphere while promoting sustainable and equitable development worldwide.[59]

Environmental NGOs, along with representatives of the most vulnerable nations such as low-lying island states, have been the standard bearers of environmental justice discourses, which highlight the inverse relationship between vulnerability to climate change, on the one hand, and contribution to the problem and capacity to respond, on the other. Environmental justice discourses embrace the protection of vulnerable species, ecosystems, communities, and future human generations and argue that the division of international responsibility for emission reductions should take account of the significant differences in historical responsibility, capacity, and vulnerability between developed and developing countries. NGO campaigns have sought to draw out and amplify the ethical implications of the scientific warnings provided by the IPCC and prominent "citizen-scientists," such as Hansen and the late Stephen Schneider, to push governments for strong emissions reduction strategies and renewable energy policies, and to negotiate an ambitious international climate treaty with clear targets and timetables and significant funding for mitigation and adaptation in developing countries. NGOs in the Global South have focused on the human dimensions of the ethical discourse and given greater emphasis to poverty eradication, the historical responsibility of developed countries, and the development needs of developing countries.

The response of the corporate world to climate change has varied significantly and predictably among firms and industry groups. For example, the renewable energy industry has emerged as climate crusaders and joined discourse coalitions with environmental NGOs in support of the transition to a low-carbon society. Meanwhile, firms and industry groups, most notably the fossil fuel industry, have used their structural power to protect their threatened interests through a range of strategies, from advertising to lobbying at the national and international levels.[60] The increasing political salience of climate change has spawned some powerful "discourse coalitions" that have sought to denigrate and de-legitimize the science of climate change, exaggerate the costs of mitigation, and resist new climate policy initiatives. In some cases, this has included disinformation and outright propaganda campaigns by particular industries, scientists with strong industry ties, and/or free market think tanks (such as the Chicago-based Heartland Institute), which have willfully exploited the lay public's lack of technical expertise on complex problems such as climate change by spreading doubt and confusion.[61]

The mass media have played a critical and generative role in the development of two waves of global and national public awareness and concern over climate change, in the late 1980s and then in 2007. Media coverage of the IPCC's Fourth Assessment Report (FAR), published in 2007, galvanized public concern and political debates. So too did the documentary *An Inconvenient Truth*, which was first screened in 2006 and went on to be screened in more than fifty countries. The film won two Academy Awards in 2007 and became the seventh highest grossing documentary in history. Indeed, the combination of coverage of the IPCC's FAR and *An Inconvenient Truth* produced a renewed wave of public concern in the run up to the important 2009 Copenhagen climate negotiations.

However, the media's role has not always been one of accurate and proportionate communication of climate science. The tendency to seek out controversy and to air both sides of an argument to ensure "balanced reporting" has had the effect of overrepresenting the views of climate denialists and generating confusion and doubt among lay publics. For instance, Maxwell Boykoff and Jules Boykoff have showed that, over a fourteen-year period from 1988 to 2002, 53 percent of articles referring to the issue in four of the United States' "prestige" newspapers gave roughly equal attention to the views of climate scientists and climate denialists, while 6 percent emphasized doubts about climate science.[62] Yet a survey of the peer-reviewed scientific literature showed that 928 articles published over the decade between 1993 and 2003 supported the scientific consensus about the human contribution to global warming, with none indicating significant dissent.[63]

Similarly in 2009, the media's appetite for sensationalism and scandal led to its coverage of the so-called Climategate Affair, which concerned the publication of e-mail correspondence purportedly showing manipulation of results by climate scientists to indicate warming trends. The e-mails were obtained by unknown hackers who had gained access to the University of East Anglia's server just weeks before the Copenhagen climate conference. Although no less than eight committees of investigation into the affair subsequently found no evidence of fraud or scientific misconduct, the widespread and intense media coverage of the story greatly assisted the climate denialists' cause and appears to have contributed to diminishing support for national climate mitigation policies in English-speaking countries, particularly the United States, in the wake of the Copenhagen conference. This was aided by the widespread coverage given to errors published in the IPCC's 2007 Fourth Assessment Report, none of which affected its core findings.

Economic discourses of climate change have been particularly influential in shaping the international negotiations and national and subnational climate policy. Whereas two decades ago, the predominant economic view supported the continuing use of cheap fossil fuels to grow and strengthen national economies—deferring mitigation until there was greater certainty about climate impacts—there is now increasing recognition that deferring action merely increases the costs of mitigation and adaptation over time while also leading to irreversible and expensive economic (as well as social and ecological) losses.[64] There is also increasing support among economists for incorporating the externalized costs of climate change into the costs of production through taxes, charges, or emission trading schemes. "Putting a price on carbon" makes fossil fuels and other GHG-generating activity more expensive and renewable energy more competitive, thereby driving technological innovation toward low- or zero-carbon alternatives. Economic prescriptions for market-based instruments for climate policy to replace "old-fashioned regulation" also fitted comfortably into the neoliberal economic discourse that rose to prominence in the 1990s.

ADJUSTING THE THERMOSTAT?
THE STRUGGLE FOR CLIMATE GOVERNANCE

Scientific, ethical, and economic discourses have all fed into the two-decade-long attempt by states to negotiate an international climate change regime to govern and manage global warming. However, as we shall see, different discourse coalitions have emerged among the various blocs in the negotiations, the most significant of which are the EU, the Umbrella Group (which includes the United States, Canada, Norway, Australia, and Japan), and China and the G77 (which includes around 132 developing countries).[65] The latter also contains important subdivisions that are increasingly threatening the unity of the developing country bloc. Although climate governance works at many levels,[66] here we confine our attention to the international efforts to negotiate a comprehensive international agreement under the auspices of the United Nations to guide the global effort to reduce emissions.

THE EVOLVING ARCHITECTURE OF INTERNATIONAL CLIMATE GOVERNANCE

The struggle for governance of the global atmospheric commons did not begin with climate change. Public alarm over radioactive fallout from the atmospheric testing of nuclear weapons in the 1950s and early 1960s led to the Partial Test Ban Treaty in 1963. Then in the mid-1980s, the discovery of "ozone holes" over the North and South Poles—the result of ozone depletion caused by a new group of synthetic gases called chlorofluorocarbons (CFCs)—led to the formulation of what is widely hailed as one of the most successful environmental treaties of the late 20th century.

The *Vienna Convention for the Protection of the Ozone Layer* was signed by the twenty major ozone-producing countries in 1985, less than a decade after the problems caused by CFCs were first noted and very shortly after the discovery of the "ozone hole." Two years later, the convention was strengthened and given content by the *Montreal Protocol on Substances that Deplete the Ozone Layer*, which stipulated control measures for the phaseout of CFC production, including a ban on trade in CFCs. The Montreal Protocol also enshrined the principle of differentiated responsibilities between developed and developing countries, based on different contribution to the problem and different capacities to respond. Developed countries, as the major producers of CFCs, were required to contribute to a multilateral fund that would cover the full incremental costs of compliance incurred by developing countries, and delayed compliance by developing countries was also permitted under certain special conditions.[67] The protocol, which opened for signature in 1987 and came into force in 1989, was eventually ratified by all

United Nations members, and by the early 1990s had a major impact on reducing the production and emission of the main ozone-depleting substances. Scientific clarity about the causes of the problem, the limited number of contributing countries and industries, the immediate availability of commercially attractive technological solutions, and the acknowledgment of differentiated responsibilities all contributed to this rapid and effective outcome.

The climate negotiators also followed the framework convention/protocol model adopted in the ozone negotiations, which involves the negotiation of a general framework treaty (containing broad objective and principles) that authorizes the parties to negotiate more detailed legal protocols to further the objectives of the treaty. However, those who believed that the success of the ozone negotiations might be replicated in the climate negotiations would be proved wrong. In the case of the climate regime, the sources of the problem were much more varied and pervasive, the science was much more complex, the solutions much more challenging, and the burden-sharing principles more contested.

FROM RIO TO KYOTO

Scientific concerns raised at Villach and by the IPCC's first assessment report, and public concern generated by its findings, were the major catalysts that prompted the negotiation of the *United Nations Framework Convention on Climate Change* (UNFCCC) at the United Nations Conference on Environment and Development ("the Earth Summit") at Rio de Janeiro in June 1992.[68] The ultimate objective of the UNFCCC is "the stabilization of greenhouse gas concentration in the atmosphere at a level that would prevent the dangerous anthropogenic interference with the climate system" (Article 2). The treaty came into force in 1994 and has been ratified by 194 states representing every recognized sovereign state in the world, plus the European Union (EU). However, this universal membership belies the tensions and conflicts associated with a treaty that many claim to be the most complex and testing treaty ever negotiated. Its early enthusiasts greatly underestimated the difficulties that would arise in tackling energy sources and industrial processes central to (conventional) economic development and associated national interests. The problems were not only geopolitical but also structural.

The UNFCCC was finalized at the same time as the negotiation of the *Rio Declaration on Environment and Development* (1992) and it embodies many of the Declaration's aspirations and principles.[69] It also reflects key tensions between the Global North and Global South that dominated the Earth Summit, including over the vexed questions of historical responsibility for environmental harm, burden sharing, the special situation and needs of developing countries, and the sovereign right to develop. The pivotal burden-sharing provision of the treaty provides that

> the Parties should protect the climate system for the benefit of present and future generations of humankind, on the basis of equity and in accordance with their common but differentiated responsibilities and capabilities. Accordingly, the developed country parties should take the lead in combating climate change and the adverse effects thereof.[70]

The convention divides member states into three different groupings: approximately 40 predominantly wealthy industrialized states made up of developed states and the Eastern European states undergoing a transition to a market economy (Annex I parties); 24 "developed" states, which reflects the OECD membership in 1992 (Annex II parties); and some 155 developing states (known as non-Annex I states). These groupings provide the basis for differentiated commitments under the UNFCCC, which are intended to reflect broad differences in historical and current emissions, per capita emission, capacity, development needs, and vulnerability. All the industrialized parties in Annex I are required to adopt policies and measures to reduce emissions, although the specific obligation to lead is restricted to developed countries.[71] Following the Montreal Protocol model, Annex I parties are also required to provide new and additional finance, and the transfer of technology, to help developing countries meet their commitments under the UNFCCC and to assist with adaptation to climatic impacts.[72] The obligations of developing countries under the UNFCCC are mainly confined to establishing national inventories of their emissions and reporting to the UNFCCC Secretariat.

While the UNFCCC laid down broad objectives and commitments, they were largely aspirational. Despite a pledge by industrialized countries at the Earth Summit to return their emissions to 1990 levels by 2000, little progress could be made without further clear and binding targets and timetables. Accordingly, the parties commenced a second phase of negotiations, which concluded with a legally binding protocol agreed by the third Conference of the Parties (COP 3) in Kyoto in 1997.[73]

The *Kyoto Protocol* (KP) maintained the commitment to "common but differentiated responsibilities" by requiring only the industrialized countries to commit to legally binding emissions reductions. These parties negotiated individually binding targets that would, if fully implemented, produce a net aggregate reduction in emissions of around 5 percent below a 1990 baseline by the end of its first five-year commitment period (2008–2012). The EU took the lead with an 8 percent reduction target; the United States followed with a 7 percent target.

However, in the lead-up to the negotiations, the Clinton administration had faced a hostile Senate, which had passed a unanimous resolution (the "Byrd-Hagel" resolution) in July 1997 declaring that it would not ratify the protocol if developing countries were not required to undertake emissions reduction obligations in the same commitment period, or if the treaty would harm the U.S. economy.[74] The grand bargain eventually struck at Kyoto was that the United States would accept emissions reduction targets without a corresponding commitment from developing countries in return for greater flexibility for Annex I parties in meeting their targets. This flexibility took the form of international emissions trading and offsetting (through the Clean Development Mechanism, Joint Implementation, and emissions trading), all of which would enable Annex I parties to take advantage of cheaper abatement options outside their territories (discussed in more detail below). The protocol also enshrined a related range of reporting and accounting rules and processes, including provisions that enabled Annex I parties to claim reductions from investing in "carbon sinks," such as forests.

The KP also further entrenched deep divisions within states and between blocs of states—divisions that would see its ratification jeopardized and the start of implementation delayed for years. The "firewall" between Annex I and non-Annex I countries in the KP was to generate increasing hostility toward the protocol inside the U.S. Congress. The Clinton administration never presented the protocol to the Senate for ratification, and when George W. Bush was took office in 2001, he promptly repudiated it for the same reasons as the U.S. Senate (while also questioning the climate science).[75] Australia also followed suit in declining to ratify the protocol, until the election of a new Labor government in 2007. The Bush administration's repudiation was to delay the protocol's entry into force for seven years.[76] The ongoing opposition of the United States to the KP (as distinct from the UNFCCC) continues to be a major impediment to the development of a second commitment period under the protocol. Canada, Japan, and the Russian Federation have also rejected or declined to commit to a second commitment period.

Environmental NGOs and scientists have also criticized the *Kyoto Protocol* as the product of political horse-trading rather than being based on scientific advice or an equitable formula for apportioning burdens according to responsibility, capacity, and development needs. (Australia, for instance, gained an exceptional target permitting an increase of 8 percent above its 1990 level of emissions by effectively blackmailing the assembled delegates with the possibility of its defection.[77])

Meanwhile the developing country bloc (the G77 plus China) and the European Union continued to insist that—under Article 3(1) of the UNFCCC—mitigation was rightly first and foremost a developed country obligation and a necessary first step in building developing bloc trust in a global climate regime. It was only through the provision of additional incentives (which further weakened the protocol's effectiveness) to win the support of Japan, Canada, and finally Russia for ratification that the protocol finally came into legal force in February 2005.

THE MARKETIZATION OF EMISSIONS

The quest for flexibility in choosing the means for meeting national emissions reduction targets has attracted strong support from many developed countries, economists, and business groups for the establishment of an international carbon market.[78] From the standpoint of firms, carbon trading and offsetting are considered superior to prescriptive regulation or a simple tax since they enable firms to find a least-cost solution to mitigation. These mechanisms were also considered to reduce the perceived threat posed to economic growth by direct regulations and are compatible with the emphasis on market-based choice central to the neoliberal economic thinking that had become dominant in the 1990s.

The protocol's flexibility mechanisms established the foundations for a form of marketized global climate governance that also supported the underlying logic of capital accumulation. It did so through the nomination of six major GHGs, the commodification and certification of emissions of those gases, the creation of an international system for exchanging emissions certificates, and the initiation of three mechanisms as the primary vehicles for "least-cost" mitigation—the Clean Development Mechanism, Joint Implementation, and emissions trading.

The Clean Development Mechanism (CDM) is an offsetting scheme that enables Annex I countries to earn tradable "certified emissions reduction" (CER) credits by investing in additional emissions reductions projects in developing countries. The CDM has also been strongly supported by developing countries because it offers them a source of new investment, the transfer of climate-friendly technologies to promote sustainable development, the improvement of livelihoods and skills, job creation, and increased economic activity.[79] Initially believed by its proponents to be unlikely to be a significant measure, it has become the core means of climate-directed investment into the major developing countries. Of the 4,369 projects listed on the CDM registry as of mid-2012, half are located in China, and approximately one-fifth in India, with most of the investment coming from the United Kingdom, Switzerland, Japan, The Netherlands, and Sweden.[80] Annual investment in registered CDM projects rose from $US40 million in 2004 to $US47 billion in 2010 and over $US140 billion in mid-2011.[81] However, critics have questioned the robustness and environmental integrity of the CDM's accounting methodologies (which require the new investment projects to produce emissions reductions that are "additional" to what would have occurred under "business as usual"), and whether the CDM has made any substantial contribution to reducing actual and prospective emissions.[82]

The second mechanism, Joint Implementation (or JI), is similar to the CDM but instead enables emissions credits to be generated by mitigation-related investment by Annex I countries in other Annex I countries (predominantly post-Soviet Central and Eastern European "economies in transition").

The KP's third mechanism is emissions trading, which allows Annex I parties that have produced more emissions than allowed under their Kyoto target to purchase "assigned amount units" from parties that have reduced their emissions more than required. The idea of a carbon emissions trading market built upon the United States' successful national sulfur dioxide cap-and-trade scheme under the U.S. Clean Air Act. The underlying logic of a cap-and-trade system is to set a tightening regulatory "cap" (the total volume of emissions to be traded in any given period) to reduce the "availability" of tradable emissions permits over time. A market in increasingly scarce and therefore increasingly expensive emissions permits is expected to increase the cost of fossil-fuel-related activities and encourage companies to invest in more financially attractive and less emissions-intensive technologies and practices.

While emissions trading had been strongly promoted by the United States prior to the Kyoto negotiations, it was initially opposed by the EU, the G77, and most environmental NGOs. The chief objection was that developed states had a moral obligation to reduce domestic emissions at source through domestic policy changes rather than pay others to reduce emissions or avoid pursuing new emissions-generating activities elsewhere. For many environmental NGOs, carbon trading and offsetting enable the evasion of national and corporate responsibility and the postponement of the necessary restructuring toward a low-carbon economy. However, during the Kyoto negotiations in 1997, the EU acceded to the United States' demands to ensure U.S. participation in the agreement and to secure the United States' expected substantial contribution—as a major emitter—to a global carbon market. The EU went on to embrace emissions trading and the international carbon market, while the United States' repudiation of the KP excluded it from this market. The EU's own regional emissions trading scheme (EU ETS), established when the KP came into force in 2005, has become the world's largest, encompassing all the twenty-seven countries of the EU plus Iceland, Liechtenstein, and Norway. The scheme, now entering its third phase, includes 72 percent of the world's volume of trade in carbon permits and 80 percent of its value. It is ironic that emissions trading has become the centerpiece of climate policy in the EU while the United States has been unable to find sufficient support in Congress to enact such a scheme and has had to resort to traditional regulation by the Environmental Protection Agency to manage greenhouse gas emissions under preexisting provisions in the Clean Air Act.

The total volume and value of global carbon trading continues to grow. The amount of carbon traded in 2011 increased by 19 percent on

2010, reaching a new high of 10.3 billion tonnes of CO_2-e and a total value of $USD 176 billion (including $148 billion in Europe)—up by 11 percent on the previous year. This is despite the ongoing influence of the global financial crisis and of the European economic downturn, which has caused a surplus in EU permits and therefore a significant depression in prices.[83] In addition to the European Union, Iceland, Liechtenstein, and Norway, national and subnational trading schemes also exist in Canada, New Zealand, Switzerland, and the United States. By 2013, there will be schemes in operation in eighteen subnational jurisdictions in Canada and the United States (including California) and, by 2015, also in seven provinces in China,[84] the Republic of Korea, and possibly Australia. However, attempts to establish national schemes in Australia and the United States have faced stiff (and in the United States, successful) opposition by business interests and associated political parties opposed to any carbon price.

FROM BALI TO COPENHAGEN

The KP's ratification initiated a third phase of regime development, at the eleventh Conference of the Parties (COP 11) in Montreal in 2005, to determine the content—including future mitigation commitments—of the protocol's second commitment period, intended for the period 2013 to 2020. But the explicit repudiation of the protocol by the United States (supported by its close ally, Australia) in 2001 generated major problems and complications for the negotiators. Not only were the KP's targets exceedingly modest relative to the scale of the problem, but the world's biggest historical emitter and biggest aggregate emitter (at the time), and two of the world's highest per capita emitters (i.e., the United States and Australia) had refused to participate and had challenged the principle of differentiated responsibilities. The situation marked the beginning of a major standoff that has continued to stalk the negotiations. The United States would not participate in any climate treaty that did not also include all major emitters (including China and India); China, India, and other major emitters in the developing world argued that the differentiated responsibilities under the UNFCCC and KP made it clear that they were under no obligation to make international commitments for so long as developed nations had failed to discharge their leadership responsibilities.

The negotiators responded to the standoff by pursuing a two-track negotiating process, whereby the parties to the KP sought to negotiate a second commitment period, while the parties to the UNFCCC (which included the United States and Australia) would begin an informal dialogue toward a long-term treaty for the post-2012 period.

In 2007, global public concern about global warming reached new heights, fueled by widespread reportage of the findings of the IPCC's Fourth Assessment Report and the impact of *An Inconvenient Truth*, and this sentiment flowed into international negotiations. At COP 13, held in Bali at the end of 2007, Australia, under a new Labor (social democrat) government, elected in part for its promise to engage with the climate issue, ratified the KP. This left the United States isolated as the only major developed country opposing the treaty. Meanwhile, China's rapid economic growth saw it overtake the United States as the world's biggest aggregate emitter in 2006, almost more than a decade earlier than predicted, although the United States remained the largest historical emitter and its per capita emissions were around four to five times higher.[85]

At the Bali negotiations, it appeared that the United States would frustrate plans to adopt a formal negotiating process to lead to timely development of a post-2012 climate regime. Intense frustration among delegates boiled over at the COP plenary, where the United States was booed and jeered for its opposition, and then applauded when it finally decided to support the Bali Action Plan to negotiate a new treaty on long-term cooperative action. This plan, intended to come to fruition in 2009 at COP 15 in Copenhagen, aimed to determine new global and national mitigation targets, establish funding arrangements for adaptation, and finalize the design and rules for an additional area of carbon marketization and offsetting—the use of financial incentives for the reduction of emissions from deforestation and forest degradation (REDD) in developing countries. Given their leadership obligations, Annex I countries were to commit to legally binding emissions targets (while ensuring comparability of effort) while developing countries agreed to pursue "nationally appropriate mitigation actions" (NAMAs) that did not amount to legally binding international commitments.

Copenhagen was the most anxiously anticipated conference of all of the COPs to date. On the one hand, the election of President Obama raised expectations of positive U.S. engagement. On other hand, the onset and severity of the global financial crisis distracted the attention of the major economies from climate negotiations, while the "Climate-gate" affair played into the hands of those who opposed a new climate treaty. These latter elements merely added to the problem of the well-entrenched standoff between the United States and major developing countries such as India and China, which persisted despite the EU's effort to play a leadership role. The formation of a new negotiating block, the BASIC group (Brazil, South Africa, India, and China) also threatened to deepen the standoff.

The Copenhagen conference came perilously close to foundering. Negotiators at its final plenary session, which continued beyond the conference's official closure for more than forty-eight hours without break, tried desperately to salvage an acceptable outcome. In the end, no second commitment period to the KP and no new legally binding treaty were agreed. Instead, a nonbinding political agreement known as "the Copenhagen Accord" was noted in the final plenary but not accepted by the COP due to the absence of consensus.[86] This agreement, the outlines of which had been brokered by an informal meeting between the United States and the BASIC group, merely "recognized" the scientific view that warming should be kept below 2 degrees, but did not make it a specific goal. Moreover, the Accord contained no near-term (2020) or long-term (2050) collective or national targets and no timetable for when global emissions would peak and then decline. Instead, the agreement endorsed a "bottom-up" process of "pledge and review" by which all states would nominate voluntary mitigation commitments through to 2020 (and choose their own baseline). It also promised significant funding from developed states of $US10 billion per annum for three years, for adaptation assistance, and the establishment of a Green Climate Fund.[87]

The Copenhagen Accord embodied the standoff between the United States and the BASIC group. The United States refused to commit to any agreement without formal mitigation commitments from all major emitters, while the BASIC group rejected the notion of binding commitments by developing countries and reiterated the principle of differentiated responsibilities and capacities and the leadership obligations of developed countries. China also refused to accept a collective target for 2050 that might compromise its development trajectory.

FROM COPENHAGEN TO DURBAN

Although the Copenhagen Accord was formally adopted a year later, at COP 16 at Cancun (2010), the standoff continued to thwart any progress on a second commitment period for the *Kyoto Protocol* or progress toward more ambitious mitigation objectives. The KP was set to expire in 2012, with no successor treaty in sight. In the lead-up to COP 17 in Durban (2011), Canada, Russia, and Japan made it clear that they saw no point in continuing the negotiations for a second commitment period in the absence of U.S. participation. Canada—unable to reach its commitments under the first commitment period—also abandoned the KP. Yet China and the G77, strongly supported by environmental NGOs, insisted on a second Kyoto commitment period given the absence of any progress on the broader post-2012 treaty.

At Durban, the EU prevented yet another derailment by agreeing to commit to a second commitment period under the KP in return for an agreement by *all* major emitters to launch negotiations for a new legally binding treaty to be signed by 2015, to come into effect in 2020. This offer was welcomed by the vulnerable developing states (especially but not only the Alliance of Small Island States), which were becoming increasingly desperate for action on mitigation, and it was eventually accepted by all major emitters. The negotiating track at Bali was wound up. A new roadmap for negotiations was agreed: the Durban Platform for Enhanced Action.

While Durban appeared to represent diplomatic progress, it produced no substantial movement toward the UNFCCC's ultimate goals.[88] The Durban Platform seeks to raise the level of mitigation ambition by recognizing the "ambition gap" between current climate science and the Copenhagen Accord's target pledges, which are unable to hold warming below 2 degrees. Yet it postponed further agreement to 2015—when the critical decade for effective action is half over—with no guarantee that a treaty containing meaningful targets will be signed then or come into legal force by 2020. As the editors of the scientific journal *Nature* summed it up: "The Durban deal may mark a success in the political process to tackle climate change, but for the climate itself, it is an unqualified disaster. It is clear that the science of climate change and the politics of climate change, which claims to represent it, now inhabit parallel worlds."[89]

WHITHER THE UNFCCC?

Critics of the climate negotiations argue that they have produced diminishing returns over time as a result of hardened and increasingly fractured negotiating blocs (many of which are framed by narrowly conceived national interests) and rivalry and mistrust, especially between the two biggest aggregate emitters. Added to this is a complex and sprawling negotiating agenda and a painfully slow process of reaching decisions that requires all COP decisions to be agreed by consensus by 195 parties, which means they can be blocked by a very small handful of countries (as occurred in Copenhagen).[90]

The UNFCCC was shaped at its inception by geopolitical divisions between the blocs of developed and developing nations, and between the United States and the EU, with former socialist states tentatively determining their position and allegiances immediately following the end of the Cold War. However, significant realignments over the two decades since 1992 have challenged the UNFCCC Annex classification system. The developing country bloc, represented by G77+China, has become increasingly differentiated in the wake of the rapid growth of the members of the BASIC group, whose interests are increasingly set apart from those of the least developed countries (LDCs) or the group of climate-threatened low-lying island nations represented by AOSIS (the Alliance of Small Island States). Some developing countries (such as Israel, Singapore, South Korea, and the United Arab Emirates) now have standards of living and GDP comparable to some Annex I countries. African and Latin American regional interests are sometimes expressed as voting blocs, occasionally reflecting the tensions between nations seeking to lead these blocs (for instance, Brazil, Mexico, and Venezuela). The oil-exporting nations, represented by OPEC, are members of the G77, but their interests and obstructionist tactics diverge dramatically from the least developed and most vulnerable states. The predominantly socialist Latin American nations in the eight-member Bolivian-led alliance (ALBA) have also pursued their own agenda. Yet now overshadowing all these divisions is China—the aspirant challenger to the United States. China's rapid growth, increasingly global economic and political power, and rising emissions profile since 1992 have made it a crucial player in the climate negotiations with a powerful veto.

On the other hand, the EU—which had expanded to twenty-seven members through the accession of a number of former Soviet states—continues to work as a bloc but without the same unity of purpose it had when it was a smaller grouping, despite the leadership efforts of Germany and the United Kingdom. Meanwhile, Russia has regained its political and economic significance and independence, as a broker for the creation of the KP and as an energy superpower. And most of the members of the Umbrella Group (with the exception of Norway) have failed to aspire to the same levels of mitigation ambition as the EU. These factors made the process of negotiation ever more complicated and the prediction of outcomes highly uncertain.

The UNFCCC negotiations, and particularly COP 15, also demonstrate the degree to which complex international agreements often depend on the geopolitical positioning of its most significant (in economic and military terms) players—the "carbon giants," the United States and China, which together account for around 45 percent of global emissions.[91] U.S. anxiety has been exacerbated by the weakening of its economy in the aftermath of the 2008 global financial crisis and China's continued dramatic economic growth. The Copenhagen Accord was substantially shaped by the United States and BASIC group, with the EU and other developing countries largely sidelined.

Finally, at and since Copenhagen, domestic political and economic interests, institutions, and circumstances have exercised a dominant influence on the international climate negotiations and their outcomes. For instance, despite President Obama's ambitions for the United States in the UNFCCC negotiations and his desire for a national emissions trading scheme to meet a defined national emissions reduction target, he was thwarted by an unsupportive Senate.[92] At Copenhagen in 2009, it was evident, even before the negotiations began, that the United States would arrive "with empty pockets." Since the 2010 Congressional elections, which delivered control of the House to the predominantly climate-skeptical Republicans and greatly reduced the Democrats' majority in the Senate, it is highly unlikely that any new climate legislation will be passed before 2014. Moreover, the U.S. Senate remains unlikely to ratify a new climate treaty that fails to contain meaningful commitments from all major emitters.

China was equally constrained in its negotiating flexibility by the long, intricate planning processes required by the Chinese Communist

Party to produce its Five Year Plans. The Twelfth Plan effectively locks in the extent of China's climate policy ambition and reflects the domestic pressures and legitimacy constraints on the Chinese Communist Party in meeting the needs of a growing and increasingly politically and economically restless population.

In all, the significant obstacles to progress have produced mounting concern that the UNFCCC negotiations seem to be incapable of producing a timely agreement that will protect the world from dangerous climate change. Increasing attention is now turning to the role of progressive "climate coalitions of the willing" (including states, cities and municipalities, local communities, regions, civil society, firms and industry groups[93]) that are prepared to lead the way toward low-carbon economies in the absence of an effective and timely international treaty, or else help build momentum for a successful treaty.

CONCLUSION—THE FUTURE
OF CLIMATE GOVERNANCE

To date, the international climate regime has failed to restrain global GHG emissions. Emissions have grown at an accelerating rate over the past two decades (figure 3.3).[94] The authors of the PBL Netherlands 2011 Report on long-term trends in global emissions write, "In 2010, total global CO_2 emissions had increased 30% since 2000 to 33.0 billion tonnes and 45% since 1990, the base year of the Kyoto Protocol. In 1990, global emissions were 22.7 billion tonnes, an increase of 45% on the 1970 level of 15.5 billion tonnes. . . . The growth rate of 45% of global CO_2 emissions in the 20 years since 1990 did not change compared to the 20 years before 1990."[95]

This growth has been generated by the increased volume of consumption associated with growing affluence, global population growth, the ongoing expansion in the aggregate volume of trade, increasing deforestation, and an increase in the use of fossil fuels to produce and transport these raw and processed materials. Indeed, the growth in production and consumption of fossil fuels has continued *despite* the global financial crisis and the subsequent downturn in the U.S. and European economies.

Despite an aspirational commitment to keep average global warming below 2 degrees, the cumulative effect of the voluntary Copenhagen

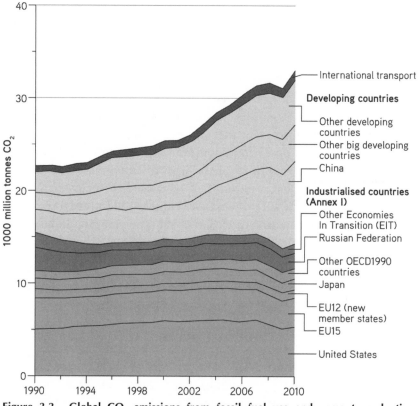

Figure 3.3. Global CO$_2$ emissions from fossil fuel use and cement production 1990–2010

Source: Olivier, J.G.J, Janssens-Maenhout, G., Peters J.A.H.W. and Wilson, J. (2011), "Long term trends in global CO$_2$ emissions." 2011 Report. The Hague: PBL/JRC, p.11.

pledges would produce warming of 3.5 to 4 degrees or more, which would clearly lead to dangerous climate change. The attempt to produce a "top-down" allocation of national targets, based on a carbon budget grounded in climate science and allocated according to an internationally agreed equitable formula, has given way to a "bottom-up" or "DIY approach" to target setting, which permits states to choose targets and policies that they find politically manageable.

As the foregoing discussion has shown, the sources of this tragedy are many and varied. Here we reflect on the key deficits and obstacles that have most contributed to the waning legitimacy of the global climate regime.

AMBITION DEFICIT

The failure of the 2020 mitigation targets nominated by almost all states at COP 15 Copenhagen to contribute to the aspirational goal of limiting global warming to 2 degrees Celsius, alongside the ongoing increase in global emissions, amounts to a major "ambition deficit" reflected in the large gap between the scientific advice and existing targets. Yet as the gap between climate science and national climate policies deepens, most governments remain unprepared to educate their publics about the scale of the problem or to pursue targets and strategies that will orchestrate the rapid decarbonization that is required to prevent dangerous warming.

BURDEN-SHARING DEFICIT

The UNFCCC's burden-sharing principles of "equity" and "common but differentiated responsibilities and capabilities" broadly acknowledge differences in relative historical contribution to the problem, aggregate emissions, per capita emissions, capacity, development needs, and relative vulnerability. They provide a starting point from which to determine an approach for the equitable allocation of national targets for mitigation and contributions to adaptation funding.[96]

A burden-sharing formula has been used successfully by the EU for the allocation of emissions reduction targets among its members to reach its collective Kyoto target, and a range of equitable and practical methods have been proposed for international burden sharing, such as the Greenhouse Development Rights Framework, which has produced a "responsibility and capacity index."[97] However, the parties to the climate convention have been unable to agree on a coherent, flexible, and implementable formula for international burden sharing that also has the flexibility to respond equitably to shifts over time in relative responsibility, capacity, and development needs. This failure reflects philosophical and ideological differences between negotiators about the nature and extent of historical and future responsibility for global warming, imbalances in negotiating power between the most responsible and the most vulnerable parties, and the shallow understanding of and ethical commitment to international responsibility evident in the political culture of most developed nations. The sheer complexity of the ethical issues associated with assigning responsibility, including the mismatch between causal responsibility, culpability, capacity, and vulnerability, contributes to what Stephen Gardiner has called a perfect moral storm that conspires to produce an overall evasion of responsibility.[98]

In the absence of such a coherent and fair formula for burden sharing, international negotiations have been dominated by special pleading by individual nations (and domestic interests within nations) seeking to minimize their responsibilities and efforts. National targets and funding contributions have been determined by political bargaining, with the "bottom-up" nomination of targets and effort based on individual nations' perceptions of their own political and economic preferences rather than fairness or global ecological requirements.

ACCOUNTABILITY DEFICITS

The ongoing increase in emissions has been enabled by a form of systemic irresponsibility and lack of accountability embedded throughout the climate governance regime from the level of the individual consumer to the meetings of the parties to the UNFCCC. Contributions to climate change are dispersed and veiled by distance and time as production/consumption chains become globally extended. End-point consumers have little awareness of how their demand for commodities contributes to growing GHG emissions. The mechanisms for calculating embodied emissions (the emissions cumulatively produced during the production of goods) are poorly developed and very few product labeling schemes exist that enable end-consumers to take responsibility for their consumption by choosing products on the basis of those embedded emissions.[99]

If states, and producers and consumers, are to be held accountable to others for their emissions, then it is necessary to establish a proper system of accounting. However, the system of national accounting developed by the UNFCCC and KP only registers the emissions from "end-point production" inside the territory of each country, not the emissions associated with consumption from imports or exports or the emissions associated with international transportation.[100] As a consequence, such accounting fails to reflect the extent to which improvements in many developed countries' domestic emissions profiles merely reflect the "offshoring" of manufacturing industries to developing countries, particularly China. If anything, over the past two decades this problem has worsened with the transfer of manufacturing from developed to developing countries, in particular to "Factory Asia." For example, approximately one-quarter of Chinese emissions are embodied in its exports.[101] Accountability for those emissions, for which consumers are ultimately responsible, has been geographically displaced to these distant producers, which generally do not have carbon pricing. Consequently, affluent consumers buy more and cheaper imported products made using higher carbon intensity energy inputs.

In the absence of a global price on carbon and in the absence of any other mechanism to restrict or register the embodiment of GHGs in globally attenuated production chains, manufacturing in developed countries with a carbon price (as in the EU) must compete against goods produced by other countries without carbon pricing. This has prompted proposals in the EU (particularly by France) for "border tax adjustments" to add an equalizing penalty to goods imported from countries without a carbon price to prevent "carbon leakage" and competitive disadvantage. Such proposals have been fiercely resisted by China and India as subverting differentiated responsibilities under the climate regime.[102] Moreover, attempts to circumvent this problem by restricting border taxes to imports from developed countries would possibly infringe the principle of nondiscrimination in the world trading system and lead to retaliation.

Finally, major fossil fuel exporters—such as Australia, Canada, Indonesia, Norway, the Russian Federation, and Saudi Arabia—have been able to increase their national wealth without taking any responsibility for the emissions associated with their exports.

THE UNFCCC'S LEGITIMACY DEFICIT

The legitimacy of any treaty depends on social judgments about the procedural fairness of the negotiating process, the substantive fairness of its principles and obligations, and its effectiveness in addressing the problem. These considerations are often grouped into "input legitimacy" and "output legitimacy." In our judgment, and that of many observers, the international climate regime falls well short of a legitimate regime.

The various deficits and flaws just described contribute to a legitimacy deficit that has diminished the authority and effectiveness of the global climate regime. The lack of a fair formula by which targets and actions can be framed and allocated amounts to an "equity deficit"; the inequalities faced by small nation parties in substantive negotiations dominated by the major economies amounts to a "democratic deficit"; the simple production-based methods of calculating national emissions inventories are unable to capture the intricacies of the globalized production and trade in emissions and produce an "accounting deficit"; and the failure of national governments to acknowledge and respond to the scale and seriousness of climate change has produced a major "ambition deficit."

As a consequence, over the past five years, the authority of the global climate regime has been eroded. Indeed, following Copenhagen and prior to the modest success of COP 17 at Durban in 2011 in establishing a negotiation process to 2015, there was real concern that the whole regime may unravel. And as a result, paradoxically, progress toward tackling global warming seems to depend even more on progress at the national level—individual national economic, administrative, and political capacities and increasingly autonomous national commitments to decarbonization—ahead of the formal evolution of global climate governance.

This trend toward delegitimization is therefore especially worrying on two counts. First, unlike during the first wave of anxiety about global warming in the late 1980s, most governments now seem less prepared to embark on ambitious restructuring toward a low-carbon economy at the national level. The institutional inertia embedded in national political systems, the structural and material power wielded by industry sectors dependent on fossil fuels, and economic and political competitiveness between nation-states in the international arena have proved to be potent retardants and in some cases obstacles to effective decarbonization policy in many countries (and especially among the Anglo-states such as Australia, Canada, and the United States). Only a few states—for instance, Germany and the United Kingdom—have overcome these obstacles to become climate leaders in terms of their own mitigation performance and in their guidance at regional and international negotiations. Many more have become laggards.[103]

Ironically, the partially successful marketization of climate governance through carbon trading and offsetting—the strong preference among developed countries to rely upon carbon pricing as their preferred policy tool, operating through a global carbon market—has worked to slow the pace of decarbonization. The attempt to solve the challenge posed by global warming to accumulation under carboniferous capitalism has merely produced a weak and unreflexive form of ecological modernization that has been more successful in commodifying emissions than reducing them. Politically, the underlying longer-term reasons for accepting such a complicated new pricing/trading are usually buried in the debate over the short-term impacts of carbon pricing.

Second, this national resistance further lessens the chance of the thing most required for effective global climate governance: a fair, coherent, integrated, and well-coordinated international effort to solve this truly global collective action problem. Yet, top-down and bottom-up initiatives should not be regarded as alternative models of climate governance. Rather, they can be mutually reinforcing. Unilateral leadership efforts at the local, national, and regional levels by state and nonstate actors help to build momentum for international agreement, while a robust international agreement provides the global direction and mutual assurance for the remaining states and other actors to join in the collective mitigation effort. Globally effective climate governance requires a coherent and integrated linking of local, national, regional, and international "levels" or "spheres."

FROM LAGGARDS TO LEADERS

What might break this logjam and overcome these pressing problems? It is increasingly feasible that rising popular concern over "extreme weather" in the United States, Europe, and elsewhere may lead to stronger political pressure from civil society for rapid, powerful, and effective climate policy performance, including revitalizing the arena of international negotiations, by governments of major emitting states. Populous developing countries such as Brazil, China, India, and Indonesia are also highly vulnerable to climate impacts, which threaten to undermine any recent progress toward higher living standards. These countries are also undergoing rapid political change through the growth of their own civil societies, which may also further transform their own participation in the global climate regime.

Under these circumstances "bottom-up decision making," the current source of failure for the institutions of global climate governance, may yet become the driver for a legitimate international climate governance regime, as climate policy innovators and leaders in both the North and the South emerge out of desperation and exasperation to drive a range of interlocking and mutually reinforcing climate-related international agreements that galvanize the UNFCCC and contribute more widely to what Robert Keohane and David Victor have termed a global "climate regime complex."[104]

In addition, the rapid and accelerating development and deployment of ever more commercially competitive renewable energy power generation and storage technologies, and the increasing energy efficiency of many technologies, are increasing the prospects for the displacement/replacement of fossil-fueled power generation. However, as the IEA has recognized, the next decade is crucial if we are to avoid locking in high-emissions technologies, as the investment horizons for large-scale power generation are decades long.[105] Continuing development of new coal and gas-fired power generation will cause significant economic and social stresses in those countries where such technological and economic lock-in occurs. Meanwhile, consumer demand for material goods may become more restrained and responsive to issues of hidden and embodied carbon. This may result from changes in monitoring and product regulation that enable proper "climate accountability," including via changes that ensure that traded embodied carbon is both fully priced and regulated. However, without such transformations and a rapid reversal of the growth trend in emissions over the next critical decade, the prospects for ecological, social, and economic stability are bleak.

CHAPTER 4

REMAKING NATURE:
BIODIVERSITY IN PERIL

THE DOOMSDAY VAULT

Buried in permafrost in the side of a mountain on the island of Spitz-bergen, in the Svalbard archipelago in the Arctic Circle, is the Svalbard Global Seed Vault. Officially opened in February 2008, the Seed Vault is designed to store backup copies of the seeds of the world's major food crops. Dubbed the "Doomsday Vault" or a "Living Fort Knox," the vault operates like a safety deposit box in a bank. The seeds are sealed and stored, at around minus 18 degrees Celsius, free of charge to public or private depositors and only the depositors or their assignees can remove the seeds. The vault was built by the government of Norway, on whose territory the vault is located, and it is managed by the Nordic Genetic Resource Centre, financed by the Global Crop Diversity Trust (an endowment fund that includes donors such as the Bill and Melinda

Gates Foundation, the Rockefeller Foundation, and Monsanto), kept secure by the Governor of Svalbard, and guided by the Food and Agricultural Organization's Global System for Plant Genetic Resources.[1]

The Svalbard Seed Vault is intended to provide a backup system to around 1,400 gene banks located in more than one hundred countries around the globe. These gene banks, in turn, provide a system of *ex situ* (off-site) conservation of valuable plant genetic resources (PGR) that are essential to maintain the resilience and productivity of the world's food crops. These PGRs include the genetic material contained in modern, scientifically bred varieties as well as material from the world's rapidly diminishing landraces—the locally adapted, traditional crop varieties selected by farmers practicing subsistence agriculture over thousands of years. The problem is that these gene banks are vulnerable to lack of resourcing, war, natural disaster, and/or climate change, with potentially devastating consequences for global food security.

Yet we should not take comfort from the Doomsday Vault. The vault, along with the system of gene banks that it is designed to back up, is one symptom of a critical ecological problem: the erosion of genetic diversity in the world's basic food crops. Genetic erosion refers to the loss of individual genes and gene-complexes in a particular species, which manifests as a reduction in the quantity of different varieties or specimens of that species. The turn to *ex situ* solutions to this problem is a clear admission that *in situ* (on site, in place) efforts to prevent genetic erosion are failing. While today's staple and other food crops have drawn on the varieties developed over millennia by farmers all over the world, the genetic variety of food crops has shrunk dramatically in the past one hundred years due primarily to the replacement of local varieties with "exotic" commercial varieties.

The Seed Vault may be seen as the culmination of a range of modernization and globalization processes—including the so-called Green Revolution in agriculture and the rise of global agribusiness—that have fundamentally transformed wild habitats and landscapes, systems of food production and consumption, and food cultures around the globe. Yet the erosion of crop genetic diversity provides just one manifestation of a much larger problem that is the subject of this chapter: the accelerating decline in the planet's biological diversity, which is the diversity or variety of life on Earth.

BIODIVERSITY

Biological diversity—or biodiversity—encompasses not just genetic diversity within particular species but also the diversity of species (animals, plants, and microorganisms) and the diversity of ecosystems.[2] All of these different forms of diversity are rapidly diminishing, producing a biodiversity crisis on a planetary scale. Seed banks, along with botanical gardens and zoos, can only ever preserve a fraction of species and their genetic material and, in any event, they cannot enable species to interact, mutate, and evolve in response to a changing natural environment. As Timothy Swanson explains, "*Ex situ* conservation maintains a one-time 'snapshot' of existing diversity; it does not provide the background against which diversity thrives and develops."[3] Yet *in situ* efforts to protect biodiversity are also failing, despite the enactment of endangered species legislation and the establishment of protected areas and national parks around the world, and despite the negotiation of a range of international treaties to protect biodiversity, the most prominent of which is the *Convention on Biological Diversity 1992*.

The major drivers of biodiversity loss are overharvesting, deforestation and habitat destruction, invasive species, pollution and environmental degradation, and, increasingly, climate change.[4] Many endemic (local, native) species will be unable to move or adapt to the range and degree necessary to survive changes in temperature and rainfall. Nor could many survive in the absence of the wholesale transplanting of the ecosystems of which they are part. It is no accident that the threatened polar bear has become the poster animal for climate activists around the world; polar bears and other species inhabiting the polar regions of the Earth simply have nowhere else to go.

The proximate causes of biodiversity loss are actions at the local level, such as catching fish; clearing land for pasture, cropland, or plantations; the effects of farms and factories releasing pollutants into the air, waterways, and oceans; and changes in local weather patterns, including temperature, rainfall, and storms. In this chapter, we seek to link these proximate causes to the deeper structural changes at work across our four domains of globalization (scientific/technological, economic, cultural, and political/governmental). This includes connecting the changing material practices wrought by these intertwined domains of globalization with changing ideas, values, and discourses about the relationship between human and nonhuman species. Population growth, a key variable in the "I=PAT" equation, is also a major driver of biodiversity loss. But changes in population growth rates cannot be understood in isolation from the four domains of globalization. For example, the key elements of population change—fertility rates, life expectancy, and net migration—are shaped by access to contraception and medicines, employment opportunities (particularly for women), educational opportunities and cultural expectations about family size and the role of women, and government regulation.

While it is clear from the fossil record that neither the long phase of modernization nor the more recent phase of globalization is uniquely responsible for biodiversity loss, we argue that they nonetheless serve as the main structural drivers behind the present acceleration of biodiversity loss, especially in the past half century. This loss is mostly unintended (a classic "negative externality"), but in some cases it has been deliberate. We also track how biodiversity loss came to be known and understood and the political, economic, and cultural responses to such loss, including efforts to put a value on biodiversity, to provide financial incentives for the protection or sustainable utilization of biodiversity, and to eliminate threats to the most vunerable and commercially valuable species. As we shall see, some of these responses—such as genetic engineering of agricultural crops to withstand climate change—represent an extension of the modernization process, while others seek to make both markets and states—the social structures of "organized irresponsibility"—more aware of, and more responsive and responsible to, the fate of nonhuman species. While there are clear incentives to preserve commercially valuable species, along with their closest wild relatives, they represent only a tiny fraction of the Earth's biodiversity. Indeed, efforts to protect and promote commercially valuable species, such as major cereal crops and livestock, are often at the expense of many wild species. Unless new social structures of "organized responsibility" can prevail at multiple levels of governance (from the local through to the global), then countless ecosystems, species, and the genetic diversity within particular species will be lost forever.

We begin with a brief overview of the depth and scale of the biodiversity crisis and then backtrack to examine how the long processes of modernization gave rise to accelerated processes of globalization to precipitate the current biodiversity crisis. Having already tracked the rise in general production, consumption, and trade in chapter 2, here we confine our focus to those dimensions of modernization and globalization that are most directly implicated in biodiversity loss: modernization and increasing international specialization and exchange in agriculture, forestry, fishing, and natural resource extraction as well as the increasing global movement of species through colonization, migration, and trade. We also track changing ideas about nonhuman species, including the emergence of the scientific understanding of the concept of a species, without which a biodiversity crisis would not be recognized, new practices such as the genetic modification of species would not be possible, and international efforts to protect biodiversity would not be under way. We then turn to the fundamental question, "Why should we care about biodiversity loss?" to examine the debates about biodiversity's worth and value, and how it should be protected. Finally, we identify the main global governance responses to the biodiversity crisis and highlight their limitations.

THE BIODIVERSITY CRISIS

Extinction is the most obscure and local of all biological processes. . . . We don't see the last butterfly of its species snatched from the air by a bird or the last orchid of a certain kind killed by the collapse of its supporting tree. . . . In order to know that a given species is truly extinct, you have to know it well, including its exact distribution and favored habitats. You have to look long and hard without result. But we do not know the vast majority of species of organisms well; we have yet to anoint so many as 90 percent of them with scientific names.[5]

As Edward O. Wilson observes, it is no easy matter to produce reliable estimates of the extent of global biodiversity, or its loss over any given time period, because we have a very patchy knowledge base against which to track change. Species extinction is the endpoint defined by the disappearance of all individuals of a particular species, and it is always harder to prove an absence than a presence. Nonetheless, generalizations can be made about those species that have been closely studied, and these studies make it clear that "extinction is proceeding at a rapid rate, far above prehuman levels" and "in many cases, the level is calamitous."[6]

The Millennium Ecosystem Assessment report on biodiversity estimates the total number of species on Earth as somewhere between five to thirty million, although only five million species have been formally described.[7] Yet the rate of species extinction has climbed dramatically over the last century, and especially since 1950. The recorded evidence of *known* extinctions over the past century indicates an increase in extinctions of approximately one hundred times the background rate (which refers to the extinction rate in the fossil record). Some of the less direct estimates put the figure at one thousand to ten thousand higher than the background rate.[8]

We noted in chapter 1 that the Millennium Ecosystem Assessment found that human activity has changed the Earth's ecosystems more rapidly and extensively over the past fifty years than in any previous time in human history. These changes have hastened the reduction of ecosystem diversity, the extinction of species, and the erosion of genetic diversity. At the time of writing, the International Union for the Conservation of Nature's (IUCN) Red List of Threatened Species has identified 3,879 animal and plant species that are critically endangered, plus a further 5,689 that are endangered, 10,002 that are vulnerable, and 4,389 that are near threatened.[9]

The evolution of life on Earth spans a period of approximately 3.5 billion years. The evolutionary process has produced a bewildering array of new species from a common ancestry, and it has seen the gradual and sometimes mass extinction of many species. However, over the long span of geological time, the rate of speciation has far outstripped the rate of extinction. The arrival of the Anthropocene—the period characterized by the wide-scale and accelerated influence of humans on the planet—is threatening to reverse this process. In effect, humans are remaking nature, but the new nature is much less diverse and resilient than the old and will become increasingly inhospitable to human and nonhuman species alike. Indeed, some leading biodiversity scientists have warned that if the calamitous rate of species extinction continues, then humans may undermine the capacity of the evolutionary process to generate new species.[10]

The Millennium Ecosystem Assessment report also makes it clear that biodiversity loss is a global problem in the sense that loss of biodiversity at local scales now spans all continents and the oceans, producing effects that are planetary in scale. In the case of terrestrial biodiversity, the report found that "while the vast majority of recorded extinctions since 1500 have occurred on oceanic islands, continental extinctions are now as common as island extinctions. Approximately 50% of extinctions over the past 20 years occurred on continents."[11]

The grand narrative of the Earth's biodiversity since the early modern period is that it has been increasingly exploited, modified, commoditized, transported, reassembled, and consumed all over the world by one particular species more than any other. In effect, *Homo sapiens* are increasingly transforming and consuming the Earth's biosphere at the expense of other species. Yet our story of biodiversity loss reveals other asymmetries as well, namely significant disparities in both the distribution and consumption of biodiversity between different regions, nations, and social classes.

The World Wildlife Fund's most recent *Living Planet Report* (2012) measures humanity's ecological footprint in terms of the consumption of "biocapacity," which is expressed in global hectares and covers croplands, land used for grazing, coastal and inland fishing grounds, and forests that provide timber and absorb carbon dioxide.[12] The report found that the rate of humanity's consumption of the Earth's biocapacity exceeded the rate at which it could be regenerated at some point in the 1970s, that by 2008 humanity was consuming the equivalent of 1.5 planets, and that by 2030, even two planets will not be enough. However, the developed countries' per capita ecological footprint is approximately three to three and half times bigger than developing countries.' With Earth's population continuing to grow, if everyone consumed at the same rates as present, then by 2050 we would need 2.9 planets.[13]

The geographic distribution of terrestrial and marine biodiversity, and biodiversity loss, is also very uneven. This can be partly explained by the fact that species diversity varies dramatically among the world's biomes (the scientific name for broad habitat and vegetation types, such as moist tropical forests, boreal forests, tundra, deserts, etc.). In the world's oceans, the richest areas of biodiversity are found in tropical coral reefs, which are under increasing threat as a result of "coral bleaching" from rising surface sea temperatures. On land, the diversity of moist tropical forests is orders of magnitude higher than any other biome, and these forests also include the greatest diversity of higher taxa (such as vertebrates). Many of the world's "biodiversity hotspots," which are "exceptional concentrations of endemic species . . . undergoing exceptional loss of habitat" are found in these regions.[14] Edward O. Wilson has made a "maximally optimistic" estimate of extinction rates in tropical forests of twenty-seven thousand species per year, seventy-four per day, and three every hour.[15]

That was in 1992. The World Wildlife Fund's Living Planet Index (LPI) of vertebrate populations shows a decline of around 33 percent between 1970 and 2008.[16] However, this average conceals a striking difference in the index for populations of terrestrial vertebrates in tropical as compared to temperate ecosystems, with the former declining by 45 percent compared to the latter increasing by an average of 5 percent.[17] This discrepancy is explained by the fact that biodiversity was much lower in temperate zones in 1970 when measurement started, and land use changes have been much more dramatic in tropical zones since 1970. The authors of the index also suggest that if the baseline for the temperate index were set earlier—several centuries back—then the long-term decline would likely be comparable to the recent decline in the tropical index.[18]

These disparities in the distribution and destruction of biodiversity highlight the central political and governance challenge facing efforts to protect biodiversity: that many of the poorest countries of the world contain the richest biodiversity that is most under threat, but the richest countries in the world have derived the greatest benefits from the exploitation of the Earth's biodiversity and general biocapacity since the Age of Empire. To understand how and why this has occurred, we therefore return to the long fuse of modernization discussed in chapter 2, with a special focus on the "ecological" side of the imperial adventure.

THE LONG FUSE OF MODERNIZATION: ECOLOGICAL IMPERIALISM

As with global warming, the understandings and actions that underpin the recent period of rapid globalization affecting biological diversity emerged slowly over the preceding five centuries. Again we see a pattern of modernization involving the interbraided influences of changing scientific knowledge and technological innovation, economic change, and deep-seated transformations in the cultural awareness that have produced a massive loss of global biodiversity while also generating a global understanding of biodiversity loss and a global political and regulatory response. We shall start with the relatively recent discovery of species before we turn to the causes of their disappearance.

DISCOVERING SPECIES

Humans had a considerable hand in wiping out some species, and co-evolving with others, well before they understood the concept of a species. Our current understanding of biological diversity separates life on Earth from the inanimate world and separates it into distinct species. This awareness is a relatively recent and thoroughly modern construct dependent on a reconfiguration of understandings of time and the processes of creation.

Although the Western study of nature dates back to classical times, from the 17th century onward new ideas arose about the origins and diversity of life on Earth. Previously, in Judaeo-Christian cosmology, all creatures were created by the hand of God, and humans originated in the Garden of Eden. Moreover, according to the Christian medieval understanding of the Great Chain of Being, all of Creation was arranged in a preordained, eternally linked hierarchy, with God at the apex and humans standing below the angels but above the beasts, plants, and minerals.

These theological and cultural certainties were demolished during the Enlightenment, when a new generation of scientific savants began to create a language and logic for thinking about "natural history," the description and classification of natural phenomena, and "natural philosophy," which investigated the relationship between natural phenomena. They puzzled over the nature and origins of fossils, which had vexed thinkers since classical times. The very relationship of these objects to life was disputed: some theories proposed that they were deceptively lifelike mineral forms, perhaps planted by God as clues or distractions, others claimed that they represented a stage of metamorphosis from inorganic to living matter, while yet others believed that they were the residues of a race of antediluvian giants. If fossils *were* traces of former life, how had they been buried, by whom, and for how long? What had happened to these now vanished creatures? If ancient shells were found on hilltops, was this the result of the Great Flood?

By the middle of the 18th century, there was widespread scientific acceptance that fossils were the remains of long dead plants and animals. "Fossils may be defined as the durable parts of animal and vegetable structures imbedded in rocks and strata by natural causes at a remote period," wrote Gideon Mantell in 1851.[19] This realization was aided by the invention of "deep" time through the emergent sciences of geology and mineralogy, which indicated that the Earth had a long history that extended well before the creation date of Sunday, 23 October 4004 BC, proclaimed by the Archbishop of Armagh James Usher on the authority of the Old Testament. Fossils were enthusiastically collected as curios and described in illustrated scientific papers widely circulated in Europe. The first step toward the "discovery" of biodiversity was the realization that there were creatures that no longer existed, whose lives and remains were affected by long and enduring earthly processes. This created a cultural space for the science of paleontology and the idea of extinction. What was still lacking, however, was the planetary overview that proved that no "lost worlds" of dinosaurs still survived, or the ability to link these lost life-forms to the present.

Simultaneously, the rich interaction between early "gentleman collectors" and the imperial and colonizing process hastened the establishment of a taxonomic science of life-forms. Colonization brought with it an enthusiasm for the wonders these places contained. New varieties of plants—some ornamental, others "useful"—were brought back as plunder from the new frontiers and traded across Europe. Botanical gardens and nurseries were established to "domesticate" these novelties. The elder and younger John Tradescant were both travellers and explorers and voracious plant collectors. Tradescant the Younger's "three trips to Virginia, in 1637, 1642 and 1654, gave south Lambeth a whole new garden flora. The haul included the bald cypress, the first tulip trees, the delightful red maple . . . the American black walnut, the red mulberry, the shagbark hickory with its long green pendulous catkins and the amazingly successful Virginia creeper."[20] More than a century later, Sir Joseph Banks embarked on an expedition to Australasia with Cook, where he found and described creatures and plants of almost indescribable strangeness—the black swan, kangaroo, and platypus and eucalypts and bottle-brushes.

This incoming tide of new species, brought by imperial trade and scientific appropriation, demanded systematization and provoked a search for order. Schema for identifying and labeling plants and animals had existed for millennia, but these were not "universal." Methods varied between localities and over time, producing uncertainty and confusion as the volume of trade and exchange in new species increased. The earliest European attempts to build specimen-based botanical gardens and herbaria, and to create accurately illustrated documentation using a robust schema for naming and classifying specimens, were, unsurprisingly, founded in 16th century Renaissance Italy, amid Europe's most dynamic centers for trade and the dispersal of knowledge through printed texts. Again, these attempts at creating knowledge were part of a cooperative scientific pursuit across Europe in the 17th and 18th centuries, aided by the use of Latin, the common language of scholars.[21] However, it is only in the mid-18th century that the Swede Carl Linnaeus defined a taxonomic method for the classification of living organisms that was eventually adopted globally. Publication of the *Species Plantarum* in 1753, and the tenth edition of his *Systema Naturae* in 1758 (first published in 1735), established the classificatory methods and nomenclature that would come to be used to definitively describe species of plants, animals, and insects. An accepted approach to identifying, naming, and communicating unambiguously about species "in the abstract" had finally been established. This was the second major discovery required to create an understanding of biodiversity and, in turn, it made possible the third transformation.

The culminating shift in understanding that transformed the Western image of nature in ways critical to the "discovery" of biological diversity was the idea of evolution, developed by Alfred Russel Wallace and Charles Darwin. The revolutionary notion that humans were connected to other species through a common ancestry, and that species were believed to have evolved over time rather than being separate, immutable, and directly fashioned in a moment of divine creation, overturned any residual notion of the Great Chain of Being and provided a starting point—along with Mendel's genetics—from which to understand speciation as a natural process. Wallace had traveled extensively and researched as a naturalist in Brazil in the late 1840s and early 1850s and then the East Indies (now Malaysia and Indonesia) from the mid-1850s to early 1860s. His publication, in 1855, of a paper on "the Law regulating the Introduction of New Species" predated and held most of the founding ideas later reflected by his colleague Darwin. The first edition of *On the Origin of Species* was published in 1859, but much of the evidence for Darwin's theory had been collected by him on his global voyage on HMS *Beagle* in the 1830s.

The colonizing process not only hastened the establishment of a taxonomic science of life. It also hastened the disappearance of many life-forms. Indeed, the global extension and intensification of resource extraction by colonization, along with technological innovation and population growth, were the major drivers behind the transformation of the Earth's biological landscape during the modern period. The technological and energy revolutions of the 18th to 20th century proceeded hand in hand with a dramatic growth in global population, which grew from some 641 million people in 1700 to 4.35 billion in 1980. Throughout this period, lightly transformed ecosystems were expropriated from indigenous peoples and converted into "productive" landscapes to meet growing demand for natural resources. According to Joel Mokyr, international trade almost doubled between 1622 and 1700 such that "by 1700, long-distance trade extended to the Caribbean, North America, and Asia. . . . Goods like sugar, spices, tea, tobacco, cod, indigo, rice and cotton, to name but a few, came from thousands of miles away."[22]

Woodlands, savannah, and native grasslands were fenced and replanted or transformed by roads; forests cleared or fragmented; wetlands drained and river systems dammed or diverted to create dryland irrigated cropland and pasture while inadvertently destroying habitat for indigenous species. J. F. Richards has estimated that, globally, 432 million hectares of grasslands, savannah, woodlands, and forests were converted into arable land in the period 1860–1919, and a further 419 million hectares in the following sixty years to 1980.[23] He writes that "European invasion of the New World, African and Australasian grasslands was the result of sudden growth in ranching or extensive commercial grazing in the second half of the 19th century. Steeply rising market demand for beef and wool in the urbanized regions of western Europe and eastern North America spurred the growth of extensive commercial sheep and cattle grazing in areas of new settlement."[24]

Deforestation occurred concurrently in both temperate and tropical regions—although initially more in the temperate. Europe lost 50 to 70 percent of its original forest cover, mostly during the early Middle Ages: for instance, the early deforestation of England was directly associated with shipbuilding and logging for fuel. North America lost about 30 percent or about 116 million hectares of forest cover, 75 percent of this in the 19th century.[25] Richards observes that, as instances of a global pattern, between 1700 and 1914, forest cover declined from 61 percent to 37 percent in European Russia; the Sila forest of southern Italy was decimated; the four million hectares of jungle in mid-19th-century Burma were reduced to a few hundred thousand hectares by 1914; and some 110,000 square kilometers of mallee woodland had been cleared for farmland in southeastern Australia.[26]

These processes were accompanied and in some instances driven by social-technological innovation. Heavy chains were dragged between bullocks to clear the stunted mallee scrub in a process known as "mallee rolling." This was greatly speeded up by the invention of bulldozers, which could haul a large iron ball between them for this purpose. The introduction of steam-driven sawmills and rail systems further hastened the destruction of forests and the processing of timber. Railroads and steam ferries moved grain, meat, timber, and fiber from the "hinterland" to cities and ports, enabling a significant increase in the volume of produce that could be moved to market and accelerating the speed of trade. Faster shipping, and canning and refrigeration technologies that became commercially viable in the 1880s, meant a wider range of foods could be transported to distant markets. Historians once dated the British agricultural revolution as occurring between 1760 and 1830 with the enclosure of the commons, the invention of the seed drill, new systems of crop rotation, and improved livestock breeding. However, more recent historical research has suggested that the Agricultural Revolution should be uncoupled from the Industrial Revolution and stretched to cover the much longer period of 1560–1880.[27] Indeed, the spread of new agricultural crops, technologies, and methods has been more of a gradual evolutionary process, propelled in part by resource demand and population growth and by the adaptive invention of new machinery (such as the stump-jump plow that helped open up the cleared but stump-littered landscapes of the Mallee to grain cropping) and species (such as drought-resistant wheat) that hastened the conquest of "new frontier" landscapes.

Similarly, humans' capacity to trap, net, shoot, and poison species grew greatly in the 19th century. Coupled in some cases with a cavalier lack of concern for the welfare of particular species, and the compounding effect of other pressures from introduced predators and diseases and the destruction of habitat, the rate of extinction leaped. Five animals—the dodo, passenger pigeon, bald eagle, bison, and certain species of whale—are now recognized as iconic examples of the effects of human rapacity on other species. The manner of extinction of the dodo may have been identical to that of hundreds of other land-bound island-dwelling bird species, which were mainly accidental victims of the introduction of pigs, rats, and other feral animals rather than of overhunting (in this case, by Portuguese sailors). However, human rapacity coupled with new technological capacities for destruction were the unambiguous cause of the demise of the passenger pigeon. A. W. Schorger comments that "no other species of bird, to the best of our knowledge, ever approached the passenger pigeon in numbers."[28] Estimates of the size of the original population of this species are impossible to make—with estimates of between three and five billion[29]—but some attempts were made to calculate the size of specific flocks, which could extend for three hundred miles in length and a mile in width in flight. In autumn 1813, near Louisville, Kentucky, the renowned naturalist James Audubon encountered a tremendous flight of passenger pigeons, which he calculated to have contained no less than "a billion, one hundred and fifteen millions, one hundred and thirty-six thousand pigeons in one flock."[30] The decline had been precipitous from 1871 to 1880, and the extinction foreseen at that time. Almost exactly a century after Audubon's calculation, in 1914, the passenger pigeon became extinct—the last known individual died in the Cincinnati Zoo—exterminated by the felling of nesting forests in Pennsylvania and by hunters and netters who, believing the supply of birds to be inexhaustible, had trapped and shot them in their millions, season after season.

The American bison, the bald eagle, and whales are notable by contrast for how close to extinction each species or group of species has been brought. Bison herds estimated to be, in total, between sixty and one hundred million strong in the mid-19th century were reduced to scattered isolated populations of a dozen individuals or less totaling perhaps two thousand in all by the end of that century. They were extinct across most of their former range, which has altered ecologically as a result.[31] They now have only returned to some 350,000 beasts in genetically depauperate herds. The recovery from overhunting or attempts at extermination, and long-term survival, of other species is even less certain.

These depredations had other consequences. Urbanization and industrialization removed people from contact with "wild nature" and led to its Romantic revaluation and appreciation.[32] This change in outlook was accompanied by an aesthetic fascination in exotic plants and animals and an emergent empathetic concern for the capacities of nonhuman species to feel pain and loss—views that have found expression in animal welfare societies and more recent arguments for animal rights. Together, these changing sensibilities would lead, in the latter part of the 19th century, to the first attempts to limit or prohibit hunting and to protect threatened iconic species—lions, seals, elephants, bison, koalas, whales—which would in turn provide the foundations for more encompassing regulatory attempts to preserve biodiversity.

ECOLOGICAL IMPERIALISM—A FORM OF UNEQUAL EXCHANGE

The Age of Empires, which began in the 1500s and reached its high point in the late 19th century, saw the colonization of not only peoples but also of nature as it accelerated the transcontinental transformation of ecosystems—a process that Crosby has called "ecological imperialism."

Crosby's biogeographic study highlights several striking features of this wave of colonization. Europeans colonized New World regions predominantly in temperate zones that were climatically similar to Europe. These regions—which Crosby calls "the neo-Europes"—were quickly transformed into major food-producing zones that now export more foodstuffs of European provenance than any other region in the world.[33] The indigenous flora and fauna were nevertheless very different from and vulnerable to colonization by European species, which spread with a vigor that made this seem a very unequal sort of exchange. As a consequence, profound and global biological changes resulted from an ongoing deliberate and accidental transcontinental exchange of species.

The separation of the great supercontinent Pangaea around 180 million years ago into the continents we know today had enabled very different patterns and paths of speciation and extinction on the resultant continents. However, since Classical times, trade and invasions between Europe and Arabia, China and India, had penetrated and then breached these natural barriers, carrying a variety of species from these places into Europe. New developments in shipbuilding, rigging, and navigational aids in the 15th century, and the establishment of new trading routes between Europe and the Far East, southern Asia, the Americas, and Australasia, extended these breaches globally.

The earlier exchanges had brought with them accidental exchanges in microorganisms that were devastating for humans in Europe. The bubonic plague was introduced to Europe in 1347 via infected fleas carried from Asia into the port of Genoa. By 1450, one-third of Europe's population had died and the resultant depopulation of the continent saw wild nature resurgent on abandoned farmland. It is believed Alexander the Great's troops introduced leprosy from India and near-Asia to Greece, from where it spread throughout Europe.

Contact with the New World in the 1490s introduced into Europe a form of yaws that mutated into syphilis (the "grand pox").[34] Meanwhile, Europeans inadvertently—and sometimes deliberately—spread lethal plagues of smallpox and seemingly harmless diseases such as influenza to the New Worlds. These sicknesses devastated, and in some places wholly exterminated, indigenous peoples—thus greatly facilitating the "success" of European invasion in Latin America and Australia.[35]

Trade, invasion, and colonization also had profound implications for all other species. The production and exchange of agricultural surpluses in the neo-Europes were achieved by a massive transmigration of seeds, animals, technologies, farming practices, people, business practices, and patterns of settlement from old Europe to the new colonies. The new environments were exceptionally hospitable to European plants and animals with few local predators and diseases to stop their "naturalization." At the same time, now staple food plants—such as tomatoes, potatoes, corn, and maize—were introduced from the New World and greatly enhanced the European diet. As Thomas Dunlap and others have noted, the leitmotif of 19th-century settlement was to remake new landscapes in the shape of the old, often by ignoring crucial ecological differences.[36] For instance, as the noted Australian historian W. K. Hancock wrote in 1930 of European settlers in Australia, "the invaders hated trees."[37] Native forests were cleared to create what appeared to resemble open European-style pasture or farmland. However, cattle and sheep quickly destroyed the fine native grasses and their hard hoofs compacted the soft soils. Plowing broke up soil structure and exposed soils to torrential rains. Massive erosion resulted, carrying away plants and topsoil and leaving gullies ten feet deep, clogging rivers, and destroying creeks and wetlands.

The deliberate introduction of European plants, birds, and animals—including by "acclimatization societies" intent on creating a pleasantly familiar environment for the new settlers—also caused havoc when these species "ran wild." The reintroduction and naturalization of horses to North and South America profoundly changed native Indian cultures as well as American ecosystems. In Australia in 1859, Thomas Austin released a dozen rabbits for hunting on his farm in southern Victoria. Within a decade, two million or more were being shot and trapped without influence on their population, and by 1900, rabbits had covered nearly the entire continent in a "grey blanket." Their burrowing added to erosion problems while their gnawing reduced native seeds and seedlings, halting regeneration and contributing to local flora extinctions. Meanwhile foxes, introduced in Australia in 1871 to make hunting more British, and cats, rats, and mice—feral escapees—had spread throughout the continent and carved a swath through native animal species, contributing greatly to the wave of extinctions that occurred among small and medium-sized mammals between 1850 and 1900.[38]

This process of translocation continues to affect the "new Europes," the "old Europe," and Asia. In 1936 scientists imported and released the cane toad (Bufo marinus), a native of South America but brought from Honolulu, in an attempt at biological control of French's cane beetle, an accidentally introduced pest, and the native greyback cane beetle, which together were infesting another introduced crop, sugar cane, in Queensland (northern Australia). The toad, a prolific breeder, failed to deal with the pest beetle. But it has now spread across much of northern Australia and is the most common vertebrate in Queensland. With its voracious appetite and its toxic skin, it has contributed directly to a new and catastrophic wave of extinctions of native mammals and reptiles wherever it has spread in Australia.[39] The eucalypt, native to Australia, was introduced to India, North America, South Africa, and Europe for its fast growing timber but has escaped to become a weed.

The Australian brushtail possum was introduced to New Zealand to create a fur industry and, in the absence of native predators, has become a pest comparable to the rabbit in Australia, with over thirty million animals harboring bovine tuberculosis and threatening native vegetation and wildlife. In all, accidental, ornamental, and inappropriate introductions of plants, animals, insects, and diseases paradoxically led to increases in overall biodiversity in some places through the introduction of exotic species while producing a net global decline in indigenous species. Indeed, the global dispersal of species appears to be accelerating and threatens to produce a "planet of weeds."[40]

SHORTENING THE BIODIVERSITY FUSE: THE GLOBAL PHASE OF MODERNIZATION

We noted earlier that the main proximate causes of species extinction today include overharvesting, deforestation and habitat destruction, invasive species, diseases (usually introduced by invasive species), pollution, and climate change. Yet the acceleration of these proximate drivers of biodiversity loss in the 20th century would not have occurred without changes in more abstract socioeconomic practices across different spatial and temporal scales. Over the past five decades, modernization in key industries such as forestry, fishing, and agriculture has been increasingly tied to processes of globalization. This includes not only trade in agricultural commodities, timber, wildlife (or parts thereof), and other natural resources but also the accelerating global diffusion of particular technologies, management systems, and forms of knowledge. In all, the industrialization of agriculture and natural resource harvesting, propelled by increasing international economic specialization and exchange, has dramatically accelerated the depletion of the Earth's biocapacity and biological diversity.

Combined processes of modernization and globalization have been facilitated by major technological transformations along every stage of global commodity chains—at the point of harvesting and resource extraction, in transportation, and for the reconstitution of nature (from selective breeding to genetic engineering)—and have increased yields, the volume, and improved the appearance of materials appearing at the point of retail.

For example, in some marine systems the modernization of the fishing industry during the course of the 20th century has seen a massive depletion of the biomass of both targeted species (especially larger fish) and those caught incidentally to as little as one-tenth of the levels prior to industrialization.[41] As fisheries in coastal areas become depleted, industrial fishing fleets have moved to deeper waters; and as fish stocks at higher rungs in the food chain become depleted, stocks of species at lower trophic levels have been increasingly targeted. Many commercial fishing vessels are now giant floating factories, with sonar technology to identify schools of fish, sophisticated harvesting systems that can trawl in deeper waters and capture massive loads, and sophisticated processing, packing, and refrigeration facilities.

According to the World Wildlife Fund's *Living Planet Report*, "Seventy per cent of commercial marine fish stocks are now threatened, with some fisheries and stocks, such as Mediterranean bluefin tuna, already on the verge of collapse."[42] Some fisheries have entirely collapsed, such as the Atlantic cod stocks off the coast of Newfoundland, which forced the closure of the cod fishing industry in 2003.[43]

Trade in fish has grown significantly during the 20th century and fish products make up around half of the exports of many developing countries.[44] Many of the areas where fisheries are being depleted are in the exclusive economic zones of low-income countries, such as Mauritania, Senegal, Gambia, Guinea Bissau, and Sierra Leone, and most of the catch is exported to wealthy markets, such as Europe.[45]

However, there are also many other pressures on the diversity of marine ecosystems, including climate change and ocean acidification, pollution, and increasing travel and trade. The latter has seen the spread of invasive alien species and disease organisms, with harmful consequences for many native marine species. For example, "the introduction of the comb jelly fish (*Mnemiopsis leidyi*) in the Black Sea caused the loss of 26 major fisheries species and has been implicated (along with other factors) in subsequent growth of the anoxic 'dead zone.'"[46] There has also been a rise in toxic algal blooms in coastal waters, which pose significant risks to marine organisms, coastal aquaculture industries, and human health. A high-level workshop convened by the International Program on the State of the Ocean in June 2011 concluded that the world's oceans may enter a phase of marine extinctions unprecedented in human history and comparable to the five mass extinctions on the geological record.[47]

The Earth's forests have been harvested, altered, and cleared by humans for thousands of years, but the overall rate of deforestation has accelerated in the past three centuries (around 40 percent), and especially the past fifty years with the introduction of more efficient harvesting technologies. In twenty-five countries, forests have now completely disappeared and another twenty countries have lost more than 90 percent of their forests.[48] Whereas forest cover in Europe diminished over many centuries, and in North America in the 19th century, deforestation in other areas of the world has occurred much more rapidly and recently. The current overall rate of forest loss is around ten million hectares per year, an area around four times the size of Belgium.[49]

Brazil is home to the earth's largest rainforest biome—the Amazon forest—which also contains one-fifth of the world's fresh water. However, since the 1960s, deforestation has grown rapidly to make way for commercial logging, cattle ranching, mining, soy bean production, and human settlement and associated infrastructure such as hydroelectric dams, roads, and highways. Despite the substantial reduction in government subsidies in the 1990s, rates of deforestation have continued, primarily due to the high profitability of private cattle ranching.[50] The "development" of the Amazon rainforest has not only led to a massive loss of biological diversity but also depleted one of the Earth's largest carbon dioxide sinks while increasing the rate of global methane emissions from livestock.

Just as the rising global demand for beef has helped to drive deforestation in the Amazon, growing demand for palm oil (used in a wide range of products, from margarine to cosmetics) has been a significant driver behind the conversion of many tropical forests to palm oil plantations, particularly in Malaysia and Indonesia, which together provide 87 percent of global supply.[51] The area of land covered by palm oil plantations increased eightfold over the past twenty years. The loss of forest cover has pushed higher-order species like the orangutans closer to extinction.

The technological developments that have enabled more efficient natural resource extraction are not autonomous processes. Rather, they are driven by public and private investment in research and development to serve social goals (feeding a growing population, ensuring national food security); cater to a rising demand for food, fiber, timber, and fuel; and maximize productivity, profits, and hence capital accumulation by private firms. Technologies are developed and applied in the context of particular social rationalities and social relations. For example, the industrialization of agriculture, forestry, and fishing has been made possible by new forms of expert knowledge (genetics, agronomy, forestry, shipbuilding, accounting, etc.), new business and management practices, and expanding markets. Mechanization in any industry requires major capital investment and demands uniformity, predictability, and repetition to maximize economies of scale. When applied to agriculture and forestry, this has seen the replacement of diverse ecosystems with monocultures; crops and trees are planted in straight, evenly spaced lines to enable the mechanical harvesting of a standardized produce or timber. Alongside the increasing movement of rural populations to large towns and cities, rural landscapes have become more homogeneous through the growth of large plantations and broad-acre farms and the development of complementary infrastructure, such as the roads and power lines that now criss-cross rural and wild areas.

We argue that the modernization process, of which "the industrialization of natural resource extraction" is a key component, is the primary structural driver of biodiversity loss. The processes of globalization across all of our four domains have exacerbated this loss by facilitating the spatial extension and intensification of the modernization process on a global scale. While industrialization has taken both communist and capitalism forms, since the end of the Cold War the global expansion and integration of capitalist markets, the unbundling of production into global supply chains, the global diffusion of new technologies (from combine harvesters to agricultural biotechnologies), the increasing movement of peoples around the world, and the development of new global rules of commerce have effectively "globalized the modernization of natural resource extraction."

To illustrate these arguments, we explore in more detail the so-called Green Revolution in agriculture, which provides a quintessential example of a modernization process that has rapidly globalized, with devastating implications for biodiversity.

THE GREEN REVOLUTION

The Green Revolution in agriculture is usually associated with the 1960s, but its roots can be traced to Mexico in the 1940s, and to the research of U.S. botanist Norman Borlaug, who developed a new, high-yielding, and disease-resistant variety of wheat. This research, in turn, built upon the pioneering work on inheritance in plant breeding carried out in the 19th century by Gregor Mendel. Funded by the Rockefeller Foundation, Borlaug's research program was designed to improve Mexico's capacity to address its own food needs. It succeeded admirably and Mexico was able to move from being a net importer to a net exporter of wheat. The success of this project prompted both governments and corporations to pour money into agricultural research to selectively breed higher-yield varieties of wheat and other basic staple crops. This included varieties that photosynthesized more efficiently and therefore grew faster, that responded to fertilizer and irrigation, and that were not sensitive to day length and could therefore grow in different seasons and regions.

The main new technologies of the Green Revolution—hybridized seeds—also required new management practices, new infrastructure (dams, irrigation systems), pesticides, herbicides, fertilizers, new agricultural machinery (such as tractors, harvesters), and greater inputs of fossil fuels. When all these inputs, systems, and infrastructure were in place (an alignment that did not always occur), these new commercial varieties produced significantly higher yields than traditional varieties. The rapid spread of these industrial technologies and methods led to a dramatic increase in cereal production around the world, particularly from the 1960s.

The Green Revolution is not the first agricultural revolution, but it is certainly the most significant one in terms of its impact on biodiversity. Since the beginning of agriculture some ten thousand to fifteen thousand years ago, farmers have drawn on the crop diversity of local landraces—local varieties of a species that had evolved in response to local conditions. Whereas seeds were once collected and planted locally by local farmers, they are now increasingly purchased from multinational seed corporations, based on crops that have been selected in the laboratory for their productivity and commercial viability. These commercial seeds have been bred (and more recently, genetically modified)

from varieties collected from all quarters of the globe to improve yield
and resistance to insects and pesticides.

The Green Revolution must be understood as a new phase of a
much longer process of agricultural modernization. The industrial
phase of this modernization process was well under way when Borlaug conducted his research insofar as machines had increasingly replaced working animals and farm laborers and fertilizer had replaced
manure. As Deborah Fitzgerald has shown in her study of the industrial ideal in American agriculture, "no single innovation created the
revolutionary context; rather, each was located within a matrix of
technical, social, and ideological relationships that both created and
sustained the change."[52] The new industrial farming technologies,
practices, and social relations were produced and reproduced through
new research and tertiary education institutions; government agencies (including aid agencies); new technocratic "agents" of agricultural modernization (scientists, engineers, economists, government
bureaucrats, bankers, accountants); new management systems, credit
systems, and business practices; and new infrastructures such as railways, roads, and power lines. The overall logic on the production side
was one of scientifically informed, rational management of nature in
the service of greater efficiency and productivity. The net effect was
to convert farms into factories.[53]

Just as the Fordist methods of industrial production had begun
in one country and quickly spread to other countries, the methods
unleashed by the Green Revolution quickly became global because
firms found them to be highly profitable and because nation-states
considered expanded food production to be essential to their national
security, either because of a desire not to be dependent on food imports
or because of a need to produce a surplus for export to build foreign exchange reserves.[54] The United States also saw the spread of high-yielding grains to developing countries as a means of diminishing the threat
of communist insurrection, a counter to the Red Revolution, which it
assisted with funding from USAID and other sources.[55] Unsurprisingly
critics from the South regarded the Green Revolution as a form of First
World food imperialism, creating new forms of material dependency.

The industrialization of agriculture was not a uniquely capitalist
development. The same rationality and similar processes were applied
when the Soviet Union replaced peasant agriculture with collective

farms, with considerable assistance from U.S. experts and U.S. industrial farm machinery imports in the late 1920s following the famine of 1921. Likewise, in China, Zhou Enlai's "Four Modernizations" campaign in 1963 included agriculture (alongside industry, national defense, and science and technology) and allowed the purchase of new industrial and agricultural machinery from the West. This modernization program was a direct response to the failure of Mao Zedong's Great Leap Forward campaign, which had led to widespread famine and mass starvation in China.

In 1970, Norman Borlaug was awarded the Nobel Peace Prize for his contribution to increased food production. Yet this was also the period of mounting criticism of the social and ecological costs of the Green Revolution. Rachel Carson had already alerted the world to the problem of bioaccumulation of pesticides in the food chain in the early 1960s, but a range of other "negative externalities" were revealed. As with any single-minded endeavor, there are often unexamined assumptions and unintended consequences. While the Green Revolution worked well for those farmers who enjoyed the appropriate infrastructure and could afford to assemble all the inputs in the new production function, it was devastating for many farmers who lacked the infrastructure, support services, and necessary capital to succeed.[56] Many farmers, particularly in developing countries, defaulted on their loans, resulting in bankruptcy and increased rural poverty.

Likewise, none of the proponents of the Green Revolution had given serious consideration to the environmental impacts and implications for biodiversity of this new farming system, such as loss of aquifers and reduced flows in rivers from major irrigation systems, the eutrophication of waterways from high fertilizer use, the contamination of soil and water from rising pesticide use, and the destruction of habitat from the extensive clearing of land for new crops. Excessive nutrient loading in farms is one of the primary drivers of change in terrestrial, freshwater, and marine ecosystems.[57] The modernization of agriculture has depleted global supplies of phosphorus (one of the planetary boundaries identified in chapter 1). By separating animals and crop production and purchasing phosphorus fertilizer (derived from nonrenewable phosphate rock), modern agriculture has broken the phosphorus cycle whereby animal manure returned phosphorus to the soil to fertilize the next crop. Reserves of phosphorus rock are dwindling and prices are escalating, with significant implications for food security.

Monocultures also proved to be more vulnerable to new pests and diseases, which led to the development and application of more pesticides—leading to diminishing returns from high-yield varieties. No one factored into the production costs the increasing dependence of modern agriculture on fossil fuels, the loss of CO_2 sinks from converting forests for agriculture land, or the significant methane emissions from livestock.

All of these problems conspired to produce a major assault on biodiversity, including the diversity of ecosystems and species but particularly genetic diversity. For example, by the end of the 20th century just fifteen crops provided 90 percent of the world's food energy intake, with just three—rice, maize, and wheat—providing 60 percent of such intake.[58] Only 20 percent of the varieties of local maize produced in Mexico in 1930 were known at the turn of the present century. In China, there were over ten thousand varieties of wheat in cultivation in 1949, but by the end of the 20th century the number of varieties had dropped tenfold to approximately one thousand varieties.[59]

The erosion of genetic diversity was not confined to cereals but extended to other crops. Take the apple. In the United States alone, approximately 86 percent of the 7,098 apple varieties documented as having been in use throughout the 19th century had disappeared by the end of the 20th century.[60] Likewise, 95 percent of the cabbage varieties, 91 percent of the field maize varieties, 94 percent of the pea varieties, and 81 percent of the tomato varieties have disappeared from U.S. farms and backyards over the same period.[61] The loss of such a significant percentage of cultivars is an indication of significant loss of crop genetic diversity. A similar story can be told in relation to agricultural livestock as a consequence of the development of standardized and high-output systems of animal husbandry. According to *Global Biodiversity Outlook 3*, "Twenty-one per cent of the world's 7,000 livestock breeds (amongst 35 domesticated species of birds and mammal) are classified as being at risk, and the true figure is likely to be much higher as a further 36 per cent are of unknown risk status."[62]

Genetic diversity has declined not only in crops and livestock but also in wild species as a result of the encroachment and fragmentation of wild habitats, primarily through land clearing but also the building of roads, railways, dams, and other infrastructure. According to the Millennium Ecosystem Assessment, "More land was converted to cropland in the 30 years after 1950 than in the 150 years between 1700 and 1850" and "cultivated systems now cover 24 percent of the Earth's terrestrial surface."[63]

The Green Revolution was launched with good intentions, and it has succeeded in expanding global agricultural output and feeding a growing population. Yet it has come at a considerable cost to global biodiversity. Indeed, it serves as a textbook case of simple modernization insofar as it is narrow-minded, technocratic, supply-oriented, insensitive to cultural and biological diversity, and generally inattentive to broader social and ecological consequences of the modernization process. Of course, not all of these consequences could have been foreseen by the early scientific pioneers, but the instrumental reason associated with a single-minded focus on increasing yields lacked the reflexivity or critical self-awareness to respond to new problems other than by the further application of instrumental reason. Despite the many criticisms of the Green Revolution, and despite the growth in sustainable farming, it is not over. It is simply no longer new or revolutionary because it has become standard practice.[64]

The accelerated phase of agricultural modernization launched by the Green Revolution provides a graphic illustration of the overlay or replacement of local place and local time with space and abstract time through the distanciated, systematic application of modern science and technology to the practices of food production, transport, and retail. Farm machinery is developed to apply to "gridded spaces" rather than local places. Crops and farm animals, and harvesting practices, are no longer unique to particular places nor responsively integrated into local ecosystems. Globalized commodity chains are increasingly disembedded from biological food chains in local ecosystems, resulting in, among other things, huge volumes of embodied nutrients and water being exported from or imported into ecosystems. Globalized food cultures (particularly the consumption of "fast foods" and highly industrially processed foods) have increasingly overlaid and in some cases displaced local food cultures. Whereas, once upon a time, peasant agriculture had been more or less self-sustaining, modern agriculture has become a more concentrated and specialized global business that produces a surplus for export.

THE SECOND GREEN REVOLUTION

Yet despite growing concern over the accumulating "side effects" of the Green Revolution, a "second" Green Revolution is under way as a result of developments in modern biotechnology, which have enabled another qualitative leap in the application of instrumental reason to food production. Modern agricultural biotechnology, which has produced "transgenic," "genetically engineered," "genetically modified" (GM) plant varieties, is qualitatively different from traditional biotechnology insofar as it seeks to "cross the species barrier" by inserting genes from a foreign species into the cells of the host organism in order to change the characteristics of the host organism.[65] As Jan van Aken explains, "no traditional breeder is able to cross a carp with a potato, or a bacterium with a maize plant."[66]

Although research on modern biotechnology began in the 1970s, the first GM plant was not produced until 1981 and the commercialization of GM crops did not take off until the mid-1990s.[67] The first generation of GM agriculture has been mainly concerned to improve yields by, for example, improving the tolerance of crops to weed-killing herbicides and insect pests. The second generation has been directed toward enhancing the shelf life, nutritional content, taste, and color of agricultural commodities in order to increase their consumer appeal.

While the first Green Revolution spread rapidly to both developed and developing countries, the spread of GM agriculture has encountered early and strong resistance in some countries and regions. Although the United States, Canada, Argentina, and more recently China have embraced this new agricultural technology, the European Union and many developing countries (most notably, India) have been more skeptical of its benefits and more cautious in granting approval for imports. This has led to a situation of "regulatory polarization" between the U.S. "science-based" approach to risk assessment and the European Union's "precautionary approach" and has culminated in a major dispute in the World Trade Organization that was resolved in the United States' favor.[68] This trans-Atlantic regulatory dispute cannot be settled by scientists or trade policy experts because it reflects different risk cultures and also different food cultures.

Proponents of GM crops have claimed that modern agricultural biotechnology can orchestrate a second Green Revolution by producing higher and better quality yields and thereby solve the problem of world hunger while also reducing the use of pesticides and herbicides.[69] For example, the genetically modified variety known as Bt corn contains a protein from the naturally occurring soil bacterium *Bacillus thuringiensis* that protects the crop from an insect known as the corn borer, which means that farmers do not have to spray their crop with insecticides.

In reply, opponents have pointed to a range of risks to biodiversity and traditional and organic agriculture. For example, they argue that some GM crops encourage the use of herbicides. For example, Monsanto has developed genetically modified varieties of "Roundup ready" soy and canola that are resistant to its own herbicide Roundup, so farmers can spray liberally and kill all surrounding weeds without killing the crop. Opponents have also raised concerns that GM plants will pass on their GM traits to wild relatives, with unknown but possibly harmful consequences for landraces and wild ecosystems.

The biggest outcry, however, has been directed against the so-called terminator gene or suicide seeds, which cause the second generation of seeds to be sterile. Devised through a cooperative research program between the U.S. Department of Agriculture and Delta and Pine Land Company, this technology has never been commercialized and is banned in many countries. The purpose behind this technology—to prevent farmers from saving and planting or selling their seeds and thereby uphold the patent rights of biotech seed companies—has been achieved through legal agreements between farmers and GM seed companies. Nonetheless, the debate over the "terminator gene" has drawn attention to the increasing power of biotech seed companies and the increasing concentration and vertical integration of the industry. According to Thomas Bernauer, in 2000 only six biotech firms—including Monsanto, Novartis, and DuPont—accounted for almost 100 percent of the GM seed market.[70]

Opponents of GM agriculture argue that it merely continues the long-term trend of genetic erosion and loss of cultivar varieties by increasing the dependence of farmers on a narrow band of crops and on the corporations selling GM seeds. These objections have helped to

spawn "the slow food movement" that celebrates local genetic diversity and local food cultures. Originating in Italy, this is now a global
movement that represents one form of organized resistance to the risks
presented by GM agriculture and the concentration of agribusiness.[71]
For farmers from Italy to Ethiopia, GM agriculture potentially threatens
the practice of saving seeds, propagating local plant varieties, and carrying on local agricultural traditions. Many transnational, regional, and
national environmental NGOs, such as Friends of the Earth, have also
conducted campaigns against GM crops.

Whereas the first Green Revolution quickly became global, opposition to GM crops has prevented their global spread. However, defend-
ers of both Green Revolutions question whether traditional or organic
methods of agricultural production are capable of feeding a growing
population, even if they concede that they may be much more conducive to the protection of global biodiversity than modern agriculture.
The answer to this question is not yet clear. However, the one thing
that is clear is that neither the first nor second Green Revolution has
solved the problem of malnutrition and world hunger, since they have
focused mainly on increasing supply and have not paid sufficient attention to the crucial issue of how food is controlled and distributed
around the world. Stepping up food production is no solution to a
growing population if those who are most in need cannot gain access
to or afford that food. Nor is it a solution if it means that subsistence
agriculture in developing countries is increasingly replaced by broad-
acre, monocultural crops for export, or if farmers become increasingly
dependent on a global agribusiness industry that has become increasingly concentrated and vertically integrated. Ultimately, a continuation
of simple, supply-side agricultural modernization is destined to become
self-defeating in the longer run: it carries too many risks to species diversity, ecosystem diversity and integrity, genetic diversity, and global
and local food security.

THE ECOLOGICAL MODERNIZATION OF AGRICULTURE

The simple modernization of agriculture has produced social and
ecological contradictions that cannot be managed merely through the
further application of instrumental reason in the context of existing
unequal global economic and political structures. In chapter 1 we

defined reflexive modernization (and reflexive globalization) as entailing the critical confrontation and transformation of the processes of knowledge generation and dissemination, the forces of production, and the relations of production and the relations of definition (who defines and manages ecological risks) in ways that are more risk-averse and more accountable to all those who may potentially suffer the consequence of unelected risks. The reflexive *ecological* modernization of agriculture would not negate the humanitarian goal of the first Green Revolution—to ensure that everyone is fed. Rather, it would seek to pursue this fundamental goal alongside other equally fundamental goals: the protection of global biodiversity, global food security, the protection of local food cultures, the empowerment of local farmers and the resilience of farming communities, and more equitable social control over the production and distribution of food. Reflexive ecological modernization recognizes that multiple ends cannot be fulfilled by a single rationality; instrumental reason has a role to play, but it should be guided by other forms of reason, including communicative reason, to enable critical debate on how to ensure the mutual fulfillment of multiple ends. Reflexivity entails accountability to all those affected by decisions to ensure that they do not, in this case, disempower or impoverish local rural communities, particularly in developing countries. Efficiency in production has many advantages but it also has its limits. For example, if food production is to protect biodiversity, life support systems, and rural livelihoods in the face of a growing population, it will need to be less dependent on fossil fuels, more diverse in its local production, and possibly more labor intensive. The ecological modernization of agriculture must draw on a range of different forms of knowledge (modern scientific as well as traditional and local, place-based knowledge) and be socially negotiated among a range of different communities and stakeholders to produce new relations of production based on a more precautionary approach to ecological and social risks. A good example is the International Institute for Environment and Development's program on "Sustaining Local Food Systems, Biodiversity and Livelihoods," which is based on participatory action research between local NGOs, local farmers, and researchers with the aim of returning control over the production of food to farmers and local communities, repairing the damage done to soils and waterways from industrial farming, and strengthening the resilience of local food systems and local food cultures.[72]

As we show in chapter 5, if this type of reflexive modernization is to be globalized, then it will also require much more socially and ecologically sensitive rules of global commerce (investment, trade) that respect the cultural and biological diversity of local places.

WHY SHOULD WE CARE?

The projected growth in both human population and the world economy is clearly on a collision course with the protection of the Earth's biodiversity. However, not all policy makers see this as a matter of high political priority. Indeed, some have greeted this prospect with the fatalistic response: biodiversity loss is the price we will have to pay to maintain economic development. Why should we care about the disappearance of species that are of no commercial use or no aesthetic appeal? Why should we care about biodiversity when people are starving? And why should we bother protecting those parts of "wild nature" for which we can invent technological substitutes or provide proxy experiences through simulation, film, or theme parks? As Martin Krieger once put it, "What's wrong with plastic trees?"[73]

The problem with these arguments is that they presuppose a zero-sum relationship between the satisfaction of human needs and the protection of diverse ecosystems, which betrays an ignorance of the wide-ranging and vital life-support services provided by diverse ecosystems. The idea that new technological developments might make nonhuman nature increasingly redundant is based on a thoroughly instrumental posture toward the nonhuman world that also grossly underestimates the complexities and multiple functions and values of diverse ecosystems.

The Millennium Ecosystem Assessment has highlighted the important links between the protection of "ecosystem services" and human well-being and development. These ecosystem services are grouped into four general categories: *supporting* (such as soil formation and regeneration, nutrient cycling); *provisioning* (such as the supply of food, water, wood, fiber, fuel, genetic resources); *regulating* (such as decomposing wastes, purifying air and water, climate, flood moderation);

and *cultural* (such as educational, recreational, spiritual, and aesthetic values).[74] The assessment has also highlighted the connections between these various ecosystem services and the constituents of human well-being, including security, health, good social relations, and freedom of choice and action.

These arguments build on the wisdom of traditional farming practices and the insights from many expanding subdisciplines in the biological and earth sciences as well as new disciplines in the social sciences and humanities, such as environmental sociology and philosophy, that emerged in the late 1970s in response to growing ecological problems.[75] Yet many environmental philosophers have questioned why we should value biodiversity only for the "services" or utility it provides human communities rather than for its own sake or its "intrinsic value." If the case for the protection of biodiversity rested exclusively on instrumental or "service"-based arguments, then particular species or particular ecosystems would be considered dispensable to the extent that they were not essential to the performance of an ecosystem service and were not commercially valuable or if technological substitutes could be found for the uses they might have otherwise provided.

As we saw in chapter 2, simple modernization is premised on a thoroughly instrumental and anthropocentric posture toward the non-human world; it is based on the conceit that nonhuman species have no other reason for being on Earth but to serve human purposes. Like racism and sexism, anthropocentrism—sometimes referred to as "human speciesism" or "human chauvinism"—is based on a set of self-serving, hierarchical dualisms of self/other and human/nonhuman that deny or denigrate difference. An ecological sensibility would reject these dualisms and acknowledge that there are differences as well as similarities and continuities between humans and other species. To the extent that nonhuman species have different "modes of being" in the world, then they should not have to be like humans, or be commercially or instrumentally valuable or aesthetically appealing to humans, before they earn the right to exist as a species.

Nonetheless, humans are dependent on a wide-range of nonhuman species for their sustenance and survival, so the core political question raised by the biodiversity crisis is how to transform the processes of modernization and globalization to ensure the mutual flourishing of human societies *and* the Earth's biodiversity. As we noted earlier, this is a particularly acute challenge given that the richest countries of the world have derived the greatest benefit from the Earth's biodiversity while the areas of richest terrestrial biodiversity are located in some of the poorest countries of the world.

GOVERNING BIODIVERSITY

The processes of globalization have not only accelerated biodiversity loss but also generated a variety of different cultural, political, and regulatory efforts to protect biodiversity. Beginning with the discovery of species, and the phenomenon of extinction, and developing through the expansion of research and education in biological science and culminating with the rise of environmental NGOs, state environmental agencies, and intergovernmental organizations and multilateral environmental agreements, the processes of modernization and globalization have produced a new ecological awareness of biodiversity as a planetary asset. We humans are now understood not only as members of particular communities or nation-states but also as members of a particular species that has profoundly transformed the distribution and abundance of other species.

The last sixty years have seen a growing array of transnational NGOs, movements, and intergovernmental organizations that have formed with the primary objective of protecting biodiversity while also safeguarding the human communities that are dependent on biodiversity. These include international organizations such as IUCN (a unique partnership between governments and state-based nature conservation organizations), the Food and Agricultural Organization, and major international environmental NGOs ranging from the World Wide Fund for Nature and Greenpeace to *La Via Campesina* (The International Peasant Movement), which formed in 1993 to represent the interests of small and medium peasant farmers, indigenous communities, landless people, and agricultural workers against the threats posed to their dependence on biodiversity by agricultural modernization and the increasing concentration of the global seed industry.[76]

Just as the causes of biodiversity loss are many and varied, so too has been the regulatory response. The traditional response at the national level has been to set aside national parks and nature reserves for habitat protection and enact various forms of legal protection such as endangered species legislation. The precedent for setting aside large areas of "wilderness" was set in the 19th century with the establishment of Yellowstone National Park in 1872, followed closely by the Royal National Park in Australia in 1879.[77] Many developed countries in the so-called New World regions with large tracts of ecologically intact land, such as North America, Australia, and New Zealand, have strong wilderness preservation movements dating from this period, and the tensions between preservationist and resource conservationist movements has remained a key axis of environmental conflict ever since.

However, the original motivation for establishing national parks was to protect "sublime nature" or pristine "scenery" for aesthetic pleasure and human health and recreation rather than to protect threatened biodiversity per se. For example, the U.S. Wilderness Act (1964) defines wilderness as "an area where the earth and community of life are untrammelled by man, where man himself is a visitor who does not remain." This idea of wilderness as a "people-less place" has been criticized in more recent decades as Eurocentric and racist by indigenous peoples, who have long inhabited these New World regions.[78] Other critics have argued that the concept of wilderness is a legacy of the Western, romantic imagination, which rests on a bifurcation between the domestic and the wild, the "native" and the "civilized," and the human and the nonhuman world. The word *wild* has different connotations in different languages, not all of which summon the same aesthetic or recreational response. The world's largest international environmental NGO dedicated to the protection of endangered species changed its name in 1986 from the World Wildlife Fund (WWF) to the World Wide Fund for Nature (although WWF is still retained in the United States and Canada) in recognition of these cultural differences.

The setting aside of ecologically intact land has also been politically controversial in the West because it seeks to "lock up natural resources" and impede the development process. However, it has been especially controversial in developing states eager to advance their prosperity through the utilization of their natural resources and control their own destiny in the postcolonial period. The protection of endangered wildlife for wealthy Western eco-tourists and the establishment of protected areas (including via "debt-for-nature" swaps and the exclusion of their original native owners) funded by Western governments or environmental NGOs have been criticized as another form of ecological colonialism that has not only displaced indigenous peoples but also undermined local livelihoods, sometimes coercively.[79]

Indeed, the rationale for establishing protected areas has evolved considerably in the latter half of the 20th century and has moved well beyond the Western preoccupation with "wilderness" or certain charismatic mammal species to include the protection of diverse ecosystems in recognition of the myriad services they provide for human development.[80] An ecosystem approach transcends the tensions between exploitation and preservation.[81] The protection of biodiversity is also increasingly recognized as a means of protecting culture diversity and sustainable livelihoods. Many wildlife conservationists and wilderness preservationist organizations have responded to these criticisms by adapting their rationales and strategies to work with indigenous peoples and other local communities dependent on biodiversity for their livelihoods.

While protected areas are one important means of protecting biodiversity, they are by no means sufficient. Indeed, some critics have argued that the idea that wild species and their habitats should be fenced off and patrolled in order to keep wildlife in and people out has created new problems and contradictions not only for the local people locked out but also the biodiversity that is locked in.[82] This is because protected areas represent only isolated fragments of biodiversity, and their establishment is often taken as a license to exploit everywhere else. This can only be avoided by a "whole-of-landscape" approach to nature conservation. Moreover, most protected areas contain genetic pools too small to sustain larger species over time and will not safeguard biodiversity from the looming threat of climate change. The bigger challenge, then, is to transform the modernization and globalization processes so that biodiversity loss is no longer a routine consequence of economic exchanges and so that biodiversity is encouraged to flourish everywhere, and not just in the designated protected areas.

COMMON HERITAGE OR COMMON CONCERN?

The growing recognition of the multiple public benefits provided by biodiversity has prompted many advocates to argue that it should be treated as a common planetary asset that is made available to all on an equitable and sustainable basis. Many have invoked the international legal principle of "common heritage of humankind," arguing that biodiversity, like the oceans, should be held in trust for the benefit of future generations rather than exploited for national or private benefit. These arguments gained official recognition in the *World Heritage Convention 1972*, which recognizes "natural heritage" as "world heritage," and the Food and Agricultural Organization's nonbinding *International Undertaking on Plant Genetic Resources 1983*, which declared that plant genetic resources were part of the "heritage of mankind" and available to all. However, the idea that biodiversity should be considered "common heritage" has encountered strong resistance from nation-states, which have strongly resisted relinquishing "permanent sovereignty" over the natural resources in their territory, and from private firms, who wish to assert their intellectual property rights and patent rights in hybridized seeds or pharmaceutical products derived from the genetic resources of nonhuman species.

These claims and counterclaims set the scene for the negotiation of the *Convention on Biological Diversity (CBD) 1992*, which serves as the centerpiece of the international effort to protect biodiversity. Before then, the international governance of biodiversity had taken the form of a wide range of ad hoc treaties designed to protect *particular species* (such as the *Whaling Convention 1946* and various regional and international treaties to protect migratory species), to address *particular threats* to biodiversity (such as the *Convention on International Trade in Endangered Species of Wild Flora and Fauna 1973*), and to establish particular *protected areas*, such as the "biosphere reserves" under the 1970 "Man the Biosphere program" or "natural heritage" under the *World Heritage Convention 1972*.

Prior to the CBD, the first systematic attempt to move beyond this patchwork approach, and from a philosophy of cure to a philosophy of prevention, was IUCN's *World Conservation Strategy 1980*.[83] Building on the Stockholm Action Plan arising from the United Nations Conference on the Human Environment held in Stockholm in 1972, this strategy sought to reconcile human development with biodiversity protection through the simultaneous pursuit of three basic objectives: the maintenance of ecological processes and life-support systems, the preservation of genetic diversity, and the sustainable utilization of species and ecosystems. The nonbinding strategy also provided a wide range of recommendations for anticipatory and cross-sectoral environmental policies and community participation in the development of conservation strategies. This was followed by the *World Charter for Nature*, adopted by the United Nations General Assembly in 1982.[84] The strategy and charter served as significant precursors to the Brundtland Report, albeit with a more pronounced focus on biodiversity and with much less influence on states or the major international economic institutions such as the World Bank Group and the International Monetary Fund.

Like the World Conservation Strategy, the CBD was based on three basic objectives: the conservation of biodiversity, the "sustainable utilization" of its components, and the fair and equitable sharing of the benefits arising from the utilization of genetic resources (including the transfer of relevant technologies [Article 1]). The CBD called on states to develop national strategies, plans, and programs to protect biodiversity and ensure its sustainable utilization, such as the establishment of protected areas and a range of other measures concerning *in situ* biodiversity protection, including respecting and protecting indigenous knowledge (Article 8). However, these obligations were couched in quite general terms and left considerable discretion to states to interpret and implement at the national level. Moreover, most of the negotiating energy, political contestation, and subsequent treaty development have focused on the rules for *utilizing* genetic resources rather than protecting biodiversity.

Major asymmetries in the global distribution of terrestrial biodiversity and the distribution of research and development capability in genetic resources shaped the CBD's provisions on the utilization of genetic resources. Biodiversity-rich developing countries wished to protect their control over their genetic resources and prevent "biopiracy"—the commercial development of genetic resources by corporations based in technologically advanced countries without compensation to the peoples or nations in whose territory the material is derived. Developed countries with strong biotech and pharmaceutical industries wished to gain access to such resources and to protect their intellectual property rights and patent rights in the genetic material they developed for commercial purposes. This tug-of-war largely sidelined the concerns of indigenous peoples and local peasant farmers, who wished to protect their traditional knowledge (especially in relation to traditional medicines and plant varieties). Whereas the International Undertaking on Plant Genetic Resources had focused on the protection of traditional farmers' rights (particularly in centers of origin and crop diversity) and declared that plant genetic resources were "common heritage," the preamble to the CBD merely declared that the conservation of biological diversity is a "common concern of humankind." The sovereign rights of states over their natural resources were upheld, and access to genetic resources was made subject to the prior informed consent of the host state. Intellectual property rights and patent rights in genetic material were recognized but partially qualified by provisions that required the fair and equitable sharing of benefits from the research and commercial utilization of genetic material on mutually agreed terms.[85] The United States strongly objected to these latter provisions on behalf of its biotech and pharmaceutical industries. While the United States later signed the CBD, it has never been ratified on the ground that it does not provide adequate protection for intellectual property rights.

The CBD contains deep-seated tensions that reflect the conflicting social forces that produced it. On the one hand, it seeks to promote the conservation and sustainable use of biodiversity. On the other hand, it provides a legal framework for the further "enclosure" of the global commons, in this case genetic resources, which is a precondition for their commodification and commercialization.[86] The commodification of biodiversity may be seen as a legacy and continuation of the "second Green Revolution" and highlights the ways in which global markets are politically constituted through international and national regulation.

The two protocols that have been negotiated under the auspices of the CBD likewise remain focused on genetic resources. The *Cartagena Protocol on Biosafety 2000* provides a prior-informed-consent regime for the safe transboundary movement of "living modified organisms," while the *Nagoya Protocol 2010* seeks to provide greater clarity and legal certainty to providers and users of genetic resources in relation to both access and benefit sharing.[87] The Nagoya Protocol sets out obligations to seek the prior informed consent of, and the sharing of benefits with, indigenous and local communities, but this obligation is only triggered where traditional rights over genetic resources are already established under domestic law, which is often not the case.

The CBD and Nagoya Protocol are primarily focused on nonagricultural genetic resources. Agricultural genetic resources had been covered by the FAO's Undertaking on Plant Genetic Resources, but this has been superseded by the *International Treaty on Plant Genetic*

Resources for Food and Agriculture 2001 (referred to as the Seed Treaty), which was negotiated after the CBD and made consistent with some of its key provisions. Like the CBD, the Seed Treaty recognizes the sovereign right of states over their plant genetic resources for food and agriculture. However, it also sets up a multilateral system of access and benefit sharing among parties to the treaty for some sixty-four key food crops and twenty-nine forage species. Farmers' rights to save and exchange seeds are acknowledged but, following the model of the CBD, the onus on securing these rights rests with national governments.[88]

Commercial interests have been even more pronounced in shaping international efforts to protect the world's forests. For example, the *International Tropical Timber Agreement 1983* (and successor agreements in 1994 and 2006), which established the International Tropical Timber Organization, provides a framework for cooperation among producers and consumers of tropical timber in order to expand and diversify the trade in tropical timber while promoting sustainable management practices and preventing illegal logging. Yet this agreement, which is essentially a commodity agreement designed to promote the expansion in the tropical timber trade, has had a minimal effect on protecting the rich biodiversity in tropical forests. Efforts to negotiate a more comprehensive, legally binding treaty to protect forests for the 1992 Earth Summit failed to garner sufficient support from states. The fallback agreement was a nonbinding *Statement on Forest Principles* that upholds "the sovereign and inalienable right" of states "to utilize, manage and develop their forests in accordance with their development needs and level of socio-economic development."[89] The statement also endorsed an open and nondiscriminatory trading system (Principle 13(a)) and closed off further opportunities for developing new rules of commerce that actively encourage sustainable forest practices through mechanisms such as trade sanctions.

The failure of states to agree to strong rules to protect forests has prompted the development of unique coalitions between business, labor, and civil society organizations to govern transnational commodity chains in timber by setting up independent certification and labeling schemes, such as the Forest Stewardship Council to promote the sustainable production of timber.[90] A similar initiative has been launched to protect fisheries under the Marine Stewardship Council. While such schemes have gained some market influence, they have not been sufficient to introduce any systematic accountability for biodiversity loss along transnational commodity chains.

While global awareness of a looming biodiversity crisis emerged well before the neoliberal phase of economic globalization, most international efforts to protect biodiversity since the late 1980s have had to contend with a dominant neoliberal economic orthodoxy that has resisted bending the rules of trade and finance in ways that actively protect biodiversity on a systematic basis. As Alexander Wood, Pamela Stedman-Edwards, and Johanna Mang argue, "The race to save biodiversity is being lost because the factors contributing to it are more complex and powerful than those forces working to protect it. At the heart of this dynamic is a global failure to understand and implement sustainable development."[91] In the next and final chapter we explore this core global governance challenge.

CHAPTER 5

GOVERNING THE PLANET

Every system of domination generates its own distinctive set of
opportunities for challenge and transformation, and neo-liberal
globalization is no exception.

—Peter Evans[1]

Our primary aim in this book has been to explore the relationship
between globalization and global environmental change from three
mutually informing perspectives: historical/sociological, critical, and
normative.

Our core historical/sociological argument is that the most recent
phase of globalization is neither the primary nor the only driver of
global environmental degradation. We have shown that global environmental degradation was clearly manifest well before the rise of neoliberal economic globalization in the 1980s, and that this degradation

was predominantly the result of a much longer wave of modernization that began with European imperial expansion in the early modern period. However, the neoliberal phase of economic globalization has dramatically accelerated and intensified environmental degradation to the point where it threatens to undermine both the broader processes of globalization and the Earth's life-support systems. The global spread of capitalist markets, aided by new communication and transport technologies, has radically accentuated the compression of space and time that is the hallmark of the modernization process. Local place and time are increasingly overlaid with abstract space and time, producing more abstract social relations along with a biophysical world that is increasingly exploited, disassembled, transported, reassembled, and consumed in different parts of the planet. These developments also have important political consequences. Growing global economic interconnectedness has produced increasing ecological disconnectedness by extending the separation between decision makers (both producers and consumers) and affected "environments." This has reconfigured the relationships between those who reap the benefits of globalization and those who suffer the social and ecological impacts across space and time.

We have also shown that globalization is a multifaceted, highly uneven, and sometimes contradictory process. While it has intensified global environmental degradation and skewed the distribution of environmental harms and risks, it has also generated a range of governance responses to such degradation, which we summarized in table 1.1.[2] The task of this concluding chapter is to assess these responses, identify the key challenges from the standpoint of our critical and normative perspectives, and suggest a way forward. As we shall see, these governance challenges cannot be underestimated.

Our core critical argument, which we illustrated in our case studies on climate change and biodiversity, is that the forces that are working to produce systemic and cumulative global environmental degradation are more complex, entrenched, and powerful than those working to protect the global environment. By "forces" we mean the various social relations of power—material, institutional/structural, and discursive— that have combined to perpetuate and normalize practices that generate environmental degradation. We see the looming global ecological crisis generated by these practices as, in part, a symptom of a political accountability crisis between those who generate and/or benefit from the production of ecological risks and those who involuntarily suffer the consequences. In short, in its neoliberal form, globalization has made it easier for more powerful social agents and social institutions to avoid or evade taking responsibility for the consequences of their decisions and actions. This has produced what Rob Nixon has called "slow violence"—the gradual and sometimes invisible spatial and temporal displacement of environmental impacts, particularly onto the most disempowered and marginal communities, as well as nonhuman species.[3] This accountability crisis lies at the heart of the failure of global environmental governance.

Finally, our core normative argument is that both the processes of modernization and globalization need to become more reflexive in ways that reverse this "slow violence" before it quickens and becomes more visible and extreme and before global tipping points are reached. Here our meaning of "reflexive" moves beyond the usual understanding of self-aware and self-critical (with the "self" standing for individuals, communities, organizations, and institutions). While this is a necessary part of reflexivity, it is also too confined and self-absorbed for our purposes in that it merely requires actors and institutions to reflect continually on the conditions of their *own* action and decisions to ensure their *own* reproduction and flourishing in complex, nonlinear, and dynamic social and ecological systems.

Our normative understanding of reflexivity is not only self-regarding but also other-regarding. That is, both agents and social structures must become more attentive to the consequences of their actions and impacts on others through space and time. Below, we argue that this requires building on but also moving beyond conventional liberal understandings of accountability and responsibility, based on individual agency, direct causation, and culpability, toward a postliberal, cosmopolitan understanding of "extended responsibility" that is more appropriate to a complex, interdependent, and globalizing world.

Before exploring what this might mean for governance, it is necessary to take stock of the global governance effort to protect the global environment thus far.

THE FAILURES OF
GLOBAL ENVIRONMENTAL GOVERNANCE

If we were asked to design a global governance system capable of protecting the global environment in a globalized world, we would not recommend an anarchic system of sovereign states based on exclusive territorial rule, supplemented by international agreements and rules based on state consent. This system is particularly ill-suited to managing ecological problems that manifest on a global scale, whether cumulative or systemic. Yet, for better and for worse, this is the system that we have inherited. It is a system that emerged in the early modern period, well before the problem of global environmental change was recognized, and it has become powerfully entrenched. It is a system that has managed to adapt slowly in response to new environmental challenges, but these adaptive efforts have thus far been faltering and insufficient. Given the diminishing time we have to avert ecological crisis, we must find a way of working more creatively with, around, above, and below this system rather than entertain the political fantasy that we can design and build new global governance institutions from scratch.

Of course the system of sovereign states is only one—albeit the most significant—component of a much larger set of governing practices and structures that together shape environmental decision making. Here it is useful to distinguish between *governance*, understood as the practice of public and private policy making, rule making, or standard setting, and *governance structures*, which provide the formal or informal framework of norms and decision-making procedures under which decisions are made and implemented.

On this broader understanding, global environmental governance encompasses not only national, subnational, and international environmental regulation but also public-private partnerships and various forms of private or "civil" regulation, including corporate environmental responsibility practices and other voluntary codes of conduct, environmental management systems, environmental policy networks, environmental certification schemes, and organized consumer boycotts. These various forms of hybrid and civil governance can sometimes complement and strengthen domestic regulation and international regimes. In other cases, they may compensate for regulatory gaps or weaknesses in state-based regulation. A prominent example is the Forest Stewardship Council discussed in chapter 4, which is a direct response to the weaknesses and gaps in international forest regulations.

A broad and critical understanding of governance helps us to identify the various social relations of power that shape social understandings, practices, and environments. These include not simply material power (the power to coerce or induce via the payment of money or resource provision) but also the regulatory and constitutive power of rules and social structures and the discursive power to define what is normal or legitimate.[4] Instead of conceptualizing governance as an abstract process that stands above society and the economy, we see it as a web of rules, relationships, practices, and understandings that both shape, and are shaped by, society and the economy.

International environmental governance is clearly only a subset of global environmental governance. However, it remains the most significant subset. Despite the debate about "the decline" of the state in the wake of economic globalization, states are still the primary gatekeepers of the global order. We therefore begin with a critical examination of environmental multilateralism, which is the traditional first port of call for those interested in understanding efforts to redress global and transboundary environmental problems.

The Paradox of Environmental Multilateralism

Environmental treaty making has been one of the biggest growth areas in multilateral cooperation among states in the past half century, and for good reason, given the spectacular growth in environmental problems during the same period. According to the International Environmental Agreements (IEA) Database Project, states have negotiated a total of more than 1,100 multilateral environmental agreements, more than 1,500 bilateral environmental agreements, and more than 250 other environmental agreements.[5] New environmental agreements accumulated at an increasing rate throughout the second half of the 20th century, with a record number being generated in the 1990s (see figure 5.1). This expanding body of treaty law is a testament to the limitations of the preexisting customary international law principle of state responsibility for environmental harm, which provides that no state may use its territory in ways that causes serious injury to the territory, property, or population of another state.[6] This principle, which has proved to be both reactive and limited in its application, focuses on adjudicating the use of territorial rights by states, rather than protecting victims or ecosystems per se.[7]

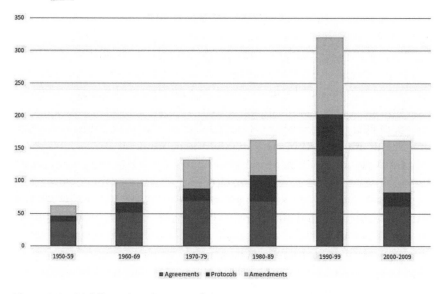

Figure 5.1. Multilateral environmental agreements

Source: Ronald B. Mitchell. 2002–2010. International Environmental Agreements Database Project (Version 2010.2). Available at: http://iea.uoregon.edu/.

At the same time, the various agencies and programs of the United Nations have played an increasingly active role in promoting environmental protection from the 1970s and sustainable development from the late1980s. This has included the facilitation of four major environmental summits, beginning with the United Nations Conference on the Human Environment held at Stockholm in 1972, which saw the establishment of the United Nations Environment Program (UNEP). However, it was the so-called Earth Summit (formally known as the United Nations Conference on Environment and Development or UNCED), held twenty years later at Rio de Janeiro in 1992, which remains the high water mark of international environmental concern, normative development, and institutional innovation. It not only served as the venue for the final negotiation and signature of the Framework Convention on Climate Change (UNFCCC) and the Convention on Biological Diversity (CBD). It also produced the United Nations Declaration on Environment and Development ("the Rio Declaration"), which provided a pithy statement of sustainable development principles, along with Agenda 21—a more detailed action plan for moving toward sustainable development. The Earth Summit also established the Commission for Sustainable Development (CSD) to oversee implementation of Agenda 21.

The two subsequent environmental summits—the 2002 World Summit on Sustainable Development held at Johannesburg in 2002 and the United Nations Conference on Sustainable Development (UNCSD or "Rio+20"), held in Rio de Janeiro in 2012—were designed to strengthen international commitment and progress toward sustainable development but neither produced any significant further progress. We assess the outcomes of Rio+20 below.

Although states are the primary actors in multilateral environmental negotiations and summits, they now attract a much wider cast of players. They depend on the expertise of the international scientific community and other professional networks, and they serve as a magnet for transnational environmental NGOs, industry groups, policy think tanks, and research organizations. At many of these negotiations, non-state actors outnumber state-based negotiating delegations and play important roles in monitoring, advising, analyzing, criticizing, and cajoling the formal negotiators and in informing wider publics of progress, or lack thereof. Many least developed states—those that are the most vulnerable to global environmental change—now depend on expertise, support, and advice from NGOs, including scientific and policy think tanks. Just as national public spheres serve as forums for critical debate about national laws and policies, these specialized transnational public spheres serve as a forum for critical debate about the negotiations, legitimacy, and effectiveness of multilateral environmental negotiations and agreements.

New global communications technologies have also enabled virtual participation in many aspects of multilateral negotiations and side-events along with more creative global environmental campaigns. The most notable is *350.org*, a global grassroots campaign to reduce atmospheric concentrations of CO_2 from current levels of around 392 to below 350 parts per million.[8] The most spectacular of 350.org's many campaigns has been the coordination of 5,200 simultaneous rallies and demonstrations in 181 countries in October 2009 in the lead-up to the Copenhagen climate conference, which has been dubbed the "most widespread day of political action in the planet's history."[9]

Yet the question remains: has this spectacular growth in environmental multilateralism—cajoled and monitored by expanding global networks of civil society actors—made a difference to the global environment? The short answer is yes, but not much. The traditional prerogative of states to develop their natural resources as they see fit has now been qualified by new environmental responsibilities, reflected in both treaty and customary international law and so-called soft law (declarations, actions plans). At the discursive level, states have repeatedly affirmed their commitment to sustainable development, along with the principles of the Rio Declaration, which include the precautionary principle, the "polluter pays" principle, and the principle of "common but differentiated responsibilities" between developed and developing countries. This has produced a modest "greening of sovereignty," paving the way for a possible further evolution in the role of states from exclusive overlords of their territory toward the idea that states are ecological trustees of their territories with environmental responsibilities not only to their citizens but also the global community.[10]

Yet despite these shifts, the global environment continues to deteriorate. As we saw in chapters 3 and 4, the UNFCCC, the Kyoto Protocol, and the Copenhagen Accord have not managed to prevent rising global emissions, while the Convention on Biological Diversity has not succeeded in slowing the rate of species extinction or the rate of erosion of genetic diversity or ecosystem diversity. And so the paradox of environmental multilateralism is that while environmental treaty output in these areas has increased, the most serious and irreversible global environmental problems facing the international community have worsened.

EXPLAINING THE PARADOX

The traditional approach of global governance scholars has been to explain this paradox by focusing on the problems that are endemic to environmental treaty making. These include the slow processes of consensus-based multilateralism exacerbated by persistent disagreements and mistrust between developed and developing countries over burden sharing, both of which give rise to the "tragedy of the global commons": fragmentation and lack of coordination and integration in the environmental treaty system, weak and/or poorly enforced treaty obligations, and persistent regulatory gaps.[11]

The source of the tragedy of the commons lies in the fact that global environmental protection is a public good but states are self-interested actors. Since the costs of taking protective action accrue to cooperating states but the gains are enjoyed by everyone, then in the absence of full information, trust, and mutual assurance that other states will do their fair share, it is more "rational" for states to defect and free ride on the actions of others than to cooperate in the collective effort, *even with full knowledge that this will make all states worse off in the long run.* Since full information, trust, mutual assurance, and agreement over what is a fair share are in short supply, then agreements are hard to negotiate and invariably suboptimal. Leadership by powerful states or groupings of states that have the motivation and capacity to furnish the costs of collective action can break this cycle. However, apart from the European Union, few developed states (or regions) have been prepared to play an environmental leadership role. Indeed, since the birth of the modern environmental movement in the 1960s, the United States has moved from an international environmental leader to laggard.[12]

Environmental treaty texts are negotiated line by line and agreed by a consensus among all parties (unless they agree—again by consensus—to establish rules that allow majority voting). Treaty provisions typically represent "lowest common denominator agreements" to encourage the wide participation that is necessary to address collective action problems. Many such provisions reflect ambiguous compromises among hardened negotiating blocs.

Persistent disagreement over burden sharing, particularly along North/South lines, has seriously hampered progress. Although the colonial era has officially ended, the legacy of that era continues to shape international environmental politics in profound ways. Developing countries have repeatedly accused developed countries of securing and maintaining their historic economic advantage and high consumption lifestyles at the expense of the developing world. As we saw in chapter 3, countries least responsible for climate change will suffer the worst impacts, but major developed country emitters like the United States have refused to commit to action to meet obligations under the international climate treaty in the absence of corresponding commitments from major developing countries with much lower per capita emissions profiles and standards of living. In chapter 4, we saw that many of the poorest countries in the world are home to the richest biodiversity, but the richest countries in the world have derived the greatest benefit from the exploitation of the Earth's species and ecosystems. In both cases, developing countries are being asked to refrain from engaging in practices (e.g., exploiting fossil fuels and forests) that enabled the developed world to acquire its economic strength, and given their unmet development needs they have been loath to exercise restraint without assistance or compensation from those with greater capacity. This is reflected in demands that developed countries assist with capacity building, provide the new and additional financial resources necessary to pursue environmental protection, and transfer the technologies that are needed to "leapfrog" over the path of "dirty" and "carbon-intensive" industrialization trodden by the developed countries.

For their part, developed countries demand that the rapidly growing developing countries should take on a greater burden-sharing role, must not be exempt from international legal obligations, and should engage in greater monitoring, reporting, and verification of the new environmental initiatives financed or supported by developed countries. For some countries, such as the United States, this demand has become a precondition for cooperation.

Most environmental treaties are negotiated in response to discrete environmental problems, rather than in response to the general global environmental predicament, and only appear when states are sufficiently motivated to make treaty commitments. Unlike multilateral trade agreements, the general approach in multilateral environmental agreements has been to provide incentives to encourage participation and compliance rather than punitive sanctions such as countermeasures or damages. The proliferation of environmental treaties, along with environmental "soft law" such as international declarations and action plans, has also produced increasing "treaty congestion," duplication, and overlap and tensions among different treaties with slightly different memberships. While this proliferation increases the points of political access for civil society actors in developed countries, it has also encouraged "forum shopping" among states and strained the capacity of many developing states to keep abreast of negotiations or to implement commitments.

Finally, although the number of environmental treaties has grown significantly, there still remain many significant regulatory gaps from the standpoint of global environmental governance. For example, there is no international legal instrument regulating the environmental activities of transnational corporations; few agreements that prevent trade in products, semifinished products, and components from unsustainable industries along transnational supply chains; no agreement that anticipates and seeks to manage the increasing physical volume of commodities produced and consumed; no agreement to assist the global movement of environmentally displaced persons; and no agreement to anticipate and regulate geoengineering.

Yet if we want a fuller understanding of the paradox of environmental multilateralism, it is necessary to look beyond these endemic problems to a set of more deep-seated, interlocking problems, the resolution of which is a condition precedent to an effective environmental treaty system. Here we single out five such problems:

1. States have failed to integrate environmental and development governance at the national level.
2. States have failed to integrate environmental and economic governance at the international level.
3. Powerful social forces continue to resist or co-opt efforts to transform economies and societies in a more ecologically sustainable direction.
4. The neoliberal economic discourse remains globally dominant, undermining sustainable development and ecological modernization discourses and practices.
5. All of the above persist because national and international accountability mechanisms remain weak and inadequate in a globalizing world.

These problems are mutually reinforcing, but as it is impossible to discuss them all at once, we treat each in turn.

ENVIRONMENT-ECONOMY INTEGRATION FAILURE AT THE NATIONAL LEVEL

If all states managed the processes of production and consumption in their territories in ways that protected their "national" environment and biodiversity and avoided any transboundary environmental spillover effects, then there would be no need for environmental multilateralism, and no need for us to write this book. However, the thoroughgoing integration of economic activity and environmental protection at the national level is yet to occur. As chapter 2 argued, economic development as a practice and ideology enabled the transformation of "pre-modern" societies into "modern" societies, and it remains a fundamental purpose of the modern state. In the postcolonial era, the distinction between "developed" and "developing" countries serves as the core binary around which states are classified. Since the development of the United Nations System of National Accounts (SNA) in the 1950s, this status is typically determined according to a state's gross domestic product (GDP). Developed countries seek to maintain or enhance their developed country status, while developing countries seek to catch up. Yet GDP was never intended to serve as a measure of national or human progress. As Robert Kennedy eloquently argued in 1968:

> Gross National Product counts air pollution and cigarette advertising, and ambulances to clear our highways of carnage. It counts special locks for our doors and the jails for the people who break them. It counts the destruction of the redwood and the loss of our natural wonder in chaotic sprawl. It counts napalm and counts nuclear warheads and armored cars for the police to fight the riots in our cities. . . . It measures everything in short, except that which makes life worthwhile.[13]

States have sponsored and regulated environmental exploitation from the early modern period onward, but it is only since the late 1960s and early 1970s that environmental protection has become an identifiable purpose in the contradictory repertoire of state activity. In developed countries, this innovation reflected the rise of the modern environmental movement, which pushed environmental issues and conflicts onto the policy agenda and led to the establishment of dedicated multipurpose environmental agencies, the rise of environmental policy professionals through expanded tertiary training, and the expansion and deepening of environmental regulation.

Even so, until the Brundtland Report's influential promotion of sustainable development in 1987, the goals of economic development and environmental protection were seen to be in fundamental tension—a view shared by governments, industry, and environmentalists (including limits-to-growth advocates) alike. States in the West and the East, and the North and the South, managed this tension in ways that gave a clear priority to the more deeply entrenched goal of economic development, pursued through conventional economic growth involving accelerating use of an increasing volume of material resources.

The Brundtland Report and the 1992 Earth Summit challenged this zero-sum relationship and defended the virtues of thoroughly integrating environmental, social, and economic development goals. Different states have responded to this challenge with a variety of political compromises, depending on their level of development, economic structure (and "variety of capitalism"), political institutions, and configuration of social forces. Most developed states articulated new, overarching sustainable development strategies or Green Plans—implemented with varying and usually very modest degrees of success—and new linkages were made between environmental policy and other policy domains.[14] In Western Europe, in particular, a new "strategy" of weak ecological modernization emerged in the 1980s. This approach highlighted the economic and environmental advantages that derived from the synergy of stricter environmental regulations, technological innovation, improvements in environmental efficiency and productivity (leading to less material-energy use, less pollution, and less waste per unit of production), and first mover advantages in international markets.[15] It also doubled as a competitive strategy, since it made both economic and ecological sense for firms to reduce resource and energy inputs and minimize pollution. Indeed, following the 2008 global financial crisis, a number of states—from Australia to South Korea to the United States—responded with green stimulus packages and defended the idea of a Green New Deal or "green growth" as an integrated response to the triple problems of environmental degradation, financial instability, and stalled economic growth.[16] The idea of the "green economy"—a rebadged means of promoting sustainable development and poverty eradication in the new Millennium—served as one of the two core agenda items at the Rio+20 Conference in 2012 and is actively supported by the OECD and UNEP.[17]

In all, these various national and international efforts provide tentative signs of increasing reflexivity when set against the longer history of environmentally indiscriminate development. They demonstrate increasing reflection upon not only instruments and policy settings but also a certain degree of (modest) realignment in the cultural hierarchy of economic and ecological goals away from the idea of balance and trade-off and toward the idea of integration. Local environmental indicators (for instance, for air and water quality) have continued to improve in most developed states, and there have been significant gains in some other environmental outcomes as well as for economic efficiency and productivity due to technological innovation. In the wake of Brundtland, it is increasingly recognized that the best indirect indicators of a government's sustainable development credentials are not their environmental policies and laws but rather their fiscal, industry, technology, infrastructure, and trade policies since environmental policies alone cannot orchestrate the necessary decoupling of economic activity from environmental degradation.

However, all is not well. The push for sustainable development in the late 1980s and 1990s was overwritten by the rise of neoliberalism, which has sought to wind back the regulatory role of the state, privatize and outsource former state functions, maximize individual choice, and increase the penetration of the market into a wider range of social spheres. In environmental policy, there has been a notable move away from the use of prescriptive regulation (often pejoratively dubbed "command and control") toward new market-based instruments such as taxes and charges and emissions-trading schemes. The latter has been a mixed blessing. The privileging of efficiency and flexibility at the level of the firm over broader environmental justice concerns has tended to hollow out national responsibility by postponing national economic restructuring in the search for cheaper abatement options elsewhere.

These shifts also coincided with a new phase of economic globalization. The Uruguay round of multilateral trade negotiations (1986–1994), which culminated in the establishment of the World Trade Organization in 1995, was the largest and most far-reaching set of negotiations in the post–World War II period and saw the liberalization in trade in a range of new areas that went beyond goods to include services (such as banking, telecommunications) and intellectual property.

As a consequence, public policies were increasingly judged in the context of comparative international competitiveness, and the state's "traditional" welfare functions and its "emergent" environmental protection functions reappeared as brakes on economic growth. Despite widespread rhetorical commitment to sustainable development, increasing or maintaining economic growth (measured as a percentage increase in GDP over a given time period and without concern about diminishing material throughputs or quality of outcomes) remains the overriding priority of governments and the key proxy measure of progress and prosperity.

This is reflected in the relative emphasis given by all states, despite the 1992 Earth Summit, to economic over environmental issues, the hierarchy of state policy goals, and the hierarchy and funding of government departments and agencies. It is also reflected in the discourses and social forces that have shaped environmental public policy and political competition among the major political parties, which have historically represented producer interests (industry, labor) rather than environmental and consumer interests.

As a result, most environmental policy gains since the late 1980s have been "supply-side" rather than "demand-side" improvements. These improvements in the "eco-efficiency of production" have been incidental to maintaining or improving competitiveness through technological innovation. Yet some of the improvements in local environmental conditions and indicators have resulted from the market-led displacement of "dirty" manufacturing to developing countries, which has reduced domestic pollution while maintaining consumption. As Tim Jackson has argued in *Prosperity without Growth*, improvements in the *relative* eco-efficiency of firms, industries, or national economies have not translated into an *absolute* decrease in material-energy consumption or pollution at the global level.[18]

In all, full national economic/environmental integration has remained elusive because governments have not been politically willing to use their regulatory, fiscal, and procurement powers to channel or constrain investment, production, and consumption to the degree that is necessary to ensure ecologically sustainable development. UNEP's report on the green economy, entitled *Towards a Green Economy: Pathways to Sustainable Development and Poverty Eradication 2011*, found that while the causes of the concurrent crises of climate change, biodiversity loss, sky-rocketing fuel and food prices, and water scarcity vary, they all reflect a "gross misallocation of capital" toward unsustainable development around the world.[19] The report found that "during the last two decades, much capital was poured into property, fossil fuels and structured financial assets with embedded derivatives. However, relatively little in comparison was invested in renewable energy, energy efficiency, public transportation, sustainable agriculture, ecosystem and biodiversity protection, and land and water conservation."[20]

The upshot is that, twenty years after the 1992 Earth Summit, no state in the world is on the path to *ecologically sustainable development*, where natural resources (including energy inputs) are not used beyond their regeneration capacity and pollution, emissions, and waste production do not threaten the health of ecosystems or otherwise jeopardize sustainable livelihoods and the maintenance of biodiversity. Since extreme poverty and extreme wealth are implicated in environmental destruction (either due to lack of alternative options or through gross overproduction or overconsumption), then ecologically sustainable development also presupposes the avoidance of extreme wealth differentials. Continuing disparities in national income within and between nation-states continue to enable an unequal appropriation of ecological space by the rich at the expense of the poor through the processes of "normal" economic exchanges (including trade), producing a skewed distribution of negative environmental impacts.

Our key point, then, is that if all or most states were able to pursue a strategy of ecologically sustainable development along the lines we have just sketched, then environmental multilateralism would be much less challenging and in some cases unnecessary. Seen in this light, environmental multilateralism may be seen as an effort to compensate for the failure of states to integrate their environment and development policies at the national level. However, as we shall see, integration at the national level has become harder rather than easier over time due to states' preoccupation with maintaining national competitiveness in an increasingly integrated and competitive international economy.

ECONOMY-ENVIRONMENT INTEGRATION FAILURE AT THE INTERNATIONAL LEVEL

Just as states have failed to integrate environmental and economic goals at the national level, so too have they failed to integrate environmental and economic regimes at the international level. As a result, the vast bulk of trade and financial flows continue to support unsustainable development. This is particularly glaring in the case of the Bretton Woods Institutions—the World Trade Organization

(WTO) and its "sister" institutions, the World Bank and International Monetary Fund (IMF).

The multilateral trading regime remains firmly fixed on facilitating trade irrespective of environmental harms or rising global emissions, despite the endorsement of sustainable development in the preamble to the Marrakesh Agreement, which established the WTO in 1994. This has undermined efforts under the UNFCCC to reduce emissions. Yet on the surface, the relationship between the UNFCCC and the agreements managed by the WTO appear to be relatively harmonious, because the parties to the UNFCCC have been at pains to avoid any rule collision by adapting the climate regime to the goals and principles of the trading regime.[21] Although the Uruguay round of negotiations concluded in 1994, two years *after* the UNFCCC was signed at the 1992 Rio Summit, there has been no corresponding effort by the members of the trading regime—all of whom are also signatories to the UNFCCC— to recalibrate the trade rules in ways that are compatible with the goal of sustainable development in general or climate protection in particular. Since the conclusion of the Uruguay round, and especially since China's accession to the WTO in 2001, the goals of the multilateral trading system have been considerably advanced under existing WTO agreements, despite the slow progress in the current Doha round. Yet this expansion in world output has led inexorably to expanding global emissions, resource consumption, and waste output, and there are no rules in the trading system that require this to be otherwise.

The WTO rules do allow for certain national restrictions on trade to protect human, animal, or plant life or health (provided they are not a disguised form of protection and are no more restrictive than is necessary), but they do not actively promote ecologically sustainable trade or the reduction of global emissions. In response to pressure, the launch of the Doha Development round of negotiations included an environmental negotiating mandate for the WTO's Trade and Environment Committee (Special Sessions), designed to enhance the mutual supportiveness of trade and environment. But very little progress has been achieved. What should have been the easiest and most straightforward negotiating item—the removal of restrictions on trade in "environmental goods"—has become bogged down over a failure by the members to agree on its meaning. Lurking behind this definitional contest lie concerns by members over who is to gain the most from what is destined to be an expanding trade in environmental and renewable energy technologies.[22]

Similarly, despite the general prohibition on subsidies, the trade rules effectively permit the use of the environment as a "free resource" in the production of export goods, which confers a competitive disadvantage on exporters that are required to internalize environmental costs. Developing countries have strongly resisted the inclusion of environmental norms from the Rio Declaration (such as the polluter-pays principle) in the trade regime, arguing that the existing trade rules are already replete with double standards that disadvantage developing countries, such as the subsidization of agriculture in the United States and the EU. At the same time, many developed states have failed in their leadership obligations under the UNFCCC due to domestic opposition to the polluter-pays principle and concerns that their industries would suffer an international competitive disadvantage and/or relocate to jurisdictions with weaker regulation.[23]

In short, while the WTO allows for certain environmental exemptions, it otherwise permits unsustainable trade and rising emissions. As a result, the liberalization of trade has led inexorably to increasing global emissions and other environmental harms. This is due to the global nature of the externality, and the fact that the increasing scale of economic activity facilitated through increasing specialization and exchange cancels out any environmental improvements flowing from new technological developments, new regulations, and shifts in the composition of trade.[24]

Yet it is too simplistic to blame the WTO or trade in general for these contradictions, given the significant overlap in the membership of the WTO and the UNFCCC. After all, it was the parties to the UNFCCC that made the decision to defer to the multilateral trading regime. They could have decided otherwise, by authorizing the use of discriminatory trade sanctions and restrictions to promote climate protection in accordance with the burden-sharing principles of the UNFCCC, which would have bound all UNFCCC parties notwithstanding the WTO. Yet despite the effectiveness of multilaterally sanctioned trade restrictions in a number of preexisting environmental treaties dealing with trade in hazardous substances (the Basel Convention), endangered wildlife (CITES), and ozone-depleting chemicals (the Montreal Protocol), the parties to the UNFCCC upheld the principles of the multilateral trading system by ruling out the use of trade sanctions as a tool of national climate policy. Instead, they agreed to cooperate "to promote a supportive and open international economic system that would lead to sustainable economic growth and development."[25]

So the problem is not trade *per se*, or the principles of the multilateral trading system, since the latter can be creatively pushed into the service of environmental protection or overridden in separate environmental agreements vis-à-vis the parties to that agreement. Rather, it is the failure of states to accept national or international regulation of a kind that would ensure ecologically sustainable trade. If all states ensured that the environmental costs of production were fully internalized by all firms operating in their jurisdiction, and otherwise managed the scale of material-energy throughput in their national economies in ways that protected biodiversity and the general carrying capacity of ecosystems, then international trade would be sustainable and states and societies would enjoy the benefits of specialization and exchange.

A similar critique of integration failure can be leveled against the World Bank and the IMF. Throughout the 1980s and 1990s, the World Bank's funding of major infrastructure projects (such as large dams, major highways, and resettlement projects) in developing countries was a major target of environmental campaigns. Among the most notorious of these projects was the Polonoroeste project in Brazil, which resulted in massive deforestation and the dislocation of indigenous and local peoples. The World Bank has since withdrawn from this project and responded to criticisms of its lending practices through internal restructuring and reform, including the introduction of environmental impact assessment of all projects, inspection panels, and greater transparency. It has also become increasingly involved in directing finance to climate-related projects. However, the lion's share of the World Bank's lending to the energy sector remains focused on fossil fuels, and it has made no effort to measure the impact of its lending on greenhouse gas emissions.[26]

Although World Bank lending for environmental projects has grown since the 1992 Rio Summit (from a very low base of around 3.5 percent in 1994 to approximately 11 percent by 2008), the vast bulk of lending is still directed toward unsustainable development.[27] For example, in April 2010 the World Bank approved a US$3.75 billion loan to South Africa to build one of the world's largest coal-fired power plants, which would draw on forty coal mines.[28] A report by the Environmental Defence Fund found that between 1994 and January 2009 the World Bank and other international public finance institutions financed the construction of eighty-eight coal-fired power plants in developing countries and economies in transition that will collectively generate more than three-quarters of the entire emissions from coal-fired plants in the European Union in 2009.[29] Moreover, the structural adjustment policies of the World Bank and IMF, which require currency devaluation, budget austerity measures, the privatization of state-owned enterprises, trade liberalization, and other measures to attract foreign direct investment and increase export revenue, have made it very difficult for indebted countries to give priority to ecologically sustainable development. Not surprisingly, environmentalists have continued to criticize the lending priorities of the World Bank and other international financial institutions such as regional development banks and export credit agencies.

Ecologically sustainable development needs all the help it can get, and it clearly cannot be managed by environmental multilateralism alone, particularly if it remains deferential to economic principles and practices that are inconsistent with environmental goals. International environmental and economic regimes need to be integrated in ways that mutually support ecologically sustainable development.

RESISTANCE AND BACKLASH

Just as existing patterns of production and consumption generate a certain pattern of benefits and burdens across classes, regions, and generations, collective efforts to restructure these activities in a more ecologically sustainable direction invariably entail a redistribution of benefits and burdens. From the standpoint of environmental justice, the internalization of the environmental costs of production and the restructuring of national economies away from unsustainable industries should not be seen as a move from a zero-burden scenario to a burdensome scenario. Rather, it is a move from an unjust and sometimes concealed set of benefits and burdens that favor powerful status quo interests to a more just and transparent distribution of greater benefits and lesser burdens, which seek to minimize the degree to which distant communities and ecosystems, in space and time, are forced to suffer unelected impacts and risks.

The problem, however, is that most of the impacts associated with ecological restructuring are usually felt in the short term, often concentrating on particular industries, regions, and classes, while most of the benefits are usually diffuse and are reaped in the medium to longer term by everyone. Ecological sustainability necessarily entails imposing a new range of constraints on private economic activity that will raise prices to reflect their full ecological and social cost. This will negatively affect the short-term profitability of some industries and the long-term viability of others as the "free ride" they have thus far enjoyed comes to an end.

Resistance from private capital, along with organized labor, in affected industries is therefore likely to be strong and politically influential in circumstances where these interests are central to the regional or national support base of the elected representatives of major political parties. For example, fifty-two senators come from U.S. states in which coal contributes to the state economy and the coal extraction industry is a major employer. This profoundly shapes U.S. Senate voting patterns on climate change issues.[30] Although the Clinton-Gore administration signed the Kyoto Protocol in 1997, no administration has presented the protocol to the Senate for ratification because of the difficulties in mustering the necessary supermajority of sixty-seven votes for treaty ratification.

In contrast, the beneficiaries of ecologically sustainable development are typically diffuse and extend beyond existing generations and the territorial boundaries of nation-states. They are therefore in a weaker position to organize and mobilize politically to secure their protection. The upshot is that, at the subnational and national levels, organized resistance from those affected by upfront costs is typically much more focused and politically potent than the campaigns of environmental NGOs and other advocates who seek to speak on behalf of diffuse and politically neglected environmental constituencies who enjoy little or no formal political representation.

The disparities in political motivation and influence between well-organized, concentrated industry interests and diffuse public interests are as old as politics.[31] However, these disparities are particularly acute in some of the highest-emitting developed countries (such as the United

States, Canada, and Australia), where extractive and emissions-intensive industries have formed influential political alliances and conducted powerful political campaigns to resist any significant encroachment on their profitability or viability through new environmental regulations.

Transnational corporations are particularly powerful actors, with capacities to shape local, national, and global environments through their investment (including in R&D in new technologies), production, retail, and marketing decisions, and through their political influence in shaping public policies and international negotiations but with limited social, ecological, and political accountability.[32] This is particularly striking in the case of transnational corporations in the oil, gas, and other extractive industries, which typically enjoy privileged access and infrastructural support for resource exploitation and less than full disclosure of government payments. For example, Transparency International's analysis of transparency in corporate reporting has found that many major oil and gas companies reveal very limited or no data on how much they pay host governments, which significantly reduces their accountability to the citizens of these countries.[33] It is no accident that many of the countries at the bottom of Transparency International's Corruption Index are rich in mineral and other natural resources yet among the poorest countries in the world.[34] Countries that are rich in oil wealth are 50 percent more likely to be governed by autocratic regimes and twice as likely to suffer civil wars.[35] This is particularly striking in oil-rich developing countries suffering the so-called oil curse, which includes not only autocratic regimes and civil conflict but also secrecy, corruption, financial volatility, and limited social and economic opportunities for women.[36]

So far, states and corporations have generally turned a deaf ear to calls by transnational environmental NGOs for a Corporate Accountability Convention, a key campaign strategy of environmentalists at the World Summit on Sustainable Development (WSSD) at Johannesburg in 2002. Instead, corporations have supported self-regulation through voluntary codes of conduct and standard setting. This response represents a mostly self-regarding rather than other-regarding form of reflexivity, designed to safeguard or enhance reputation and brand name.

Meanwhile, environmental NGO strategies toward corporations have evolved considerably over the past four decades, expanding from the traditional strategies of lobbying governments to regulate corporations or directly confronting corporations to working cooperatively with corporations in setting such standards and providing their conditional endorsement, becoming shareholders, and championing "green industry leaders."[37] Savvy environmental NGOs have recognized that some industries are important allies in the quest for ecologically sustainable development, particularly in sustainable energy systems, sustainable food and fiber production, closed-loop manufacturing firms, the recycling industry, insurance, and ethical investments. Building broad-based political alliances of this kind is essential to building the necessary public support for a transformation toward an ecologically sustainable economy.

DISCURSIVE CO-OPTATION

So far, we have highlighted some of the institutional impediments to global environmental protection at the national and international levels and identified the key economic actors that have played a significant role in resisting stronger environmental regulation. Institutions set the rules that govern social interactions, and powerful economic actors have greater influence in shaping these rules than other social actors by virtue of the resources they command and their structural power as owners of capital. However, structural and material power do not exhaust the forms of power at play in reproducing unsustainable development. Here we focus on discursive power, or the power delivered via control over the production of systems of meaning and signification. This is a more socially diffuse form of power that structures the constitution of subjectivity and social relations according to particular forms of knowledge, social values, and goals.

While repeatedly reaffirmed by governments, industry, and environmentalists as the overarching discourse for reconciling environmental, social, and development goals, sustainable development also remains a highly contested, weakly implemented, and constantly mutating discourse. Indeed, it has joined the ranks of essentially contested concepts such as "security," "justice," and "the national interest."[38] Although the language of sustainability has become deeply entrenched as a universal good, it serves as a floating signifier with no clear or fixed meaning, enabling "sustainable environment" to mutate into "sustainable economic growth" or "green growth." The discursive politics of sustainable development are essentially a struggle between contending social forces to fix this meaning. This includes a struggle between different forms of knowledge; different constructions of interests, risk, and responsibility; and different constructions of subjectivity.

Discourses define what is normal, legitimate, and desirable and what is not, with varying degrees of success. A hegemonic discourse is one that has emerged as the overwhelming, defining discourse in a particular social field (such as among policy professionals or governments), especially when it enjoys a widely "taken-for-granted" status among particular publics and is no longer contested. However, discourses are inherently unstable and they typically mutate over time in response to contestation. Hegemonic discourses often co-opt aspects of counter-hegemonic discourses in order to maintain legitimacy and weaken the challenger, leading to a splintering and realignment of challenging discourses. This is clearly evident in the evolving discourse of sustainable development vis-à-vis the dominant discourse of neoliberalism.

"Sustainable development" quickly achieved dominance as an international "meta-environmental discourse" in the immediate aftermath of the publication of the Brundtland Report in 1987. But by 1992, at the Earth Summit, it had been reinterpreted in more capitalist market-friendly terms to embrace the liberalization of trade and finance and the promotion of market policy tools over so-called command-and-control regulation. It may be argued that two decades on, by Rio+20 in 2012, the term had exhausted itself, overcome by policy failure and the search for more fashionable and energetic mobilizing concepts. In his detailed analysis of the evolution of global environment and development discourses since the Stockholm conference in 1972, Steven Bernstein concluded that

> Rio institutionalized the view that liberalization in trade and finance is consistent with, and even necessary for, international environmental protection, and that both are compatible with the overarching goal of sustained economic growth. Thus, the Earth Summit embraced, and perhaps even catalyzed, the new economic orthodoxy then sweeping through the developing world.[39]

This was encapsulated in the Rio Declaration 1992, Agenda 21, the Convention on Biological Diversity, and the UNFCCC. In effect, the key environmental treaties designed to tackle biodiversity loss and climate change were adapted to fit neoliberal economic globalization in ways that papered over deep-seated contradictions between the trajectory of the global economy and the health, integrity, and resilience of the Earth's ecosystems.

However, increasing global financial instability since 2008, along with the growing incidence of climate-related disasters around the world, has undermined the legitimacy of deregulated or weakly regulated markets and prompted renewed questioning of the broader neoliberal consensus. While the initial limits-to-growth discourse never gained a footing in governmental and environmental policy professional circles during the 1970s and 1980s and was countered by that of sustainable development in its muted form, a discourse emphasizing planetary boundaries and tipping points has gathered increasing momentum among not only Earth scientists and transnational environmental NGOs but also major international organizations.[40] The Group of Twenty (G20) major economic powers responded to these pressures by employing the new discourse of "green growth" and "the green economy" in the run up to Rio+20.[41]

Whereas sustainable development had been largely co-opted and neutralized by neoliberalism in the 1990s, there are now signs that neoliberalism is facing an emerging legitimacy crisis. Deregulated global markets and the externalization of ecological costs can no longer be viewed as the "normal" way of doing business. As the World Bank report on *Inclusive Green Growth: The Pathway to Sustainable Development* put it, the market failures and institutional failures that are producing unsustainable development now "threaten the long-term sustainability of growth and progress made on social welfare."[42] This creates an important opportunity for discursive shifts toward more reflexive forms of modernization and globalization that are essential precursors to governance reforms, but with the ever-present possibility of further attempts to reincorporate and neutralize "Limits-to-Growth II."

DEMOCRATIC ACCOUNTABILITY DEFICITS

A central argument of this book has been that the routine production and skewed distribution of ecological risks arise from and reflect a crisis of accountability. This applies, first and foremost, to market transactions that externalize ecological and social costs. As Nicholas Stern, author of *The Economics of Climate Change: The Stern Review* put it, climate change "is the greatest example of market failure we have ever seen."[43] Climate change, along with other forms of irreversible global environmental change such as biodiversity loss, also represents one of the greatest examples of *regulatory* failure by states, which multilateralism has only partially been able to redress. This has prompted some frustrated critics (often scientists) to argue that liberal democracy must yield to the authoritative rule of experts to avoid climatic and other ecological catastrophes. Others have warned that—like it or not—authoritarianism is likely to intensify in the face of resource scarcity and environmental decline in a warming world.[44] Our argument, in response, is that these market and regulatory failures are a sign that democracy needs to be deepened, extended, and adapted to an interdependent world—not abandoned.

Many anti-globalization critics and democrats have argued that multilateralism suffers even greater democratic deficits than those occurring at the national level. Increasing international interdependence has seen the rise of international regimes and organizations that operate under a delegated authority, which means that they are internally accountable only to their members but only weakly accountable to broader publics that are affected by their rules and decisions.[45] In other words, multilateralism is best understood as "executive multilateralism," since negotiations are conducted by the political executive of states, with minimal involvement or scrutiny by citizens.[46] According to these critics, states may be seen as more or less democratic according to whether they hold free and fair elections, but multilateral regimes and organizations are typically only designated as more or less legitimate.[47]

Moreover, not all states are democratic in form or substance (e.g., China and Russia), and there are significant asymmetries in the size, capabilities, and negotiating power among states. And so Robert Dahl has argued that international institutions lie well below any threshold of democracy, which he understands to mean popular control over governmental policies and decisions, made possible by a system of civil and political rights.[48] These arguments form a significant strand in U.S. civic nationalism, which has been played out in the form of resistance to the incursion of externally generated, treaty-based norms and the defense of the United States' right to author its own laws on its own terms in accordance with the U.S. Constitution. The U.S. Senate exercises this right when it invokes its constitutional power to refuse ratification of treaties signed by the executive when the multilateral norms they embody are considered to be out of step with American policies or values.

While acknowledging the weak and indirect lines of accountability between international regimes and affected publics, we must not assume the existence of a simple binary of "good" (i.e., democratic) states versus "bad" (i.e., undemocratic) multinational regimes. Although multilateral regimes do not qualify as democratic institutions according to Dahl's test of direct popular control, they can nonetheless embody certain democratic values and virtues, such as due process, deliberation, and diverse regional representation. They can prompt states to think about transboundary and planetary concerns, not just national concerns. They can sometimes enhance democracy at the national level by helping to empower general over rent-seeking special interests, empower minority rights, and improve the epistemic quality of deliberation and promote participation at the domestic level.[49] Moreover, bureaucrats working for multilateral institutions, such as the General-Secretary of the United Nations or the Secretary of the UNFCCC, are typically more strongly motivated to represent global and transnational concerns and collective interests than democratically elected prime ministers or presidents whose primary responsibility is toward their state-bounded communities. Critically, multilateralism provides an important "supplementary structure of rule" that compensates for the inadequacies of exclusive territorial rule.[50] Moreover, multilateralism has evolved considerably since the end of World War II, moving away from the club model of executive multilateralism that dominated the period of embedded liberalism and moving toward a more complex form that increasingly acknowledges the important role played by nonstate actors in agenda setting, negotiating, debating and challenging, monitoring, and enforcement.[51]

When we turn to examine the liberal democratic state, we also find significant democratic deficits. Abraham Lincoln's famous Gettysburg address of 1863 described representative democracy in its liberal form as "government of the people, by the people, for the people," but they are not all the same people (voters, political representatives, citizens) and there are many more people beyond the nation who may be affected by decisions made within the nation. Liberal democratic states have generally demonstrated their superiority over authoritarian states in matters of environmental protection and environmental justice, but they nonetheless suffer from a range of representation, accountability, and institutional deficits that enable them to externalize ecological costs in the same way as firms. For example,

- Liberal democratic states formally represent only the citizens of territorially bounded nation-states, but their decisions affect a much broader, neglected "environmental constituency" comprising "foreigners," future generations, and nonhuman species.
- Political representatives and political leaders typically make decisions framed by short-term electoral cycles rather than long-range, ecological horizons.
- Diffuse public interests are usually disadvantaged in the policy-making process when pitted against well-organized interest groups with a direct material or financial stake in policy outcomes; meanwhile, socially and economically marginalized groups and classes are usually not only the most affected by environmental impacts but also the most politically disempowered.
- Many environmental problems are complex and require specialized knowledge, which tends to disenfranchise the lay public from informed debate on environmental issues.
- Economic globalization is compromising the political autonomy and steering capacity of states in relation to domestic environmental management.

The transnational and transtemporal character of global environmental change directs attention to these major democratic deficits at the heart of the modern state and challenges the idea of democracy based on a fixed *demos* and a defined territory. However, the primary challenge to territorially based democracy arises not from globalization per se but rather from the boundary problem that is inherent in democracy itself, which globalization has merely helped to expose.[52] The liberal nationalist and civic republican claim that only the "people" or "the nation" constitutes the legitimate source of authority has always been vulnerable to the argument that there is no democratic means for determining who the people are, or who should be deemed to belong to the nation, for the purposes of self-rule.

While state boundaries cannot be erased, the practice of territorial rule can certainly become more responsible to the needs of wider communities. As we argue below, overcoming this ecological accountability deficit requires new ways of redressing the profound disconnect between those who make decisions that generate ecological risks (primarily investors, producers, and consumers but also governments), those who have expert knowledge of such risks (primarily scientists), the ecological victims who suffer (typically the most marginal and least represented constituencies in time and space), and those who must take political responsibility for such risks (political representatives). Reflexive modernization and globalization require the development of reflexive public and private governance structures that bring these disparate parties onto the radar of decision making. Below we suggest this can be done through the development of the idea and practice of "extended responsibility" across spatial and temporal boundaries through the institutionalization of new forms of accountability, representation, and deliberation at all levels of economic, social, and ecological governance.

REFLEXIVE MODERNIZATION, REFLEXIVE GLOBALIZATION

We have identified modernization as the initial and primary driver of global environmental change, and the recent neoliberal phase of economic globalization as an intensifier of this process. Since both are multifaceted and multiscalar processes, it follows that the governance response must also be multifaceted and multiscalar. This demands *both* reflexive modernization and reflexive globalization. In both cases, governance structures must become "geared towards continual learning in the course of modulating ongoing developments, rather than towards complete knowledge and maximization of control."[53] Reflexive governance brings the challenges of complexity and uncertainty to the forefront of decision making, which requires principles, processes, and procedures that enable deliberation, self-correction, and readjustment of both policy instruments and policy goals in response to feedback from social and ecological systems.[54]

Unfortunately the dominant global discourse of "good governance" promoted by major international institutions such as the

United Nations, the World Bank, and the OECD does not take us very far in this direction. While there is nothing objectionable about the familiar set of good governance principles—such as the rule of law, the absence of corruption, transparency, participation, account-ability, efficiency, and effectiveness—we argue that they need to be developed and adapted to a globalizing world.[55]

Discourses of risk, responsibility, and accountability are intimately connected to particular configurations of knowledge and power, and they shift over time according to shifting "relations of definition" prompted by counterhegemonic discourses. The first step toward more reflexive globalization, then, is to challenge dominant constructions of acceptable risk, accountability, and responsibility. The second step is to build support for governance reforms that deepen and extend accountability and responsibility. Since we have claimed that the global ecological crisis reflects a crisis of accountability, we single out this principle for special treatment.

FROM ACCOUNTABILITY TO EXTENDED RESPONSIBILITY

Markets have no in-built mechanisms of accountability toward third parties negatively affected by market transactions, since the profit motive drives firms to privatize gains and socialize costs in the absence of regulation. The neoliberal discourse of deregulated, unfettered markets and economic freedom serves to depoliticize decision making and therefore limit accountability in the very domain that most typically generates diffuse yet cumulative ecological impacts and injustices. Decisions to invest, produce, and consume are essentially considered individual and private matters, unless those who are negatively affected by commercial transactions can prove damage, causation, and dereliction of a legal duty under the common law. The growth of environmental regulation and treaties may be seen as a collective effort to limit the degree to which firms can enjoy an environmental free ride at the public's expense, but we have seen that this regulatory effort has been inadequate. Here, we show that this inadequacy derives from an idea and practice of accountability that is no longer adequate for a globalizing world.

The principle of accountability is central to the governance of international organizations, liberal democratic states, and modern corporations. While it has different meanings in different contexts, the conventional understanding requires governing bodies or decision makers to report, explain, justify, and answer to a particular constituency for past or prospective decisions, actions, or inactions. Governance structures with *formal* lines of accountability are usually linked to a fixed constituency defined by their status (e.g., shareholder) or membership (such as a citizen of a state or state member of an international organization) that grants a delegated authority to the governing body, which then becomes accountable to the constituency for the exercise of that authority. Holding governing bodies accountable depends on transparency and a right to know, and it is further enhanced if the relevant constituency has an opportunity to make their voices heard in the decision-making process.

The problem with this conventional membership-based model of accountability is that, like markets, it has no in-built mechanisms for preventing decision makers from unfairly externalizing and displacing costs through space and time onto "outsiders." It is based on the pretense that no one else is affected by decisions made by the governing body, or if they are, then they are not formally recognized and do not matter. We believe this model needs to be enriched and supplemented with mechanisms that ensure enlarged accountability and responsibility to wider communities at risk in space and time that are affected by the decisions of states, international organizations, and corporations.

There are, of course, legal remedies that may be sought against individuals, corporations, or states by negatively affected third parties with the relevant legal standing where direct environmental or physical harm can be proved. Yet the legal grammar of responsibility remains rooted in notions of individual agency, direct causation, and culpability. As a consequence, it obscures the structural character of global environmental harms and risks—which are becoming increasingly complex, incalculable, and uninsurable. Climate change, biodiversity loss, and other forms of global environmental change demand a new, postliberal account of accountability that moves beyond a focus on responsibility for particular events in the context of existing rules and toward a critical understanding of the historical conditions and social structures that systematically produce environmental injustices across space and time.[56]

Whereas accountability presupposes the existence of a constituency that can defend its own interests, extended responsibility seeks to bring into view those constituencies that may not be in such a position. A classic example is the case of a trustee or guardian, who takes on the responsibility to look after the interests of others who are not in a position to represent themselves. We argue that governance structures must increasingly allow for "ecological guardianship" on behalf of wider environmental constituencies. For this to occur, existing mechanisms of accountability must be strengthened with new mechanisms of extended responsibility, adapted to suit different types of governance. Governance will become more reflexive through a rich plurality of both kinds of mechanisms, including electoral and nonelectoral, vertical and horizontal, membership-based and "affectedness-based," reputational and market-based.[57]

The 1992 Rio Declaration already provides a range of principles that would enable much more reflexive environmental governance. These include the precautionary principle (Principle 15); the polluter-pays principle (Principle 16); common but differentiated responsibilities (Principle 7); and intra- and intergenerational equity and access to information, participation, and justice (Principle 10), which seek to enhance responsibility and accountability, both ex-post to an identifiable and directly affected constituency and ex-ante by anticipating and preventing ecological harmful consequences. While these principles have been endorsed by most states, they remain largely aspirational and only weakly implemented. They are also qualified by other principles in the Declaration that reinforce sovereign rights over territory (Principle 2) and uphold an open and growing international economy as the default position in the absence of international environmental consensus (Principle 12). Even so, the systematic institutionalization of the more reflexive principles would make a profound difference to the processes and outcomes of modernization and globalization, and none more so than the precautionary principle.

THE PRECAUTIONARY PRINCIPLE

The precautionary principle provides that "where there are threats of serious or irreversible damage, lack of full scientific certainty shall not be used as a reason for postponing cost-effective measures to prevent environmental degradation."[58] This principle is particularly adept at catching global risks (such as climate change and loss of biodiversity) that develop over long lead times and spatial scales, produce serious and irreversible consequences, and therefore affect a wide class of victims who are given no opportunity to exercise any informed consent to the practices that generate the risks. In this sense, it transcends the simple model of accountability discussed above by enabling the practice of extended responsibility that befits a global risk society. In effect, the principle provides a simple and effective form of "proxy" representation for, and accountability to, the "neglected environmental constituency" by removing the systematic bias in economic and political decision making against long-term public interests.

The principle has been criticized for paralyzing decision making since there are risks on every side of a decision.[59] Yet this criticism is based on a misunderstanding of the conditions that trigger the principle. The precautionary principle does not prevent risk-taking decisions, it does not apply to all risks, and it cannot be invoked on the basis of flimsy evidence. Rather, it works as an evidentiary rule and is only triggered when credible evidence is raised that a particular decision may produce serious and/or irreversible ecological damage. Only in these circumstances does the onus shift to the proponent of a new development, technology, trade, or investment agreement to demonstrate that no such damage is likely, and if this cannot be demonstrated, then preventative measures must be taken, which may mean not proceeding with the proposal.

Below, we identify a range of renovations that could be made to existing governance structures that would enable richer ecological information, wider forms of accountability, and extended responsibility. We begin with the processes of consumption and production and then move to the state and then to international governance.

REFORMING ENVIRONMENTAL GOVERNANCE

REFLEXIVE CONSUMPTION

Whereas the practices of consumption and citizenship were once considered separate economic and political domains, with quite different logics, they have increasingly merged such that ecologically responsible consumption has become a form of "ecological citizenship." Consumers (which include individuals as well as firms, organizations, and governments acting as purchasers) are becoming more proactive in their choices about what they consume—or do not consume—and how they dispose of the wastes associated with their consumption. Increasingly they are choosing to recycle their waste, become vegetarians, limit the carbon footprint of their consumption (including by buying local produce where this is the low-carbon option), and restrict or forgo carbon intensive forms of travel to reduce emissions. Some of these choices are underpinned by economic incentives (for instance, waste levies and carbon pricing). Others are shaped by cultural drivers and new sources of environmental information to assist informed consumer choice, such as voluntary and mandatory certification, eco-labeling, and fair trade schemes that encourage wholesalers, retailers, and consumers to better understand the environmental consequences of their purchasing decisions. Likewise, green procurement practices by firms can discipline the practices of suppliers, especially when the purchasing decisions are made by large corporations. Together, these "local" practices of "extended consumer responsibility" help to reduce environmental impacts along global commodity chains.

REFLEXIVE PRODUCTION

The flip side of "extended consumer responsibility" is "extended producer responsibility," which requires the manufacturer to take environmental responsibility for its product throughout its entire life cycle—from "cradle to grave," from resource extraction to end use, and to take back the product for disposal, reclamation, or recycling.

The corporate social responsibility movement represents an attempt to extend the environmental and social responsibilities of corporations. For example, the United Nations Global Compact invites corporations and other organizations ranging from universities to municipalities to commit to a set of ten principles that embody the United Nations core human rights, environment, labor, and anti-corruption standards. The three environmental principles in this list are: commitment to a "precautionary approach; taking initiatives to promote greater environmental responsibility; and encouraging the development and diffusion of environmentally friendly technologies."[60] Other voluntary initiatives include the Global Reporting Initiative (GRI), a nonprofit organization that provides a sustainability reporting framework for companies and organizations; the ISO 26000 standard on social responsibility; and the "UNEP Statement of Commitment by Financial Institutions on Sustainable Development."[61] However, these initiatives remain merely voluntary and their uptake is limited.

A more effective means to extend the responsibility of corporations would be to formally require accountability to external stakeholders affected by corporate decisions, so that that the board of directors is no longer only accountable to shareholders.[62] The principle of accountability to external stakeholders, along with extended producer responsibility, could be components of a UN-sponsored Corporate Social Responsibility and Accountability Convention.[63]

GREENING NATIONAL GOVERNANCE

It should be clear from our critique of "integration failure" at the national level that states are the linchpins in global governance and that greening the state is an essential component of greening global governance. By "greening the state" we mean reforming both the *practice* of governance by states (i.e., policy and law making) and the *structures* of governance (the institutional framework in which policy and law are made and implemented) in ways that are more ecologically responsible in the extended sense of the term.

In greening the *practice* of governance, reforming economic policies is key. Instead of adapting environmental policies to suit the dominant economic discourse of neoliberalism, economic policies need to be consistent with *ecologically* sustainable development. This entails a more thoroughgoing integration of economic and environmental policies.

In the lead-up to Rio+20, many international organizations and some governments argued that this integration could be achieved through "green growth" or "the green economy." However, like "sustainable development," there are no agreed definitions of these terms.[64] For UNEP, a green economy is one where "growth in income and employment are driven by public and private investments that reduce carbon emissions and pollution, enhance energy and resource efficiency, and prevent the loss of biodiversity and ecosystem services." For the World Bank, which focuses on developing countries, green growth "is efficient, clean, and resilient—efficient in its use of natural resources, clean in that it minimizes pollution and environmental impacts, and resilient in that it accounts for natural hazards and the role of environmental management and natural capital in preventing physical disasters."[65] For the OECD, green growth is intended to provide the operational policy agenda for "fostering the necessary conditions for innovation, investment and competition that can give rise to new sources of economic growth—consistent with resilient ecosystems."[66]

However, those governments that have actively enlisted the rhetoric of green growth see it merely as another opportunity for economic growth. This is despite the fact that many of the major reports prepared for Rio+20, such as those of UNEP and the OECD, make it clear that green growth is merely one prong in a more comprehensive strategy of ecologically sustainable development. These reports also acknowledge the depth of malfunctioning markets in failing to account for environment resources, assets, and ecosystem services. They call for the removal of direct and indirect "perverse environmental subsidies" that encourage the exploitation of fossil fuels, forests, and fisheries and for the full incorporation of ecological and social costs into prices so they reflect the true cost of production. They even provide a belated acknowledgment of the environmental critique of GDP as an indicator of progress (which has been in circulation for nearly four decades) and call for the development of new indicators for measuring progress that replace GDP as a surrogate measure of welfare.[67] All of the reports now acknowledge that the costs of environmental damage will mount in the absence of anticipatory action. Even the World Bank has conceded the self-defeating character of the "grow now, clean up later" argument that is implicit in the Environmental Kuznets Curve discussed in chapter 2.[68]

Yet even the more enlightened discourses of green growth, if pursued as a singular policy, still suffer from the same fatal flaw as the discourse of ecological modernization: while green growth can accelerate the *relative* decoupling of economic activity from environmental degradation through greater energy and resource efficiency, it cannot lead to absolute decoupling because it is still premised on the idea of perpetual economic growth and therefore a physically expanding economy. Nor do these discourses grapple with the "rebound effect" (or "take-back" effect)—in which the higher incomes achieved via increases in eco-efficiency are redeployed to pay for more consumption and production, and hence more material-energy use.

The only way to shift from the relative to the absolute decoupling of economy activity and resource depletion, environmental degradation, and rising emissions is through the establishment of ecological ceilings or safe sustainability boundaries.[69] These planetary boundaries or "guardrails" would provide the safe operating space and core target corridors for human development.[70] This will require the development of a broad scientific and political consensus on the nature and limits of planetary boundaries, which will be an intensely political process, given significant scientific uncertainty, political disagreement about acceptable risks, and significant inequalities in the distribution of income, wealth, and opportunity within and between countries. For instance, in the climate domain, a broad but shallow political consensus has been reached over a "2 degree guardrail" and this may yet shape future international climate negotiations.[71] Ecological boundaries would need to be negotiated and continually adjusted at multiple scales through international and regional negotiation and agreement, and national and local regulation, in order to safeguard ecosystem resilience at multiple scales. This is the only way to prevent the global economy from reaching dangerous ecological tipping points that carry the risk of abrupt, nonlinear, and irreversible changes that could be devastating for human civilization. As we saw in chapter 1, the most significant planetary boundaries are climate change, ozone depletion, land use change, freshwater use, biological diversity, ocean acidification, nitrogen and phosphorus inputs to the biosphere and oceans, aerosol loading, and chemical pollution.[72]

Moreover, "growing" new, ecologically sustainable industries has to go hand in hand with "de-growing" and phasing-out old, unsustainable industries, which is a major political challenge in the absence of a widespread community understanding of the risks associated with perpetuating such industries.

In short, reflexive governance in pursuit of ecologically sustainable development is far more politically demanding than the green growth discourse suggests, and avoiding options that are not "win-win" solutions will not produce the necessary transition to a genuinely sustainable economy. This cannot be accomplished without a rich flow of environmental information, critical public debate, and adaptive social learning and policy making. This requires, in turn, a significant shift not only in the practice of governance (including major shifts in economic philosophy, goals, policies, and measures) but also the *structures* of governance.

We have already noted the various democratic deficits and institutional failures of liberal democratic states, which create a strong bias against the representation of long-term public interests like ecological sustainability. We also reject the complacent rejoinder that this reflects "public opinion" and "the will of people" since these are merely artifacts of the communicative contexts, institutions, procedures, and different voting methods that are used to summon and measure them, just as policy and law making are shaped by the constitutional and political institutional context.[73] Instead, we argued that actually existing liberal democracy—seen as the gold standard of governance at the state level—is too "thin" to safeguard the ecological conditions for human flourishing. Rather than abandoning liberal democracy, as some eco-authoritarians have argued, we argue that it needs to be deepened and extended through procedural innovations that summon more public-spirited and ecologically responsible decision making that is sensitive to wider communities at risk.

Most green political theorists argue that deliberative or "discursive" democracy is especially suited to dealing with complex, variable, and transboundary ecological problems and concerns, provided the communicative context is relatively undistorted. Deliberation—the ongoing, critical public testing and exchange of ideas and arguments—facilitates reflexivity, self-correction, and social learning.[74] While voting enables the representation of territorially bounded constituencies, such deliberation enables the ongoing "representation of discourses," including cosmopolitan discourses that speak on behalf of transnational and global interests.[75] The process of anticipating and addressing objections raised by others can steer the public opinion formation and decision making toward understanding of and support for longer-term, generalizable interests. A vibrant national and transnational civil society, made up of a wide variety of public interest advocacy groups and a diverse and independent media, plays a vital role in challenging structures of authority that define, assess, and manage risks. New global communications technologies provide one of the positive contributions of globalization in this respect.

Deliberative democracy clearly presupposes the traditional repertoire of constitutionally guaranteed civil and political rights—such as freedom of speech, assembly, movement, and so forth. However, if liberal democracies are to become more ecologically responsible, then their governance structures need to incorporate environmental values and rights. As Tim Hayward has argued, the case for *procedural* environmental rights is "all but unanswerable" while the moral case for substantive environmental rights is unimpeachable insofar as a basic environmental minimum is a precondition for democratic decision making.[76] Such procedural rights would include a right to accurate (up-to-date, peer-reviewed) environmental information, the right to be informed of risk-generating proposals, third-party litigation rights, and a right to participate in environmental impact assessment processes. While more than seventy countries now have environmental constitutional provisions, most of these are not expressed in terms of enforceable rights.[77]

However, not all of the above reforms need to occur at the constitutional level. They can also be achieved through administrative and regulatory reforms that ensure greater integration between different government agencies, greater public participation in policy making, and new mechanisms to ensure the more systematic representation of environmental concerns. The latter can take a variety of different forms, such as the establishment of an Office of Environmental Defender, a Commissioner for the Environment (such as in New Zealand), or a Parliamentary Commissioner for Future Generations (such as in Hungary).[78] These mechanisms of "proxy representation" help to provide a fairer balance between immediate, concentrated, and well-organized economic interests and long-term, diffuse public environmental interests. Clearly, the green democratic state is not a neutral state—but then again neither is the liberal democratic state. Both shape and reflect different social values and different conceptions of moral and political community.

State governance structures must not only incorporate new mechanisms of enlarged representation and extended responsibility. Given the complexities and uncertainties associated with long-term sustainability planning, these structures must be capable of ongoing adaptive learning while modulating ongoing developments, rather than operating in the expectation of "complete knowledge" and "total control."[79] There are unavoidable tensions and trade-offs between the persistence and purposefulness that are required to achieve an overarching strategy of ecologically sustainable development, on the one hand, and the flexibility, participation, trial-and-error policy experimentation, and adaptation that are required to enable effective and democratic social learning, on the other. This suggests the need for "polycentric" governance structures that combine both leadership and governance hierarchies that sustain focus and commitment, without being too rigid, alongside participatory planning, decentralized networks, and self-regulation to enable experimentation and adaptive learning.[80]

Clearly, the governance reforms that we have suggested cannot happen without societal and political mobilization. They require much more than a committed environmental movement to generate the requisite levels of popular understanding and social and political support. The building of an effective counterhegemonic discourse of ecological sustainability that breaks the dominance of neoliberalism needs a broad-based political coalition that includes environmental NGOs, unions, scientists, policy professionals, social justice advocates, religious organizations, universities, industry associations, and major firms. Yet despite all the signs that point to such a need, this is clearly a tall order: developed states and their societies are still constructed around the politics and desire for more rather than less conventional economic growth, while many developing states lack the institutions of civil society and the state capacities to meet their basic needs and functions.

GREENING INTERNATIONAL GOVERNANCE

Many observers had hoped that the Rio+20 conference in 2012 would provide a new "constitutional moment" for reforming both the practice and structures of global environmental governance, on a par with the immediate post–World War II period when the United Nations, the International Monetary Fund, the World Bank, and the General Agreement on Tariffs and Trade (GATT) were born.[81] However, Rio+20 proved to be a squandered opportunity. Although the attendance at Rio+20 (approximately forty-four thousand) was more than double that of the 1992 Earth Summit (approximately seventeen thousand), there were fewer heads of state (notable absences included Barack Obama, Angela Merkel, and David Cameron) and it failed to produce the same level of political commitment and institutional innovation.[82]

The summit was organized around two key agenda items: "the green economy in the context of sustainable development and poverty eradication" and reform of the global environmental architecture, generating considerable excitement about the possibilities of innovation. As we noted above, most of the major economic and environmental organizations (such as the World Bank, the OECD, and UNEP) produced reports for Rio+20 that demonstrated a significant evolution in thinking about the relationship between market economies and environmental degradation since the 1992 Earth Summit. Yet the same cannot be said for governments. The heavily watered-down outcome document, titled "The Future We Want," turned out to be a triumph of diplomatic artifice, full of reaffirmations of previous commitments but precious few new concrete commitments. Most of the hard work in areas such as sustainable consumption and production, finance, and technology transfer was simply passed on to the UN General Assembly. However, one modest outcome was the establishment of a working group to develop a process for developing a set of Sustainable Development Goals to complement the Millennium Development Goals.[83]

Rio+20 has been roundly condemned by environmental and anti-poverty NGOs; many governments have also admitted that the outcome was disappointing, and former Norwegian prime minister and chair of the Brundtland Commission, Gro Harlem Brundtland, criticized the document for failing to recognize planetary boundaries and tipping points.[84]

The key paragraphs in the Outcome Document on the green economy amounted to nothing more than a vague wish list and effectively left it to the discretion of individual states to determine what vision, approach, and measures to implement according to national circumstances.[85] The phrase "economic growth" appeared twenty times, usually with the adjective "sustained and inclusive" or "sustained, inclusive, and equitable" but not "green" or "ecological." The parties also reaffirmed international trade as an engine for development and sustained economic growth.[86] However, the parties did manage to agree on calling upon the UN Statistical Commission to launch a work program to develop broader progress measures "to complement" rather than replace GDP.[87]

The watered-down document reflects many of the persistent and long-standing tensions between developed and developing countries.

The key champion of the idea of green growth, the EU, found little support among the G77 or China. Developing countries made it clear that they did not want any new "conditionalities" attached to their development and did not wish to make any international undertakings in the absence of further assistance with capacity building, financing, and technology transfer.[88]

The outcome on governance reform is only marginally more encouraging. The reform of the architecture of international environmental governance has been the subject of increasing debate since the 1992 Earth Summit. The United Nations system was established well before environmental concerns had emerged as a major political preoccupation, yet the environmental institutional reforms since the end of World War II have been relatively modest and have not enjoyed high status. UNEP, established in 1972, remains the environmental centerpiece and green conscience of the UN system. Although its role is to promote international environmental cooperation, coordination, and policy guidance, it is merely a subsidiary program, not a specialized UN agency. It does not report directly to the UN General Assembly, only through the Economic and Social Council, which restricts its independent voice. UNEP's Governing Council does not enjoy universal membership; rather, fifty-seven members are elected by the General Assembly for four-year terms. It has a very small budget and relies on voluntary contributions, which means that the major donors are able to exert greater control. Likewise, the Commission for Sustainable Development (established at the 1992 Earth Summit) has not enjoyed a high status or been effective in hastening the implementation of sustainable development despite its wide stakeholder consultations.

Rio+20 certainly generated a creative outpouring of innovative ideas and debate about the reform of the UN system. These ranged from relatively modest proposals, such as strengthening and upgrading UNEP, to more ambitious proposals, such as establishing a World Environment Organization (WEO), a Sustainable Development Council or Trusteeship Council to exercise trusteeship over the global commons, an International Environmental Court, a Global Parliament for the Environment, an Ecological Security Council, and a UN Commissioner for Future Generations.[89]

The case for a WEO arose early in the 1990s out of the environmental critique of the WTO and was largely modeled on that organization.

This entailed bringing all multilateral environmental treaties under the WEO umbrella to avoid fragmentation and improve coordination, holding biennial ministerial conferences, and establishing a binding dispute resolution system.[90] The Sustainable Development Council has been proposed as a replacement for the Commission for Sustainable Development, to oversee the implementation of sustainable development in the UN.

Given our critique of integration failure, we see greatest merit in the establishment of a Sustainable Development Council. However, as critics have noted, proposals for reforms to the UN structure of governance do not address the fundamental problem, which is the failure of states to live up to the compact made at the 1992 Earth Summit.[91] If this commitment were to be genuinely renewed and implemented at the national level, then a new WEO or Sustainable Development Council would no longer be necessary. As we argued above, the paradox of environmental multilateralism cannot be resolved simply by more environmental multilateralism. Rather, it requires a shift in thinking in national capitals toward a new guiding economic philosophy that moves beyond perpetual, indiscriminate growth in material-energy throughput in the economy to a new model of the green economy based on ecologically positive or benign growth, which necessarily entails the contraction and disappearance of ecologically destructive growth. This shift is a condition precedent to successful governance reforms.

So to what did Rio+20 agree? The parties invited the General Assembly to adopt a resolution to strengthen and upgrade UNEP by establishing universal membership of the UNEP's Governing Council and more stable and increased financial resources.[92] They also agreed to replace the Commission for Sustainable Development with a high-level political forum to follow up on the implementation of sustainable development.[93] The international financial institutions were called upon to "mainstream" sustainable development, while the WTO was merely enjoined to get on with the business of the Doha round, including the negotiations on environmental goods and services.[94]

The compromise on UN reform reflected the lack of political support for major institutional innovation by key players. The United States opposed the establishment of any new UN organs and, as Maria Ivanova has rightly predicted, "without a real financial commitment and a genuine effort to address the underlying concerns of developing countries, no reform initiative would pass through the voting bloc of the G-77 and China.[95]

After two years of work on the draft text, a steady buildup of major reports on the ailing and possible terminal health of the global environment since the 1992 Earth Summit, and the development of an increasingly sophisticated critique of the neoliberal economic consensus emanating not only from the NGO community but also key international organizations, the Rio+20 outcome—"The Future We Want"—struggles to deserve the name.

FUTURE CHALLENGES TO A GREEN WORLD ORDER

Clearly, there is no shortage of ideas and opportunities to transcend the dominant discourse and practice of neoliberal globalization and transform outdated corporate and state governance structures in ways that would safeguard the global environment. It should be equally clear that there are considerable challenges facing the project of reflexive modernization and reflexive globalization. We conclude by singling out the key challenges—geopolitical, demographic, economic, and ethical/discursive—that stand in the way of the development of a green world order.

It is widely argued that the end of the Cold War has seen a significant geopolitical shift from a perilous but superficially stable bipolar world divided between the United States and the Soviet Union, to a brief interregnum of unipolarity with the United States as the singular global superpower, and now, with the rise of China, India, and Brazil and the reemergence of Russia, to a potentially much less stable period of multipolarity. Some critics have suggested we are now living in a "G-Zero" world, in which no major power or group of powers has the motivation or leverage to drive any significant international agenda.[96] Many globalization scholars have pointed to a simultaneous "shift of power" away from states toward markets and nonstate actors following neoliberal globalization and the increasing influence of transnational nonstate actors and networks.

Together, these developments have made the practice of multilateralism in general, and environmental multilateralism in particular, much more challenging. The Chinese economy has grown at around 10 percent per year over the past three decades, which has transformed

China from a poor country to the world's second largest economy after the United States.[97] The rapid economic growth of India, Brazil, and Indonesia, Korea, Mexico, Russia, and Turkey has seen a discernible shift in the economic center of gravity away from the so-called West as well as new strains on the unity of the China/G77 grouping as the gap between the rapid developers and least developed countries grows. At the same time, the economies of the United States and Western Europe have threatened to unravel in the wake of the 2008 global financial crisis and the crisis in the Eurozone.

One common narrative explaining the failure of international environmental cooperation maintains that the rising powers in the East and the South (particularly the so-called BASIC group—China, India, Brazil, and South Africa) have failed to assume environmental responsibilities that are commensurate with their new economic power. According to this argument, the world has changed since the 1992 Earth Summit, particularly with the rise of the BASIC group. The developed versus developing country divide, along with the whole idea of the Third World, has become outmoded, just as the reference to the Second World has faded out. The argument for special treatment, or differentiated responsibilities by these particular developing countries, is therefore becoming less tenable and they should no longer hide behind their poor, given their rapidly growing middle class.

While few would deny the importance of cooperation by the BASIC countries, and their obligation to take responsibility for the rising consumption of their middle class, there is another narrative that is less flattering to the traditional Western powers. The emerging economies are catching up with the developed world, but only 31 percent of people in Latin America and 13 percent of people in Asia are part of the "global middle class." In any event, as Andrew Hurrell and Sandeep Sengupta have pointed out, Brazil, India, and China did not "emerge" as political players after Rio; they were key players at Rio and had a major hand in shaping the various Rio agreements in ways that acknowledged the importance of addressing poverty and the needs of the developing world. The most significant development since Rio has been the extent to which certain Western states, led by the United States, have succeeded in unpicking those agreements.[98] In the two decades following Rio, the United States has made no substantial concessions, while the BASIC group have increasingly taken on new environmental responsibilities by undertaking a range of national measures for which they have received very little acknowledgment in Washington.

According to Hurrell and Sengupta, the failure by developed countries to fulfill the commitment they made at Rio in 1992, and U.S. revisionism vis-à-vis those commitments, underpins the slow progress and profound lack of trust that have characterized environmental negotiations ever since.[99] Instead of singling out the outdated "firewall" between developed and developing countries as the heart of the problem, this analysis suggests that the biggest obstacle to international environmental cooperation has been the absence of environmental leadership by the most powerful state in the world, which has failed to assume responsibilities that are commensurate with its historical contribution to ecological problems and its capacities to address these problems.[100] We concur. Despite the efforts of the European Union to fill this void, these disagreements continue to hold back institutional innovation and they are responsible for the modest outcomes of environmental summitry since Rio 1992.

The globalization and transnationalization of capitalism has made reflexive governance increasingly necessary but also increasingly difficult. Economic globalization was largely orchestrated by states through national and international regulatory change, although some states had a stronger orchestrating role, while many others served as followers or victims. However, it has proved much harder to reregulate markets than deregulate them, despite the considerable suffering wrought by environmental problems and financial crises. The expanding culture of capital accumulation, speculation, and consumerism in the advanced and newly emerging economies has vastly overshadowed the rise of environmental activism, green political parties, green consumerism, and ecological citizenship. Likewise, we have seen that the expansion of multilateral, regional, and bilateral trade agreements has, for the most part, undermined the reach and effectiveness of multilateral, regional, and bilateral environmental agreements and private and civil environmental regulation. Weak capital controls and debt-fueled consumption are bad for stability and bad for the environment yet states appear to have a diminishing collective capacity and motivation to redirect economic globalization down a more reflexive path. The removal of restrictions on the movement of goods, services, labor, and investment has made all states more nervous of playing an environmental leadership or pioneering role for fear of losing competitive advantage. While fears of a "race to the bottom" have been overplayed, and the win-win discourses of ecological modernization and "green growth" have highlighted the competitive advantages of being a first mover, there have been very few states that have seized the opportunity to play a leadership role, which is the first step in breaking the collective action problem. Yet fears of short-term competitive disadvantage in the developed countries of the world appear paltry when compared to underdevelopment in many parts of the developing world and the one billion people living in abject poverty.

Rapid economic growth in Asia and elsewhere has been accompanied by major demographic changes, which include not only a growing population in the developing world but also increasing urbanization. In 2011, for the first time in China's long history, more people were living in cities and towns than in the countryside, requiring greater economies of scale in food production.[101] The world's population is expected to grow from seven billion to around nine billion people by 2050, and most of this growth will be in the developing world. If all the citizens of this more crowded world are to enjoy sustainable livelihoods, then it is clear that they cannot consume at the rate of the average European or North American. Yet growing demand and supply constraints will see rising prices for commodities, fuel, and food, possibly kicking off a resurgence of economic nationalism and protectionism rather than international economic cooperation. The 2011 Human Development Report found that the distribution of income has worsened at the country level in much of the world while Official Development Assistance falls well below what is needed to close the development gap. However, this gap needs to be closed on the basis of a fresh development model that addresses sustainability and equity together while respecting ecological thresholds.[102]

There is an old Chinese saying that if you keep heading in a particular direction, you might get there. This book has argued that the latest phase of neoliberal globalization will get us there much faster than the early phase of modernization, and the "there" is a tragic place of great suffering and loss that none of us would willingly choose. As Paul Gilding argued in his book *The Great Disruption*, ecological collapse cannot give birth to a new ecological shining star, movement, or world order—it will be too late for that.[103] Reflexive modernization and globalization must be generated before the possibility of political choice is foreclosed by the new and much less hospitable "planetary environment" that we have produced.

NOTES

CHAPTER 1: A WORLD FIT FOR US ALL

1. John R. McNeil, *Something New Under the Sun: An Environmental History of the Twentieth-Century World* (New York: W. W. Norton and Co., 2000), 4.

2. The data is from the World Bank and World Development Indicators, at data.worldbank.org/data-catalog/world-development-indicators?cid=GPD_WDI.

3. Daniel C. Esty, Marc Levy, Tanja Srebotnjak, and Alexander de Sherbinin, *2005 Environmental Sustainability Index: Benchmarking National Environmental Stewardship* (New Haven: Yale Center for Environmental Law & Policy, 2005), 40. At www.yale.edu/esi/ESI2005_Main_Report.pdf. For updates, see http://sedac.ciesin.columbia.edu/data/collection/esi/.

4. At www.unep.org/geo/pdfs/geo5/Measuring_progress.pdf.

5. The latest *State of the World* report and data on *Vital Signs* can be accessed at www.worldwatch.org; the assessment reports of the Intergovernmental Panel on Climate Change can be accessed at www.ipcc.ch/; and WWF's

Living Planet Report can be accessed at wwf.panda.org/about_our_earth/all_publications/living_planet_report/.

6. Rachel Carson, *Silent Spring* (London: Houghton and Mifflin, 1962).

7. Gloria L. Manney et al., "Unprecedented Arctic Ozone Loss in 2011," *Nature* 478 (2011): 469–75.

8. Alan Robock, "20 Reasons Why Geoengineering May Be a Bad Idea," *Bulletin of the Atomic Scientists* 64, no. 2 (2008): 14–18, 15.

9. Johan Rockström et al., "Planetary Boundaries: Exploring the Safe Operating Space for Humanity," *Ecology and Society* 14, no. 2 (2009): Art. 32. At www.ecologyandsociety.org/vol14/iss2/art32/.

10. Will Steffen and David Griggs, "Climate Change in a Complex World: Compounding Crises," paper presented at the conference on "Four Degrees or More? Australia in a Hot World" held at the University of Melbourne, 12–14 July 2011.

11. For a useful typology of four key discourses on globalization and the environment, see Jennifer Clapp and Peter Dauvergne, *Paths to a Green World: The Political Economy of a Global Environment,* 2nd ed. (Cambridge: MIT Press, 2011).

12. Karen L. O'Brien and Robin M. Leichenko, *Environmental Change and Globalization: Double Exposures* (Oxford: Oxford University Press, 2008).

13. Modified from Michael Barnett and Raymond Duvall, "Power in International Politics," in *Power in Global Governance,* ed. Michael Barnett and Raymond Duvall (Cambridge: Cambridge University Press, 2005).

14. Barnett and Duvall, "Power in International Politics," 3.

15. Fredric Jameson, "Future City," *New Left Review* 21 May–June (2003): 65-79, 76.

16. Ulrich Beck, "Politics of Risk Society," in *The Politics of the Risk Society,* ed. Jane Franklin (Cambridge: Polity Press, 1998), 9–22, 21.

17. Michael Jacobs, *The Green Economy: Environment, Sustainable Development and the Politics of the Future* (London: Pluto Press, 1991), chapter 3.

18. Ulrich Beck, *The Risk Society: Towards a New Modernity* (London: Sage, 1992), 40.

19. Peter Dauvergne, *The Shadows of Consumption: Consequences for the Global Environment* (Cambridge: MIT Press, 2008).

20. See, for example, Alf Hornborg, "Towards an Ecological Theory of Unequal Exchange: Articulating World System Theory and Ecological Economics," *Ecological Economics* 25, no. 1 (1998): 127–36; and Andrew Jorgenson and Brett Clark, "Ecologically Unequal Exchange in a Comparative Perspective," *International Journal of Comparative Sociology* 50 (2009): 211–14.

21. Ulrich Beck, *Ecological Politics in an Age of Risk* (Cambridge: Polity Press, 1995), 2, 63–65.

22. K. Arrow, B. Bolin, R. Costanza, P. Dasgupta, C. Folke, C. S. Holling, B-O. Jansson, S. Levin, K-G. Mäler, C. Perrings, and D. Pimental, "Economic Growth, Carrying Capacity, and the Environment," *Science* 268 (1995): 520–21.

23. Fred P. Gale, "Economic Specialization versus Ecological Diversification: The Trade Policy Implications of Taking the Ecosystem Approach Seriously," *Ecological Economics* 34 (2000): 285–92.

24. David Held, Anthony McGrew, David Goldblatt, and Jonathan Perraton. *Global Transformations: Politics, Economics and Culture* (Stanford: Stanford University Press, 1999), 1.

25. Jan Aart Scholte, *Globalization: A Critical Introduction*, 2nd ed. (Houndsmill, Basingstoke: Palgrave, 2005), 54–59.

26. Roland Robertson, *Globalization: Social Theory and Global Culture* (London: Sage, 1992), 173–74, 183.

27. William McKibben, *The End of Nature* (New York: Random House, 1989), 58.

28. Frederick H. Buttel, Ann P. Hawkins, and Alison G. Power, "From Limits to Growth to Global Change: Constraints and Contradictions in the Evolution of Environmental Science and Ideology," *Global Environmental Change* 1, no. 1 (1990): 57–66.

29. Stephen Yearley, "Globalization and the Environment," in *The Blackwell Companion to Globalization*, ed. George Ritzer (Malden: Blackwell Publishing, 2007), 239–53.

30. B. J. Turner II, Roger E. Kasperson, William B. Meyer, Kirstin M. Dow, Dominic Golding, Jeanne X. Kasperson, Robert C. Mitchell, and Samuel J. Ratick, "Two Types of Global Environmental Change: Definitional and Spatial-Scale Issues in their Human Dimensions," *Global Environmental Change* 1, no. 1 (1990): 14–22.

31. Held et al., *Global Transformations*, 15.

32. David Held and Anthony McGrew, *The Global Transformation Reader: An Introduction to the Globalization Debate*, 2nd ed. (Cambridge: Polity, 2003), 4.

CHAPTER 2: A SHORT HISTORY OF GLOBALIZATION AND THE ENVIRONMENT

1. Rachel Carson, *Silent Spring* (London: Houghton and Mifflin, 1962).

2. Walter W. Rostow, *The Stages of Economic Growth: A Non-Communist Manifesto* (Cambridge: Cambridge University Press, 1960).

3. Donella H. Meadows, Dennis L. Meadows, Jørgen Randers, and William W. Behrens III, *The Limits to Growth: A Report to the Club of Rome's Project on*

the Predicament of Mankind (London: Earth Island Limited, 1972); Edward Goldsmith and Robert Allen (with Michael Allaby, John Davoll, and Sam Lawrence), *A Blueprint for Survival* (London, Penguin Books, 1972).

4. Garrett Hardin, "The Tragedy of the Commons," *Science* 162, no. 3859 (1968): 1243–48; Garrett Hardin, *Exploring New Ethics for Survival: The Voyage of the Spaceship Beagle* (New York: Viking Press, 1972); Garrett Hardin, "Commentary: Living on a Lifeboat," *BioScience* 24, no. 10 (1974): 561–68; Paul R. Ehrlich, *The Population Bomb* (New York: Ballantine Books, 1968); William Ophuls, "Leviathan or Oblivion?" in *Toward a Steady State Economy*, ed. Herman E. Daly (San Francisco: Freeman, 1973), 215–30; and Robert L. Heilbronner, *An Inquiry into the Human Prospect* (New York: Norton, 1974).

5. See, for example, H. S. D. Cole, Christopher Freeman, Marie Jahoda, and K. L. R. Pavitt, *Thinking about the Future: A Critique of The Limits to Growth* (London: Chatto and Windus, 1973).

6. Donella H. Meadows, Dennis L. Meadows, and Jørgen Randers, *Beyond the Limits: Global Collapse or a Sustainable Future* (London: Earthscan Books, 1992); and Donella H. Meadows, Dennis L. Meadows, Jørgen Randers, and William W. Behrens III, *Limits to Growth: The Thirty Year Report* (London: Chelsea Green Publishing, 2002).

7. Graham M. Turner, "A Comparison of The Limits to Growth with 30 Years of Reality," *Global Environmental Change* 18 (2008): 397–411.

8. Goldsmith et al., *A Blueprint for Survival.*

9. Sara Parkin, *Green Parties: An International Guide* (London: Heretic Books, 1989).

10. Paul R. Ehrlich and John P. Holdren, "Impact of Population Growth," *Science* 171 (1971): 1212–17.

11. Barry Commoner, *The Closing Circle: Nature, Man, and Technology* (New York: Knopf, 1971); and Barry Commoner, "A Bulletin Dialogue: On 'The Closing Circle' — Response," *Bulletin of the Atomic Scientists* 28, no. 5 (1972): 17, 42–56.

12. Anthony Giddens, *The Consequences of Modernity* (Oxford: Polity Press, 1990); Peter Christoff, "Ecological Modernisation, Ecological Modernities," *Environmental Politics* 5, no. 3 (1996): 476–500.

13. UNPD (United Nations Population Division), *The World at Six Billion* (undated), 6. At www.un.org/esa/population/publications/sixbillion/sixbilpart1 .pdf.

14. Alfred W. Crosby, *Ecological Imperialism: The Biological Expansion of Europe 900–1900* (Cambridge: Cambridge University Press, 1986).

15. Geoffrey Bolton, *Spoils and Spoilers: A History of Australians Shaping Their Environment* (Sydney: Allen and Unwin, 1981), 81.

16. Domenico Sella, "European Industries, 1500–1700," in *The Sixteenth and Seventeenth Centuries*, The Fontana Economic History of Europe: Volume 2, ed. Carlo M. Cipolla (Glasgow: Collins Books, 1974).

17. Anthony J. Venables, "Economic Geography," in *The Oxford Handbook of Political Economy*, ed. Barry R. Weingast and Donald A. Wittman (Oxford: Oxford University Press, 2006), 747.

18. John Darwin, *The Empire Project: The Rise and Fall of the British World-System 1830–1970* (Cambridge: Cambridge University Press, 2009), 114.

19. Darwin, *The Empire Project*, 114.

20. Eric J. Hobsbawm, *Industry and Empire—The Pelican Economic History of Britain: Volume 3* (Melbourne/London: Penguin Books, 1968), 136–37.

21. Immanuel Wallerstein, *The Modern World System: Capitalist Agriculture and the Origins of European World Economy in the Sixteenth Century* (New York: Academic Press, 1974).

22. Friedrich Engels, "Socialism, Utopian and Scientific," in *Marx, Engels, Lenin, Four Classic Texts on the Principles of Socialism* (London: Allen and Unwin, 1960), 144.

23. Eric J. Hobsbawm, *Age of Extremes: The Short Twentieth Century 1914–1991* (London: Michael Joseph, 1994), 200.

24. In saying Europe-centered, we are not suggesting that Europe was the simple source of all ideas from where they spread outward, but rather that Europe-in-the-World, already exchanging ideas with and through other regions, became for a while the center of a globalizing process.

25. Hobsbawm, *Age of Extremes*, 201.

26. Lynn White Jr. "The Historical Roots of Our Ecological Crisis," *Science* 155, no. 3767 (1967): 1203–7, 1205.

27. Val Plumwood, *Feminism and the Mastery of Nature* (London: Routledge, 1993).

28. Max Weber, "Science as a Vocation," in *From Max Weber: Essays in Sociology*, translated and edited with an introduction by H. H. Gerth and C. W. Mills (Oxford: Oxford University Press, 1958), 129–56.

29. Robert Hughes, *The Shock of the New* (New York: Random House, 1981).

30. Hughes, *The Shock of the New*, 15.

31. Cited in Raymond Williams, *Keywords*, 2nd ed. (New York: Oxford University Press, 1983), 89.

32. Williams, *Keywords*, 89.

33. Richard Grove, *Green Imperialism: Colonial Expansion, Tropical Island Edens and the Origins of Environmentalism, 1600–1860* (Cambridge: Cambridge University Press, 1995), 474.

34. John Gascoigne, *Science in the Service of Empire: Joseph Banks, the British State and the Uses of Science in the Age of Revolutions* (Cambridge: Cambridge University Press, 1998).

35. Donald Worster, *Nature's Economy: A History of Ecological Ideas*, 2nd ed. (New York: Cambridge University Press, 1994), x.

36. Peter Hay, *Main Currents in Western Environmental Thought* (Sydney: University of New South Wales Press, 2002), 4–11.

37. Venables, "Economic Geography," 747.

38. Peter Marsh, "China Noses Ahead as Top Goods Producer," *Financial Times*, 13 March 2011.

39. WTO-UNEP, *Trade and Climate Change: A Report by the United Nations Environment Programme and the World Trade Organization* (Geneva: World Trade Organization, 2009), 48.

40. UNEP (United Nations Environment Program), *Keeping Track of Our Changing Environment: From Rio to Rio +20* (Nairobi: United Nations Environment Program, 2011), 15.

41. Thomas Oately, *The Global Economy: Contemporary Debates* (New York: Pearson/Longman, 2005), 397.

42. OECD, *Measuring Globalization: OECD Economic Globalization Indicators 2010* (Paris: OECD, 2010), 8.

43. Data for 1950–1964 compiled by Worldwatch Institute from U.S. Department of Defense and U.S. Department of Energy data; 1965–2009 data from BP, *Statistical Review of World Energy June 2010* (London: BP, 2010).

44. Data compiled by Earth Policy Institute with bicycle data compiled by Gary Gardner for "Bicycle Production Reaches 30 Million Units," in *Vital Signs 2009* (Washington, D.C.: Worldwatch Institute, 2009), 53–54; car production for 1950–1970 from *Signposts 2002* (Washington, D.C.: Worldwatch Institute 2004); car production for 1971–2007 from *World Motor Vehicle Data 2008* (Southfield, Mich.: Ward's Automotive Group, 2008), 239–42.

45. Data from Lester R. Brown, *World on the Edge: How to Prevent Environmental and Economic Collapse* (New York: Norton and Company, 2011).

46. Data from Brown, *World on the Edge*.

47. WTO, *World Trade Report 2011, The WTO and Preferential Trade Agreements: From Coexistence to Coherence* (Geneva: World Trade Organization, 2011).

48. IMF, *Changing Patterns of Global Trade, Prepared by the Strategy, Policy, and Review Department*, International Monetary Fund, 15 June 2011, 18. At www.imf.org/external/np/pp/eng/2011/061511.pdf.

49. John Gerard Ruggie, "International Regimes, Transactions, and Change: Embedded Liberalism in the Postwar Economic Order," *International Organization* 36, no. 2 (1982): 379–415, 385.

50. Robert Cox, "Critical Political Economy," in *International Political Economy: Understanding Global Disorder*, ed. Björn Hettne (Halifax, Nova Scotia: Fernwood Publishing, 1995), 39.

51. Philip Cerny, "Paradoxes of the Competition State: The Dynamics of Political Globalisation," *Government and Opposition* 36, no. 2 (1997): 251–74, 259.

52. World Commission for Environment and Development (WCED), *Our Common Future* (Oxford: Oxford University Press, 1987).

53. WCED, *Our Common Future*, 43.

54. Steven Bernstein, *The Compromise of Liberal Environmentalism* (New York: Columbia University Press, 2002).

55. Richard York and Eugene A. Rosa, "Key Challenges to Ecological Modernisation Theory: Institutional Efficacy, Case Study Evidence, Units of Analysis and the Pace of Eco-Efficiency," *Organization and Environment* 16, no. 3 (2003): 273–88; see also Christoff, "Ecological Modernisation, Ecological Modernities."

56. Erns U. von Weizsäcker, *Factor Four: Doubling Wealth, Halving Resource Use—A Report to the Club of Rome* (London: Earthscan, 1997).

57. Peter Dauvergne, *The Shadows of Consumption: Consequences for the Global Environment* (Cambridge: MIT Press, 2008).

58. Thomas Princen, "Consumption and Its Externalities: Where Economy Meets Ecology," *Global Environmental Politics* 1(3) (2001): 11-30, 19.

59. Zygmunt Bauman, *Consuming Life* (London: Polity Press, 2007), 28.

60. See, for example, Tim Jackson, *Prosperity without Growth: Economics for a Finite Planet* (London: Earthscan, 2009), chapter 6 ("The Iron Cage of Consumerism").

61. Bauman, *Consuming Life*, 11.

62. Vance Packard, *The Hidden Persuaders* (London: Longmans, Green, 1957); Stuart Ewen, *The Captains of Consciousness: Advertising and the Social Roots of Consumer Culture* (New York: McGraw Hill, 1977).

63. Bauman, *Consuming Life*, 53.

64. UNWTO (UN World Tourism Organization), "International Tourism 2010: Multi-speed Recovery." At 85.62.13.114/media/news/en/press_det.php?id=7331&idioma=E.

65. WTO-UNEP, *Trade and Climate Change*, 60.

66. UNEP, *Keeping Track of Our Changing Environment*, 49.

67. Faith Campbell, "The Hidden Costs of Trade: Invasive Species as a Trade 'Externality,'" *Bridges Trade BioRes Review* 5, no. 3 (November 2011). At ictsd.org/i/news/biosreview/117729/.

68. IMF, *Changing Patterns of Global Trade*.

69. Jan Ott Andersson and Mattias Lindroth, "Ecologically Unsustainable Trade," *Ecological Economics* 37 (2001): 113–22.

70. James Rice, "Ecological Unequal Exchange International Trade and Uneven Utilization of Environmental Space in the World System," *Social Forces* 85, no. 3 (2007): 1369–92; Andrew K. Jorgenson and Brett Clark, "Ecologically Unequal Exchange in Comparative Perspective: A Brief Introduction," *International Journal of Comparative Sociology* 50, no. 3–4 (2009): 211–14; Andrew K. Jorgenson, Kelly Austin, and Christopher Dick, "Ecologically Unequal Exchange and the Resource Consumption/Environmental Degradation Paradox: A Panel Study of Less-Developed Countries, 1970–2000," *International Journal of Comparative Sociology* 50, no. 3–4 (2009): 263–84; Steven Davis and Ken Caldeira, "Consumption-Based Accounting of CO_2 Emissions," *PNAS* 107, no. 12 (23 March 2010): 5687–92; and Glen P. Peters, Jan C. Minx, Christopher L. Weber, and Ottmar Edenhofer, "Growth in Emission Transfers via International Trade from 1990 to 2008," *PNAS* 108, no. 21 (24 May 2011): 8903–8.

71. Muthukumara Mani and David Wheeler, "In Search of Pollution Havens? Dirty Industry in the World Economy," *Journal of Environment and Development* 7, no. 3 (1998): 215–47; Jennifer Clapp, "What the Pollution Haven Debate Overlooks," *Global Environmental Politics* 2, no. 2 (2001): 11–19; Smita B. Brunnermeier and Arik Levinson, "Examining the Evidence on Environmental Regulations and Industry Location," *The Journal of Environment Development* 13, no. 1 (2004): 6–41; and Mariana Spatareanu, "Searching for Pollution Havens: The Impact of Environmental Regulations on Foreign Direct Investment," *The Journal of Environment & Development* 16, no. 2 (2007): 161–82.

72. See, for example, Pascal Lamy, "Trade Can Be a Friend, and Not a Foe of Conservation," speech delivered at the Symposium on Trade and Sustainable Development within the Framework of Paragraph 51 of the Doha Ministerial Declaration. Geneva, 10–11 October 2004. At www.wto.org/english/news_e/sppl_e/sppl07_e.htm.

73. Jagdish N. Bhagwati, *In Defense of Globalization* (New York: Oxford University Press, 2007), 155–58.

74. Norman Myers and Jennifer Kent, *Perverse Subsidies: How Tax Dollars Can Undercut the Environment and the Economy* (Washington, D.C.: Island Press, 2001), xvii.

75. OECD, *Methodologies for Environmental and Trade Reviews*, OECD/GD(94)103 (Paris: OECD, 1994).

76. WTO-UNEP, *Trade and Climate Change*, 53.

77. S. Managi, A. Hibiki, and T. Tsurumi, "Does Trade Liberalization Reduce Pollution Emissions," Research Institute of Economy, Trade and Industry (RIETI) Discussion Paper Series 08-R-013, 2008.

78. WTO-UNEP, *Trade and Climate Change*, 53.

79. Peter J. Marcotullio, Eric Williams, and Julian Marshall, "Faster, Sooner, and More Simultaneously: How Recent Road and Air Transportation CO_2 Emission Trends in Developing Countries Differ From Historic Trends in the United States," *The Journal of Environment & Development* 14, no. 1 (2005): 125–48.

80. Herman E. Daly, *Beyond Growth* (Boston: Beacon Press, 1996).

81. Gaylord Nelson, *Beyond Earth Day: Fulfilling the Promise* (Madison: University of Wisconsin Press, 2002), 18.

CHAPTER 3: AN OVERHEATED PLANET

1. *Global warming* refers to the overall increase in average global temperature, but also involves complex changes to the planet's climatic systems. We use the terms *global warming* and *climate change* interchangeably in this chapter to mean anthropogenic (i.e., human-induced) changes in climatic conditions.

2. See http://keelingcurve.ucsd.edu.

3. See Michael C. MacCracken, Frances Moore, and John C. Topping, eds., *Sudden and Disruptive Climate Change* (London: Earthscan Books, 2008), especially the chapter by Barry A. Pittock, "Ten Reasons Why Climate Change May Be More Severe than Projected," 11–28.

4. Jos G. J. Oliver, Greet Janssens-Maenhout, and Jeroan A. H. W. Peters, *Trends in Global CO_2 Emissions; 2012 Report* (The Hague: PBL Netherlands Environmental Assessment Agency; Ispra: Joint Research Centre, 2012), 18.

5. Hans J. Schellnhuber, Wolfgang Cramer, Nebojsa Nakicenovic, Tom Wigley, and Gary Yohe, *Avoiding Dangerous Climate Change* (Cambridge: Cambridge University Press, 2006); WGBU (German Advisory Council on Global Change), *Solving the Climate Dilemma: The Budget Approach* (Berlin: German Advisory Council on Global Change, 2009); and Malte Meinshausen, N. Meinshausen, William Hare, S. C. B. Raper, K. Frieler, R. Knutti, Dave J. Frame, and M. R. Allen, "Greenhouse-Gas Emission Targets for Limiting Global Warming to 2 °C," *Nature* 458 (2009): 1158–62, doi:10.1038/ nature08017.

6. IPCC, *Managing the Risks of Extreme Events and Disasters to Advance Climate Change Adaptation—A Special Report of Working Groups I and II of the Intergovernmental Panel on Climate Change. Summary for Policymakers* (Cambridge: Cambridge University Press, 2012), 1–19; Jean-Pierre Gattuso and Lina Hansson, eds., *Ocean Acidification* (Oxford and New York: Oxford University Press, 2011); and NAS (National Academy of Sciences, U.S.),

Ocean Acidification: A National Strategy to Meet the Challenges of a Changing Ocean (Washington, D.C.: National Academy of Sciences Press, 2010).

7. John Houghton, "Global warming is now a weapon of mass destruction: It kills more people than terrorism, yet Blair and Bush do nothing," *The Guardian*, 28 July 2003.

8. National Climatic Data Center, "Global Analysis—Annual 2012." At www.ncdc.noaa.gov/sotc/global/2012/13 (accessed 17 April 2013).

9. Christopher C. Burt, "Weather Extremes," 2 January 2013. At www .wunderground.com/blog/weatherhistorian/comment.html?entrynum=112.

10. National Oceanic and Atmospheric Administration, "Arctic Report Card: Update for 2012." At www.arctic.noaa.gov/reportcard/ (accessed 14 January 2013).

11. Australian Government, Bureau of Meteorology, "Australia in Summer 2012–2013." At www.bom.gov.au/climate/current/season/aus/summary.shtml (accessed 17 April 2013).

12. Janet Larsen and Sara Rasmussen, "2011—A Year of Weather Extremes, with More to Come," 1 February 2012 (IPS). This article was originally published by the Earth Policy Institute. Data and additional resources at www .earth-policy.org.

13. World Bank, *Turn Down the Heat: Why a 4C Warmer World Must Be Avoided, A Report for the World Bank by the Potsdam Institute for Climate Impact Research and Climate Analytics* (Washington, D.C.: World Bank, 2012), xiii. At climatechange.worldbank.org/sites/default/files/Turn_Down_the_heat_ Why_a_4_degree_centigrade_warmer_world_must_be_avoided.pdf.

14. David D. Zhang, Harry F. Lee, Cong Wang, Baosheng Li, Qing Pei, Jane Zhang, and Yulun An, "The Causality Analysis of Climate Change and Long-Term Human Crisis," *PNAS Early Edition* (2012). At www.pnas.org/cgi/ doi/10.1073/pnas.1104268108 (accessed 12 February 2012).

15. Karl Marx and Friedrich Engels, *The Manifesto of the Communist Party* (London: Penguin Books, 1967 [1848]).

16. John Hatcher, *Before 1700: Towards the Age of Coal*, The History of the British Coal Industry, Volume 1 (Oxford: Oxford University Press, 1993), 55; E. A. Wrigley, *Continuity, Chance and Change: The Character of the Industrial Revolution in England* (Cambridge: Cambridge University Press, 1988), 54.

17. Barbara Freese, *Coal: A Human History* (London and New York: Penguin Books, 2003), 95.

18. Michael. W. Flinn, *1700–1830: The Industrial Revolution*, The History of the British Coal Industry, Volume 2 (Oxford: Oxford University Press, 1984), 442.

19. Carl N. Degler, *The Age of the Economic Revolution 1876–1900* (Glenview: Scott Foreman, 1977), 29; S. H. Schurr, B. C. Netschert, V. F. Eliasberg,

J. Lerner, and H. H. Landsberg, *Energy in the American Economy* (Baltimore: Johns Hopkins Press, 1960), 69, quoted in Barbara Freese, *Coal*, 137.

20. Industrial and domestic coal use became so intensive in certain cities that it contributed to heavy, sometimes life-threatening, smogs in major Victorian cities like London and Manchester, and in the United States in Pittsburgh and Chicago. By the late 19th century, new "smoke abatement" laws and regulations to govern industrial air pollution were being implemented in these places as part of a general response to public pressure to make cities healthy and livable spaces. These innovations provided early models of pollution control that were communicated and copied internationally as similar problems emerged in industrializing countries worldwide in the 19th and 20th centuries. See Freese, *Coal*, 73.

21. See: www.eia.gov/countries/cab.cfm?fips=CH.

22. U.S. Department of Energy (US DoE), *Transportation Energy Data Book*. At cta.ornl.gov/data/chapter8.shtml.

23. OICA (International Organization of Motor Vehicle Manufacturers), *OICA Production Statistics 2012*. At oica.net/category/production-statistics/ (accessed 12 April 2013).

24. See Thomas Princen, "Leave It in the Ground: The Politics and Ethics of Fossil Fuels and Global Disruption," International Studies Association Annual Conference, Montreal, 16–19 March 2011.

25. IEA (International Energy Agency), *Oil Market Report*, 13 June 2012. At homrpublic.iea.org/archiveresults.asp?formsection=full+issue&formdate=2012&Submit=Submit.

26. William Watson, Nicholas Paduano, Tejasvi Raghuveer, and Sundar Thapa, *U.S. Coal Supply and Demand: 2010 Year in Review* (Washington, D.C.: U.S. Energy Information Administration, 2011). At 205.254.135.7/coal/review/pdf/feature10.pdf (accessed 20 June 2012).

27. Michael Klare, *Blood and Oil* (New York: Metropolitan Books, 2004), xiii–xiv. See also Matthew Paterson, *Automobile Politics: Ecology and Cultural Political Economy* (Cambridge: Cambridge University Press, 2007).

28. Simon Bromley, *American Hegemony and World Oil* (Cambridge: Cambridge University Press, 1991); Simon Bromley, "The United States and the Control of World Oil," *Government and Opposition* 40, no. 2 (2005): 225–55.

29. U.S. Energy Information Administration, *Annual Energy Outlook 2013*. At www.eia.gov/forecasts/aeo/IF_all.cfm#petroleum_import (accessed 18 April 2013).

30. Zhe Daojiong, "China's Energy Security and Its International Relations," paper presented at Third IISS Global Strategic Review, Geneva, 16–18 September 2005. At www.silkroadstudies.org/new/docs/CEF/Zha_Daojiong.pdf.

31. IEA, *Energy Subsidies: World Energy Outlook* (2012). At www.worldenergyoutlook.org/subsidies.asp.

32. T. A. Boden, G. Marland, and R. J. Andres, *Global, Regional, and National Fossil-Fuel CO_2 Emissions* (Oak Ridge, Tenn.: Carbon Dioxide Information Analysis Center, Oak Ridge National Laboratory, U.S. Department of Energy, DOI: 2011). 10.3334/CDIAC/00001_V2011.

33. R. A. Houghton, "The Annual Flux of Carbon to the Atmosphere from Changes in Land Use 1850–1990," *Tellus* 51b (1999): 298–313.

34. T. Barker, I. Bashmakov, L. Bernstein, J. E. Bogner, P. R. Bosch, R. Dave, O. R. Davidson, B. S. Fisher, S. Gupta, K. Halsnæs, G.J. Heij, S. Kahn Ribeiro, S. Kobayashi, M. D. Levine, D. L. Martino, O. Masera, B. Metz, L. A. Meyer, G.-J. Nabuurs, A. Najam, N. Nakicenovic, H.-H. Rogner, J. Roy, J. Sathaye, R. Schock, P. Shukla, R. E. H. Sims, P. Smith, D. A. Tirpak, D. Urge-Vorsatz, and D. Zhou, "Technical Summary," in *Climate Change 2007: Mitigation*, Contribution of Working Group III to the Fourth Assessment Report of the Intergovernmental Panel on Climate Change, ed. B. Metz, O. R. Davidson, P. R. Bosch, R. Dave, and L. A. Meyer (Cambridge: Cambridge University Press, 2007), 27. The authors also noted that "these figures should be seen as indicative, as some uncertainty remains, particularly with regards to CH4 [methane] and N2O [nitrous oxide] emissions (error margin estimated to be in the order of 30-50%) and CO_2 emissions from agriculture and forestry with an even higher error margin."

35. Barker et al., "Technical Summary," 27.

36. See Paul N. Edwards, *A Vast Machine: Computer Models, Climate Data, and the Politics of Global Warming* (Cambridge, Mass.: The MIT Press, 2010).

37. See, for instance, Tim Flannery, *The Weather Makers: How Man Is Changing the Climate and What It Means for Life on Earth* (Melbourne: Text Publishing, 2005); James Roger Fleming, *Historical Perspectives on Climate Change* (Oxford: Oxford University Press, 1998); Spencer R. Weart, *The Discovery of Global Warming* (Cambridge, Mass.: Harvard University Press, 2003).

38. For instance, in 1784 Montesquieu wrote , "We have already observed that great heat enervates the strength and courage of men, and that in cold climates they have a certain vigor of body and mind which renders them capable of long, painful, great and intrepid actions" (quoted in Fleming, *Historical Perspectives*, 16).

39. See Jan Golinski, *British Weather and the Climate of the Enlightenment* (Chicago: University of Chicago Press, 2007).

40. Fleming, *Historical Perspectives*, 41 and 44.

41. Svante Arrhenius, "On the Influence of Carbonic Acid in the Air upon the Temperature of the Ground," *Philosophical Magazine* 5, no. 41 (1896): 237–76.

42. Arrhenius's predicted 4 degrees Celsius increase is remarkably close to more recent predictions by the Intergovernmental Panel on Climate Change. However, many would argue that this was merely a coincidental outcome, given the crudeness of Arrhenius's underlying model. See Svante Arrhenius, *Worlds in the Making: The Evolution of the Universe* (New York: Harper and Brothers, 1908), 52.

43. G. S. Callendar, "The Artificial Production of Carbon Dioxide and Its Influence on the Atmosphere," *Quarterly Journal of the Royal Meteorological Society* 64 (1938): 223–40.

44. Like Arrhenius before him, Callendar welcomed this change as a potential benefit to humanity, increasing plant growth and the northern extension of agriculture, and possibly delaying a new Ice Age. See G. S. Callendar, "The Composition of the Atmosphere through the Ages," *The Meteorological Magazine* 74, no. 878 (March 1939).

45. Gilbert N. Plass, "Effects of Carbon Dioxide Variation on Climate," *American Journal of Physics* 24, no. 5 (1956): 377–80.

46. Plass, "Effects of Carbon Dioxide Variation," 387.

47. Roger Revelle and Hans E Suess, "Carbon Dioxide Exchange Between Atmosphere and Ocean and the Question of an Increase of Atmospheric CO_2 during the Past Decades," *Tellus* 9, no. 1 (1957): 19.

48. An additional comment can be made about how evolving technological capacities contributed to the development of this global scientific narrative about climate. From the 1950s onward, technological developments in the capacity to survey the planet and to manipulate data—through the advent and use of satellites and the development of computers with the capacity to run elaborate climatic models—enabled the articulation of complex climate scenarios based around an increasing number of interactive factors. These developments were also influenced by the tensions of the Cold War. Concerns were raised in the 1960s about the use of weather as a weapon and about climatic implications for national security. Artificial satellites were quickly used to generate new knowledge of planetary atmospheric, terrestrial, and marine conditions. They were simultaneously contributors to a fierce ideological and technological struggle for supremacy between the leading states of the capitalist and socialist worlds—signaled, for instance, by the launch of the world's first satellite, the Russian Sputnik 1, as part of the International Geophysical Year in 1957. The United States launched its first meteorological satellite, TIROS 1, on 1 April 1960, and its first successful photo-reconnaissance satellite, Discovery 14, in August that year. The first results of a general circulation model (GCM) were presented in 1975, and the first GISS global temperature analysis was published in 1981, analyzing

surface temperatures at meteorological stations from 1880 to 1985. As Edwards notes, full global consolidation of technical work on climate change did not really begin until 1992, with the establishment of the Global Climate Observing System, created to support the UN Framework Convention on Climate Change (see Edwards, *A Vast Machine*, 15).

49. EPP (Environmental Pollution Panel), *Restoring the Quality of Our Environment*, report of President's Science Advisory Committee (Washington, D.C.: U.S. Government Printing Office, 1965).

50. NAS (National Academy of Sciences, U.S.), *Weather and Climate Modification Problems and Prospects*, vol. 1, final report of the Panel on Weather and Climate Modification, NAS-NRC Publication 1350 (Washington, D.C.: NAS Press, 1966).

51. NAS (National Academy of Sciences, U.S.), *Energy and Climate*, Geophysical Study Committee (Washington, D.C.: NAS Press, 1977).

52. NAS (National Academy of Sciences, U.S.), *Carbon Dioxide and Climate: A Scientific Assessment*, Report of an Ad Hoc Study Group on Carbon Dioxide and Climate, Woods Hole, Massachusetts, 23–27 July 1979 (Washington D.C.: National Academy of Sciences, 1979).

53. CEQ, in Bert Bolin, *A History of the Science and Politics of Climate Change: The Role of the Intergovernmental Panel on Climate Change* (Cambridge: Cambridge University Press, 2007), 34.

54. WMO (World Meteorological Organization), *Report of the International Conference on the Assessment of the Role of Carbon Dioxide and of Other Greenhouse Gases in Climate Variations and Associated Impacts*, Villach, Austria, 9–15 October 1985, WMO No.661. At www.scopenvironment.org/downloadpubs/scope29/statement.html.

55. Bolin, *A History of the Science and Politics of Climate Change*, 40.

56. IPCC (Intergovernmental Panel on Climate Change), *Principles Governing IPCC Work* (1988). At www.ipcc.ch/pdf/ipcc-principles/ipcc-principles.pdf (accessed 17 February 2012).

57. While Fleming (*Historical Perspectives*, 118 and 131) suggests that "global warming was on the public agenda in the late 1940s and early 1950s," its occasional mentions in the popular press in the 1950s do not compare with the high salience of climate debate in the late 1980s.

58. Philip Shabecoff, "Global Warming Has Begun, Expert Tells Senate," *New York Times*, 24 June 1988.

59. www.climatenetwork.org/about/about-can.

60. See, for example, Peter Newell and Matthew Paterson, "A Climate for Business: Global Warming, the State and Capital," *Review of International Political Economy* 5, no. 4 (1998): 679–704; and David Levy and Peter Newell,

eds., *The Business of Global Environmental Governance* (Cambridge, Mass.: The MIT Press, 2005).

61. See, for example, Aaron M. McCright and Riley E. Dunlap, "Anti-reflexivity: The American Conservative Movement's Success in Undermining Climate Science and Policy," *Theory, Culture & Society* 27, no. 2–3 (2010): 100–133; Naomi Oreskes and Erik Conway, *Merchants of Doubt* (New York: Bloomsbury Press, 2010); and Riley E. Dunlap and Aaron M. McCright, "Organized Climate Change Denial," in *The Oxford Handbook of Climate Change and Society*, ed. J. S. Dryzek, R. B. Norgaard, and D. Schlosberg (Oxford: Oxford University Press, 2011), 144–60.

62. Jules Boykoff and Maxwell Boykoff, "Balance as Bias: Global Warming and the U.S. Prestige Press," *Global Environmental Change* 15, no. 2 (2004): 125–36.

63. Naomi Oreskes, "Beyond the Ivory Tower: The Scientific Consensus on Climate Change," *Science* 306, no. 5702 (2004): 1686. DOI:10.1126/science.1103618. PMID 15576594.

64. Nicholas Stern, *The Economics of Climate Change: The Stern Review* (Cambridge: Cambridge University Press, 2007); Ross Garnaut, *The Garnaut Climate Change Review* (Cambridge: Cambridge University Press, 2008). However, significant trans-Atlantic differences have emerged over the construction of economic cost-benefit analyses and appropriate discount rates.

65. The complete list of Umbrella Group members are the United States, Canada, Australia, Norway, Iceland, Japan, the Russian Federation, and Ukraine. This group evolved out of an alliance known as JUSCANZ, made up of Japan, the United States, Canada, Australia, and New Zealand.

66. See, for instance, Harriet Bulkeley and Peter Newell, *Governing Climate Change* (London: Routledge, 2010).

67. Mathew J. Hoffman, *Ozone Depletion and Climate Change: Constructing a Global Response* (Albany: State University of New York Press, 2005), 120.

68. *United Nations Framework Convention on Climate Change*, United Nations, 1992. FCCC/INFORMAL/84 GE.05-62220 (E) 200705. At unfccc.int/resource/docs/convkp/conveng.pdf.

69. *The Rio Declaration on Environment and Development* (1992). At www.unesco.org/education/information/nfsunesco/pdf/RIO_E.PDF.

70. UNFCCC, Article 3(1). The convention also acknowledges the development needs, and the special vulnerability to climate change, of developing countries (Preamble, Article 3(2), 3(3), and 4(5)). In terms of specific commitments, Article 4(2)(a) requires developed countries to undertake policies and measures that demonstrate that they are taking the lead in reducing emissions. Article 4(3) also requires them to provide the financial resources

(including technology transfer) to enable developing countries to meet their commitments. The principle of CBDR was also articulated in Principle 7 of the Rio Declaration.

71. UNFCCC, Article 4(2)(a).

72. UNFCCC, Article 4(2) and Article 12(1).

73. The Kyoto Protocol to the United Nations Convention on Climate Change, United Nations, 1998. At unfccc.int/resource/docs/convkp/kpeng.pdf.

74. The Byrd-Hagel Resolution was passed unanimously (95–0) by the U.S. Senate on 25 July 1997, during the 105th Congress. When the U.S. Senate rejected the protocol, it argued that the KP was contrary to the United States' national economic interest and was environmentally flawed—its exemption for developing country parties being seen as inconsistent with the need for global action on climate change.

75. The United States—then clearly the world's biggest GHG emitter—objected that developing countries such as China and India had made no commitment to reduce their emissions despite the prospect of them becoming significant aggregate GHG contributors over coming decades.

76. Joanna Depledge, "Against the Grain: The United States and the Global Climate Change Regime," *Global Change, Peace and Security* 17, no. 1 (2005): 11–28.

77. Peter Christoff, "From Global Citizen to Renegade State: Australia at Kyoto," *Arena Journal* 10 (1998): 113–28.

78. At the 2005 World Economic Forum, twenty-three multinational corporations, including British Airways, BP, Ford, Toyota, and Unilever, formed the G8 Climate Change Roundtable Group. In June 2005, the group published a statement affirming the need for action on climate change and stressing the importance of market-based solutions. It called on governments to establish "clear, transparent, and consistent price signals" through a long-term policy framework that would include all major producers of GHGs. At www.weforum.org/pdf/g8_climatechange.pdf.

79. UNFCCC, *The Benefits of the Clean Development Mechanism* (2011), 5. At cdm.unfccc.int/about/dev_ben/pg1.pdf.

80. At cdm.unfccc.int/Statistics/index.html.

81. UNFCCC, *The Benefits of the Clean Development Mechanism*, 6.

82. See Matthew Paterson, "Selling Carbon: From International Climate Regime to Global Carbon Market," in *The Oxford Handbook of Climate Change and Society*, ed. J. S. Dryzek, R. B. Norgaard, and D. Schlosberg (Oxford: Oxford University Press, 2011), 616; and UNFCCC, *The Benefits of the Clean Development Mechanism*.

83. Andre Kossoy and Pierre Guinon, *The State and Trends of the Carbon Market 2012* (Washington, D.C.: World Bank, 2012).

84. Kossoy and Guinon, *The State and Trends*.

85. Netherlands Environmental Assessment Agency, "China Now No. 1 in CO_2 Emission; USA in Second Position." At www.pbl.nl/en/dossiers/Climatechange/moreinfo/Chinanowno1inCO2emissionsUSAinsecondposition.

86. The Copenhagen Accord, *Report of the Conference of the Parties on Its Fifteenth Session, Held in Copenhagen from 7 to 19 December 2009 Addendum Part Two: Action Taken by the Conference of the Parties at Its Fifteenth Session*, Decision 2/CP.15 (2009). At unfccc.int/resource/docs/2009/cop15/eng/11a01.pdf.

87. See also: Peter Christoff, "Cold Climate in Copenhagen: China and the United States at COP15," *Environmental Politics* 19, no. 4 (2010): 637–56.

88. Draft decision -/CP.17, Establishment of an Ad Hoc Working Group on the Durban Platform for Enhanced Action (advanced unedited version). At unfccc.int/files/meetings/durban_nov_2011/decisions/application/pdf/cop17_durbanplatform.pdf.

89. Editorial, "The Mask Slips," *Nature* 480, no. 292 (14 December 2011).

90. Robyn Eckersley, "Moving Forward in the Climate Negotiations: Multilateralism or Minilateralism?" *Global Environmental Politics* 12, no. 2 (2012): 24–42.

91. Olivier, Janssens-Maenhout, and Peters, *Trends in Global CO_2 Emissions*.

92. The Waxman-Markey Bill, which included a national cap-and-trade scheme, had passed the House of Representatives on June 2009 (219 votes for, 212 against). However, efforts to pass a similar bill in the Senate were abandoned due to the lack of an effective majority.

93. See, for instance, Chukwumerije Okereke, Harriet Bulkeley, and Heike Schroeder. "Conceptualizing Climate Governance Beyond the International Regime," *Global Environmental Politics* 9 (2009): 58–78.

94. In 2009, Canadell et al. reported that combined emissions from fossil fuels and land use changes increased by over 3 percent per year since 2000, up from 1.9 percent per year over the period 1959–1999. Emissions from fossil fuels and cement production in 2008 were some 40 percent higher than 1990. Indeed, the rate of increase in concentrations of atmospheric CO_2 in the atmosphere has itself grown—rising from around 3.1 gigatonnes of CO_2 per annum in the decade 1990–2000 to around 4.1 gigatonnes per annum in the period 2001–2008. See J. G. Canadell, P. Ciais, S. Dhakal, C. Le Quere, A. Patwardhan, and M. R. Raupach, *The Human Perturbation of the Carbon Cycle. The Global Carbon Cycle II* (UNESCO-SCOPE-UNEP Policy Brief Series, November 2009—No. 10), 3. Olivier et al. report that, after a brief decline in 2009 and 2010 because of the global recession, global emissions have resumed their upward trend and, with growth of 5 percent per annum, more than compensated for the slowdown in those two years. "Since 2002 an accelerated global annual CO_2 growth rate is seen as a consequence of the industrialization of China."

See: Jos G. J. Olivier, Greet Janssens-Maenhout, Jeroen A. H. W. Peters, and Julian Wilson, *Long-Term Trend in Global CO₂ Emissions; 2011 Report* (The Hague/Bilthoven: PBL Netherlands Environmental Assessment Agency, 2012).

95. Olivier, Janssens-Maenhout, Peters, and Wilson, *Long-Term Trend in Global CO₂ Emissions*, 12.

96. See, for example, Edward Page, "Distributing the Burdens of Climate Change," *Environmental Politics* 17, no. 4 (2008): 556–75.

97. Paul Baer, Tom Athanasiou, Sivan Kartha, and Eric Kemp-Benedict, *The Greenhouse Development Rights Framework*, revised 2nd ed. (Berlin: Heinrich Böll Foundation, Christian Aid, EcoEquity, and the Stockholm Environment Institute, 2008). See also CAN International, *CAN Fair Sharing Effort Principles Position Paper*, 22 September 2011. At gdrights.org/publications/.

98. Stephen Gardiner, *A Perfect Moral Storm: The Ethical Tragedy of Climate Change* (New York: Oxford University Press, 2011).

99. And so, for instance, the value in terms of emissions savings associated with upgrading to a more energy-efficient car or refrigerator may be outweighed by the total emissions involved in producing that new object.

100. This problem is highlighted by the struggle that negotiations have encountered in bringing "bunker fuels"—fossil fuels used in the international transport of humans and goods—to account under the regime.

101. Davis and Caldeira claim China's export-oriented emissions comprised some 22.5 percent of the total in 2004. Stephen J. Davis and Ken Caldeira, "Consumption Based Accounting of CO₂ Emissions," *Proceedings of the National Academy of Science of the United States of America (PNAS)* 107 (2010): 5687–92; Glen P. Peters, Jan C. Minx, Christopher L. Weber, and Ottmar Edenhofer, "Growth in Emission Transfers via International Trade from 1990 to 2008," *Proceedings of the National Academy of Science of the United States of America (PNAS)* 108 (2011): 8903–8. See also IEA, *World Energy Outlook 2007* (Paris: International Energy Agency, 2007); Tao Wang and Jim Watson, "Who Owns China's Carbon Emissions?" *Tyndall Centre Briefing Note No. 23* (Norwich: Tyndall Centre, 2007); Tao Wang and Jim Watson, "China's Carbon Emissions and International Trade: Implications for the Post 2012 Regime," policy analysis paper for submission to *Climate Policy*, Sussex Energy Group and Tyndall Centre for Climate Change Research SPRU, 25 February 2008.

102. This shift has been driven by lower labor costs rather than cost savings associated with the absence of emissions mitigating regulations in "carbon pollution havens."

103. See Peter Christoff and Robyn Eckersley, "Comparing State Responses," in *The Oxford Handbook of Climate Change and Society*, ed. J. S. Dryzek, R. B. Norgaard, and D. Schlosberg (Oxford: Oxford University Press, 2011).

104. Robert O. Keohane and David G. Victor, "The Regime Complex for Climate Change," Discussion Paper 10-33, The Harvard Project on Interna-

tional Climate Agreements, January 2010. At: papers.ssrn.com/sol3/papers
.cfm? abstract_id=1643813.

105. "Four-fifths of the total energy-related CO_2 emissions permissible by
2035 in the 450 Scenario are already 'locked-in' by our existing capital stock
(power plants, buildings, factories, etc.). If stringent new action is not forth-
coming by 2017, the energy-related infrastructure then in place will generate
all the CO_2 emissions allowed in the 450 Scenario up to 2035, leaving no room
for additional power plants, factories and other infrastructure unless they are
zero-carbon, which would be extremely costly." IEA, *World Energy Outlook 2011
Executive Summary* (2011). At www.worldenergyoutlook.org/media/weoweb
site/2011/executive_summary.pdf.

CHAPTER 4: REMAKING NATURE:
BIODIVERSITY IN PERIL

1. See Norwegian Ministry of Agriculture and Foods, Svarlbard Global
Seed Vault, at www.regjeringen.no/en/dep/lmd.html?id=627.

2. Article 2 of the *Convention on Biological Diversity 1992* defines "biological diversity" to mean "the variability among living organisms from all sources
including, inter alia, terrestrial, marine and other aquatic ecosystems and the
ecological complexes of which they are part; this includes diversity within species, between species and of ecosystems." At www.cbd.int/.

3. Timothy M. Swanson, "Wildlife and Wildlands, Diversity and Development," in *Economics for the Wilds: Wildlife, Wildlands, Diversity and Development*, ed. Timothy M. Swanson and Edward Barbier (London: Earthscan,
1992), 1–14, 4.

4. Millennium Ecosystem Assessment, *Ecosystems and Human Well-Being:
Synthesis* (Washington, D.C.: Island Press, 2005), 68.

5. Edward O. Wilson, *The Diversity of Life* (London: Penguin, 1992), 243.
The process of naming species takes time, but also has a lighter side. The
humble Australian horsefly has just been named *Scaptia (Plinthina) beyonceae*,
in honor of American singer Beyoncé. "It was the unique dense golden hairs on
the fly's abdomen that led the researcher to choose this particular name. It was
also discovered in 1981, the year of Beyoncé's birth but it took three decades of
expert consultation before it was finally categorized and named." See "Beyoncé
Fly Goes from Hummer to Bummer," *The Age*, 14 February 2012, 3.

6. Wilson, *The Diversity of Life*, 243.

7. Rashid Hassan, Robert Scholes, and Neville Ash, eds., *Ecosystems and
Human Well-Being, Volume 1. Current State and Trends* (Millennium Ecosystem
Assessment Series) (Washington, D.C.: Island Press, 2005), chapter 4 ("Biodi-
versity"), 77–122, 79.

8. Hassan et al., *Ecosystems and Human Well-Being*, 79.

9. IUCN Red List. At www.iucnredlist.org/ (accessed 1 March 2012).

10. Norman Myers, "The Biodiversity Crisis and the Future of Evolution," *The Environmentalist* 16 (1996): 37–47, 37.

11. Hassan et al., *Ecosystems and Human Well-Being*, 79.

12. WWF, *Living Planet Report 2012: Biodiversity, Biocapacity and Development* (Gland: WWF International, 2012). At wwf.panda.org/about_our_earth/all_publications/living_planet_report/2012_lpr/.

13. WWF, *Living Planet Report 2012*, 100.

14. Norman Myers, Russell A. Mittermeier, Cristina G. Mittermeier, Gustavo A. B. da Fonseca, and Jennifer Kent, "Biodiversity Hotspots for Conservation Priorities," *Nature* 403 (2000): 853–58, 853.

15. Wilson, *The Diversity of Life*, 268.

16. WWF, *Living Planet Report 2012*, 18.

17. WWF, *Living Planet Report 2012*, 23.

18. WWF, *Living Planet Report 2012*, 22.

19. Gideon Algernon Mantell, *Petrifactions and Their Teachings, or A Handbook to the Gallery of Organic Remains of the British Museum* (London: Henry Bohn, 1851), 2.

20. David Stuart, *The Plants That Shaped Our Gardens* (London: Francis Lincoln Press, 2002), 30.

21. See, for example, Anna Pavord, *The Naming of Names: The Search for Order in the World of Plants* (London: Bloomsbury Press, 2005).

22. Joel Mokyr, *The Enlightened Economy: Britain and the Industrial Revolution 1700–1850* (London: Penguin Books, 2011), 18.

23. J. F. Richards, "World Environmental History and Economic Development," in *Sustainable Development of the Biosphere*, ed. W. C. Clark and R. E. Munn (Cambridge: Cambridge University Press, 1986), 55.

24. Richards, "World Environmental History and Economic Development," 67.

25. Anatoly Shvidenko, Charles Victor Barber, and Reidar Persson (coordinating lead authors), "Forest and Woodland Systems," in *Millennium Ecosystem Assessment, Ecosystems and Human Wellbeing, Volume 1. Current State and Trends*, ed. Rashid Hassan, Robert Scholes, and Neville Ash (Washington, D.C.: Island Press, 2005), chapter 21, 585–621, 589.

26. Richards, "World Environmental History and Economic Development," 59–61.

27. J. V. Beckett, *The Agricultural Revolution* (Oxford: Basil Blackwell, 1990), 9.

28. A. W. Schorger, *The Passenger Pigeon: Its Natural History and Extinction* (reprinted) (New Jersey: The Blackburn Press, 1955), 199.

29. Schorger, *The Passenger Pigeon*, 204.

30. Schorger, *The Passenger Pigeon*, 201.

31. William T. Hornaday, *The Extermination of the American Bison*. From the Report of the National Museum (Smithsonian Institute), 1886–1887 (Washington, D.C.: Government Printing Office, 1889), 369–548.

32. Keith Thomas, *Man and the Natural World: Changing Attitudes in England 1500–1800* (London: Allen Lane Press, 1983).

33. Alfred Crosby, *Ecological Imperialism: The Biological Expansion of Europe, 900–1900* (Cambridge: Cambridge University Press, 1986), 7.

34. Sheldon Watts, *Epidemics and History: Disease, Power and Imperialism* (New Haven, Conn.: Yale University Press, 1997).

35. Judy Campbell, *Invisible Invaders: Smallpox and Other Diseases in Aboriginal Australia 1780–1880* (Melbourne: Melbourne University Press, 2002).

36. Thomas R. Dunlap, *Nature and the English Diaspora: Environment and History in the United States, Canada, Australia and New Zealand* (Cambridge: Cambridge University Press, 1999).

37. W. K. Hancock, *Australia* (London: Heinemann, 1930), 33.

38. Eric. C. Rolls, *They All Ran Wild: The Enthralling Story of Pests on the Land in Australia* (Melbourne: Angus and Robertson, 1969).

39. Tim Low, *Feral Future: The Untold Story of Australia's Exotic Invaders* (Ringwood: Viking Press, 1999).

40. David Quammen, "Planet of Weeds: Tallying the Losses of Earth's Animals and Plants," *Harper's Magazine* 297, no. 1781 (October 1998): 57–59.

41. Millennium Ecosystem Assessment, *Ecosystems and Human Well-Being*, 67.

42. WWF and ZSL, *Indicator Fact Sheet 1.2.1*, Living Planet Index (2010), 55. At www.zsl.org/science/research-projects/indicators-assessments/index,134,ZI.html.

43. Millennium Ecosystem Assessment, *Ecosystems and Human Well-Being*, 12.

44. Millennium Ecosystem Assessment, *Ecosystems and Human Well-Being*, 59.

45. Millennium Ecosystem Assessment, *Ecosystems and Human Well-Being*, 63.

46. Millennium Ecosystem Assessment, *Ecosystems and Human Well-Being*, 90.

47. Details of the high-level workshop can be found at www.stateoftheocean.org/ipso-2011-workshop-summary.cfm. For a summary of the workshop, see Michael McCarthy, "Oceans on Brink of Catastrophe," *The Independent*, 21 June 2011. At www.independent.co.uk/environment/nature/oceans-on-brink-of-catastrophe-2300272.html.

48. Shvidenko et al., "Forest and Woodland Systems," 587.

49. Shvidenko et al., "Forest and Woodland Systems," 587.

50. Sergio Margulis, *Causes of Deforestation of the Brazilian Amazon*, World Bank Working Paper 22 (Washington, D.C.: The World Bank, 2004).

51. WWF and ZSL, *Indicator Fact Sheet*, 57.

52. Deborah Fitzgerald, *Every Farm a Factory: The Industrial Ideal in American Agriculture* (New Haven, Conn.: Yale University Press, 2003), 5.

53. Fitzgerald, *Every Farm a Factory*.

54. John H. Perkins, *Geopolitics and the Green Revolution: Wheat, Genes and the Cold War* (New York: Oxford University Press, 1997).

55. Perkins, *Geopolitics and the Green Revolution*, 259.

56. Ignacy Sachs, "Towards a Second Green Revolution?" in *The Green Revolution Revisited: Critique and Alternatives*, ed. Bernhard Glaeser (London: Allen and Unwin, 1987), 193–98.

57. Millennium Ecosystem Assessment, *Ecosystems and Human Well-Being*, 69.

58. Food and Agricultural Organization (FAO), "Staple Foods: What Do People Eat?" in *Dimensions of Need: An Atlas of Food and Agriculture* (Rome: Food and Agricultural Organization, 1995). At www.fao.org/docrep/u8480e/U8480E07.htm#Staple%20foods%20What%20do%20people%20eat.

59. FAO, *The State of the World's Plant Genetic Resources for Food and Agriculture* (Rome: The Food and Agricultural Organization of the United Nations, 1997), 34.

60. FAO, *The State of the World's Plant Genetic Resources for Food and Agriculture*, 35.

61. FAO, *The State of the World's Plant Genetic Resources for Food and Agriculture*, 35.

62. Convention on Biological Diversity, "Global Biodiversity Outlook 3: Biodiversity in 2010—Genetic Diversity." At www.cbd.int/gbo3/?pub=6667&section=6710.

63. Millennium Ecosystem Assessment, *Ecosystems and Human Well-Being*, 2, 3.

64. Perkins, *Geopolitics and the Green Revolution*, 258.

65. Modern biotechnology is defined in Article 3(i) of the *Cartagena Protocol on Biosafety* as "the application of: a) in vitro nucleic acid techniques, including recombinant deoxyribonucleic acid (DNA) and direct injection of nucleic acid into cells or organelles, or b) fusion of cells beyond the taxonomic family, that overcome natural physiological reproductive or recombination barriers and that are not techniques used in traditional breeding and selection." At bch.cbd.int/protocol/text/.

66. Jan van Aken, *Centres of Diversity: Global Heritage of Crop Varieties Threatened by Genetic Pollution* (Berlin: Greenpeace International, 1999), 8.

67. European Communities, *Measures Affecting the Approval and Marketing of Biotech Products* (DS291, DS292, DS293), first written submission by the European Communities, Geneva, 17 May 2004, 12.

68. Thomas Bernauer, *Genes, Trade, and Regulation: The Seeds of Conflict in Food Biotechnology* (Princeton, N.J.: Princeton University Press, 2003); Robyn Eckersley, "A Green Public Sphere in the WTO?: The *Amicus Curiae* Interventions in the Trans-Atlantic Biotech Dispute," *European Journal of International Relations* 13 (2007): 329–56.

69. Per Pinstrup-Anderson and Ebbe Schiøler, *Seeds of Contention: World Hunger and the Global Controversy over GM Crops* (Baltimore: Johns Hopkins University Press, 2000).

70. Bernauer, *Genes, Trade, and Regulation,* 32.

71. See www.slowfood.com/.

72. International Institute for Environment and Development (IIED), "Sowing Innovation for Sustainable Food," *Reflect and Act* (January 2012). At pubs.iied.org/pdfs/G03229.pdf.

73. Martin H. Krieger, "What's Wrong with Plastic Trees?" *Science* 179, no. 4072 (1973): 446–55.

74. Millennium Ecosystem Assessment, *Ecosystems and Human Well-Being,* vi.

75. Environmental philosophers have defended the value of wild ecosystems on a variety of similar grounds: wild ecosystems provide a *silo* of genetic diversity; a *cathedral* for spiritual renewal; a *laboratory* for scientific inquiry; a *gymnasium* for recreation; and an *art gallery* or place of aesthetic wonder. See William Godfrey-Smith, "The Value of Wilderness," *Environmental Ethics* 1 (1979): 309–10; and Warwick Fox, *Toward a Transpersonal Ecology: Developing New Foundations for Environmentalism* (Boston: Shambhala, 1990).

76. See www.viacampesina.org. See also Action Group on Erosion, Technology and Concentration (formerly the Rural Advancement Foundation International), www.etcgroup.org/en/about.

77. Roderick Nash, *Wilderness and the American Mind,* 3rd ed. (New Haven, Conn.: Yale University Press, 1982), 108.

78. Mark Dowie, *Conservation Refugees: The Hundred-Year Conflict between Global Conservation and Native Peoples* (Cambridge, Mass.: MIT Press, 2009).

79. Nancy Lee Peluso, "Coercing Conservation," in *The State and Social Power in Global Environmental Politics,* ed. Ronnie Lipschutz and Ken Conca (New York: Columbia University Press, 1993); Alexander Wood, Pamela Stedman-Edwards, and Johanna Mang, *The Root Causes of Biodiversity Loss*

(London: Earthscan, 2000), 5–6; Charles Geisler, "Your Park, My Poverty," in *Contested Nature—Promoting International Biodiversity and Social Justice in the Twenty-first Century*, ed. Brechin et al. (Albany: SUNY Press, 2003).

80. See, for example, the protected area philosophy and management practices of the IUCN. At iucn.org.

81. Charlotte Epstein, "The Making of Global Environmental Norms: Endangered Species Protection," *Global Environmental Politics* 6, no. 2 (2006): 32–54, 41.

82. Thomas Birch, "The Incarceration of Wildness—Wilderness Areas as Prisons," *Environmental Ethics* 12, no. 1: 3–26; Dowie, *Conservation Refugees*, xvii.

83. John McCormick, "Origins of the World Conservation Strategy," *Environmental Review* 10, no. 3 (1986): 177–87.

84. Article 1(2) declared that "the genetic viability on the earth shall not be compromised; the population levels of all life forms, wild and domesticated, must be at least sufficient for their survival, and to this end necessary habitats shall be safeguarded." United Nations General Assembly, A/RES/37/7, 48th plenary, 28 October 1982.

85. See Articles 15(5) and 15(7) Convention on Biological Diversity. At www.cbd.int.

86. Christoph Gorg and Ulrich Brand, "Global Environmental Politics and Competition Between Nation-States: On the Regulation of Biological Diversity," *Review of International Political Economy* 7, no. 3 (2000): 371–98.

87. Host states are to provide clear rules and procedures for prior informed consent and mutually agreed terms, and for the fair and equitable sharing of benefits, including R&D on genetic resources and subsequent applications and commercialization. See the *Nagoya Protocol 2011* at www.cbd.int/abs/doc/protocol/nagoya-protocol-en.pdf.

88. Stuart Coupe and Roger Lewins, *Negotiating the Seed Treaty* (Bourton on Dunsmore, Rugby, Warwickshire: Practical Action Publishing, 2007), 20–21.

89. United Nations General Assembly (UNGA), "Report of the United Nations Conference on Environment and Development, 3–14 June 1992, Annex III, Non-Legally Binding Authoritative Statement of Principles for a Global Consensus on the Management, Conservation and Sustainable Development of All Types of Forests," 14 August 1992; A/CONF.151/26 (Vol. III), Principle 2(a)).

90. Fred Gale and Marcus Haward, *Global Commodity Governance: State Responses to Sustainable Forest and Fisheries Certification* (London: Palgrave, 2011).

91. Wood, Stedman-Edwards, and Mang, *The Root Causes of Biodiversity Loss*, 81.

CHAPTER 5: GOVERNING THE PLANET

1. Peter Evans, "Is an Alternative Globalization Possible?" *Politics and Society* 36, no. 2 (2008): 298.

2. See page 28.

3. Rob Nixon, *Slow Violence and the Environmentalism of the Poor* (Cambridge, Mass.: Harvard University Press, 2011).

4. Michael Barnett and Raymond Duvall, "Power in International Politics," *International Organization* 59 (Winter) (2005): 39–75.

5. Ronald Mitchell, International Environmental Agreements Database Project (Version 2012.1). At iea.uoregon.edu.

6. *Trail Smelter* Case (United States v Canada) 3 R Int'l Arbitration Awards, 1905.

7. Robyn Eckersley, *The Green State: Rethinking Democracy and Sovereignty* (Cambridge, Mass.: The MIT Press, 2004), 217–19.

8. At www.350.org.

9. CNN, "All Over the World Today, '350' Signs," 24 October 2009. At newsroom.blogs.cnn.com/2009/10/24/all-over-the-world-today-350-signs.

10. These arguments are developed in Eckersley, *The Green State*. See also Karen Litfin, ed., *The Greening of Sovereignty in World Politics* (Cambridge, Mass.: The MIT Press, 1998); and Robert Falkner, "Global Governance and the Greening of International Society," *International Affairs* 88. no. 3 (2012): 503–22.

11. See, for example, Adil Najam, Mihaela Papa, and Nadaa Taiyab, *Global Environmental Governance: A Reform Agenda* (Winnipeg: International Institute for Sustainable Development, 2006).

12. Robyn Eckersley, "Global Environment," in *US Foreign Policy*, 2nd ed., ed. Mick Cox and Doug Stokes (Oxford: Oxford University Press, 2012), 351–74.

13. Remarks of Robert F. Kennedy at the University of Kansas, 18 March 1968, John F. Kennedy Presidential Library and Museum. At www.jfklibrary. org/Research/Ready-Reference/RFK-Speeches/Remarks-of-Robert-F-Kennedy-at-the-University-of-Kansas-March-18-1968.aspx.

14. William M. Lafferty and James R. Meadowcroft, *Implementing Sustainable Development: Strategies and Initiatives in High Consumption Societies* (Oxford: Oxford University Press, 2000).

15. Maarten A. Hajer, *The Politics of Environmental Discourse: Ecological Modernization and the Policy Process* (Oxford: Clarendon Press, 1995).

16. See, for instance, Korea's commitment to green growth. web.worldbank.org/WBSITE/EXTERNAL/TOPICS/EXTSDNET/0,,contentMDK:23187028~pagePK:64885161~piPK:64884432~theSitePK:5929282,00.html.

17. OECD, *Towards Green Growth*, 2011. At www.oecd.org/greengrowth; UNEP, *Towards a Green Economy: Pathways to Sustainable Development and Poverty Eradication*, 2011. At www.unep.org/greeneconomy.

18. See Tim Jackson, *Prosperity without Growth* (London: Earthscan, 2009), especially chapter 5 on "The Myth of Decoupling."

19. UNEP, *Towards a Green Economy*, vi.

20. UNEP, *Towards a Green Economy*, vi.

21. Trade disputes have arisen over some of the unilateral measures introduced by states to reduce their emissions.

22. This is evident in the mutual antagonism between China and the United States over what are claimed to be unwarranted renewable energy support subsidies, which saw the United States apply duties on imported solar panels from China in 2012 as a retaliatory measure against what they regarded as "dumping" to the detriment of the U.S. solar panel industry. See ICTSD, "China-US Sparring over Renewable Energy Intensifies," *Bridges Weekly Trade News Digest* 16, no. 21 (30 May 2012). At ictsd.org/i/news/bridgesweekly/134029.

23. Calls within the EU by countries such as France to impose a general "carbon tariff" on imports from "carbon havens" so as not to disadvantage European firms or prompt industry relocation have so far been resisted by the European Commission and most member states due to expected intense opposition from other countries. The European Union's first tentative step to impose impositions at the border—the inclusion of emissions from aviation in its regional emissions trading scheme—has drawn strong protests from the airline industry and from the United States, China, and India.

24. WTO-UNEP, *Trade and Climate Change: A Report by the United Nations Environment Programme and the World Trade Organization* (Geneva: World Trade Organization, 2009).

25. See Articles 3(5) and 4(2)(a) of the UNFCCC.

26. Kirk Herbertson, "Greening the International Financial Institutions (IFIs): Finance for the Next Decade's Sustainable Development," World Resources Institute for the Stakeholder Forum, 2012, 9–10. At www.stakeholderforum.org; and Christian Aid, "Why the World Bank—and Why Now?" At www.christianaid.org.uk/ActNow/climate-justice/world-bank/background.aspx; and Bretton Woods Project, "World Bank Clings to Fossil Fuels, Stumbles on Clean Energy," www.brettonwoodsproject.org/art-566379.

27. Jennifer Clapp and Peter Dauvergne, *Paths to a Green World: The Political Economy of the Global Environment* (Cambridge, Mass.: The MIT Press, 2011), 205.

28. Herbertson, "Greening the International Financial Institutions," 4.

29. Bruce Rich, *Foreclosing the Future: Coal, Climate and Public International Finance* (New York: Environmental Defense Fund, 2009). At www.edf. org/climate/report-foreclosing-future. See also Sustainable Energy and Economy Network USA, International Trade Information Service, US Halifax Initiative, Canada; and Reform the World Bank Campaign, Italy, *The World Bank and the G7: Changing the Earth's Climate for Business: An Analysis of the World Bank Fossil Fuel Project Lending since the 1992 Earth Summit*, June 1997; and Peter Newell, "The Political Economy of Global Environmental Governance," *Review of International Studies* 34 (2008): 507–29, 518.

30. Dana R. Fisher, "Bringing the Material Back In: Understanding the U.S. Position on Climate Change," *Sociological Forum* 21, no. 3 (2006): 467–94, 480.

31. See Mancur Olsen, *The Logic of Collective Action: Public Goods and the Theory of Groups* (Cambridge, Mass.: Harvard University Press, 1965).

32. See, for example, Mathias Koenig-Archibugi, "Transnational Corporations and Public Accountability," in *Global Governance and Public Accountability*, ed. David Held and Mathias Koenig-Archibugi (Oxford: Blackwell Publishing, 2005), 110–35.

33. Transparency International, *Transparency in Corporate Reporting: Assessing the World's Largest Companies* (Berlin: Transparency International, 2012). For an analysis of the Extractive Industries Transparency Initiative, see Virginia Haufler, "Disclosure as Governance: The Extractive Industries Transparency Initiative and Resource Management in the Developing World," *Global Environmental Politics* 10, no. 3 (2010): 53–73.

34. Transparency International's 2012 Corruption Perceptions Index is available at www.transparency.org/cpi2011.

35. Michael L. Ross, *The Oil Curse: How Petroleum Wealth Shapes the Development of Nations* (Princeton: Princeton University Press, 2012).

36. Ross, *The Oil Curse*.

37. Peter Newell, "Civil Society, Corporate Accountability and the Politics of Climate Change," *Global Environmental Politics* 8, no. 3 (2008): 122–53.

38. The phrase "essentially contested concept" was first introduced by Walter Gallie to refer to abstract, qualitative, and highly valued but also highly complex concepts the interpretation of which cannot be settled by appeal to evidence or reason. See W. B. Gallie, "Essentially Contested Concepts," in W. B. Gallie, *Philosophy and the Historical Understanding* (London: Chatto & Windus, 1964), 157–91. See also William Connolly, *The Terms of Political Discourse* (Lexington, Mass.: Heath, 1974).

39. Steven Bernstein, "Liberal Environmentalism and Global Environmental Governance," *Global Environmental Politics* 2, no. 3: 1–16. See also

Bernstein, *The Compromise of Liberal Environmentalism* (New York: Columbia University Press, 2001); and Chukwumerije Okereke, *Global Justice and Neoliberal Environmental Governance* (Abingdon: Routledge, 2008).

40. See, for example, UNEP, *Towards a Green Economy*, 15. At www.unep.org/greeneconomy; UNDP; Ulrich Hoffman, "Some Reflections on Climate Change, Green Growth Illusions and Development Space," Discussion Paper No. 205, United Nations Conference on Trade and Development (UNCTAD), December 2011; OECD, *Towards Green Growth* (Paris: OECD, 2011); OECD, *Inclusive Green Growth for the Future We Want*, OECD Work of Relevance to Rio+20, June 2012. At www.oecd.org/dataoecd/11/54/50480040.pdf; IEA, *World Energy Outlook 2011*. At www.iea.org/weo/; The World Bank, *Inclusive Green Growth: The Pathway to Sustainable Development* (Washington, D.C.: International Bank for Reconstruction and Development, 2012). At web.worldbank.org/; The United Nations Secretary-General's High Level Panel on Global Sustainability, *Resilient People, Resilient Planet: A Future Worth Choosing* (New York: United Nations, 2012). At www.un.org/gsp.

41. For example, the communiqué of the Group of Twenty (G20) meeting of finance ministers and central bank governors in February 2012 directed the OECD, World Bank, and the United Nations to prepare a report detailing options for including green growth and sustainable development policies into structural reform agendas, tailored to specific country conditions and level of development. International Institute for Sustainable Development Reporting Services, "G20 Finance Ministers and Chancellors Discuss Green Growth." At climate-l.iisd.org/news/g20-finance-ministers-and-chancellors-discuss-green-growth.

42. The World Bank, *Inclusive Green Growth*, xi.

43. Nicholas Stern, *The Economics of Climate Change: The Stern Review* (Cambridge: Cambridge University Press, 2007), 1.

44. David Shearman and J. W. Smith, *The Climate Change Challenge and the Failure of Democracy* (Davenport, Conn.: Praeger, 2007); Mark Beeson, "The Coming of Environmental Authoritarianism," *Environmental Politics* 19, no. 2 (2010): 276–94.

45. Robert O. Keohane, "Global Governance and Democratic Accountability," in *Taming Globalization: Frontiers of Governance*, ed. David Held and Daniel Archibugi (London: Polity, 2003), 130–59, 142.

46. Michael Zürn, "Global Governance and Legitimacy Problems," *Government and Opposition* 39, no. 2 (2004): 261–87.

47. Allen Buchanan and Robert O. Keohane, "The Legitimacy of Global Institutions," *Ethics and International Affairs* 20, no. 4 (2006): 405–37.

48. Robert Dahl, "Can International Organizations be Democratic? A Skeptical View," in *Democracy's Edges*, ed. Ian Shapiro and Casiana Hacker-Cordon (Cambridge: Cambridge University Press, 1999).

49. See Robert Keohane, Stephen Macedo, and Andrew Moravcsik, "Democracy-Enhancing Multilateralism," *International Organization* 63, no. 1 (2009): 1–31.

50. John G. Ruggie, "Multilateralism: The Anatomy of an Institution," *International Organization* 46, no. 3 (1992): 561–98; and Ruggie, "Territoriality and Beyond: Problematizing Modernity in International Relations," *International Organisation* 47, no. 1 (1993): 144–73.

51. See, for example, Luk Van Langenhove, "The Transformation of Multilateralism Mode 1.0 to Mode 2.0," *Global Policy* 1, no. 3 (2010): 263–70.

52. Sofia Näsström, "What Globalisation Overshadows," *Political Theory* 31, no. 6 (2003): 808–34.

53. Jan-Peter Voß, Dierk Bauknecht, and René Kemp, eds., *Reflexive Governance for Sustainable Development* (Cheltenham, UK: Edward Elgar, 2006), 7.

54. See Tim Cadman, *Evaluating the Quality of Global Governance: A Theoretical and Analytical Approach*, Earth Systems Governance Working Paper No. 20, Lund and Amsterdam, February 2012.

55. For example, the United Nations defends the principles of good governance as promoting equity, participation, pluralism, transparency, accountability, and the rule of law, in a manner that is effective, efficient, and enduring. See www.un.org/en/globalissues/governance.

56. See Chad Lavin, *The Politics of Responsibility* (Urbana: University of Illinois Press, 2008).

57. See, for example, Karin Bäckstrand, "The Accountability of Networked Climate Governance: The Rise of Transnational Climate Partnerships," *Global Environmental Politics* 8, no. 3 (2008): 74–102.

58. Principle 15, The Rio Declaration on Environment and Development 1992. At www.unep.org/Documents.multilingual/Default.asp?DocumentID=7 8&ArticleID=1163. For a comprehensive discussion, see Kerry H. Whiteside, *Precautionary Politics* (Cambridge, Mass.: The MIT Press, 2006).

59. Cass Sunstein, *Laws of Fear: Beyond the Precautionary Principle* (Cambridge: Cambridge University Press, 2005).

60. United Nations Global Compact. At www.unglobalcompact.org.

61. www.globalreporting.org/; www.unpri.org/; www.iso.org/iso/social_responsibility; www.unepfi.org/statements/statement/index.html.

62. "External stakeholders" might include representatives of workers, environmental NGOs, environmental ombudspersons, or relevant government environmental agencies, and local municipalities in the jurisdiction in which the company operates, all of which are given the opportunity to ask questions, raise concerns, and challenge decisions in annual board meetings.

63. According to a discussion paper promoted by the Dialogue on a Convention for Corporate Social Responsibility, such a treaty would also require "all listed and large private companies to implement sustainability issues

into their management and throughout their supply chains, and to integrate sustainability information within the reporting cycle." See Gustavo Ferroni, *Corporate Social Responsibility and Rio+20: Time to Leap Forward*, Vitae Civilis, Discussion Paper, March 2012, produced for the Dialogue on a Convention for Corporate Social Responsibility. At www.csradialogue2012.org.

64. www.earthsummit2012.org/conference/themes/green-economy-pov erty-eradication/971-green-econ-definition.

65. World Bank, *Inclusive Green Growth*, 30.

66. OECD, "Towards Green Growth," 11 (Box 0.1).

67. UNEP, *Toward a Green Economy*, 16.

68. World Bank, *Inclusive Green Growth*, 30–34.

69. Frank Biermann, "Planetary Boundaries and Earth Systems Governance: Exploring the Links," *Ecological Economics* 81 (2012): 4–9.

70. Biermann, "Planetary Boundaries and Earth Systems Governance," 5.

71. Biermann has suggested that different governance mechanisms would be required for systemic and cumulative environmental problems. Systemic problems, such as climate change, require more overarching, centralized mechanisms such as inclusive treaties based on a global grand bargain. Cumulative problems, such as forest and biodiversity protection, might allow, in the first instance, for more fragmented and localized responses (measures to combat deforestation, biodiversity loss), provided the countries facing the most significant biodiversity loss are provided with assistance. Biermann, "Planetary Boundaries and Earth Systems Governance," 7.

72. Johan Rockström et al., "Planetary Boundaries: Exploring the Safe Operating Space for Humanity," *Ecology and Society* 14, no. 2 (2009): 32. At www.ecologyandsociety.org/vol14/iss2/art32.

73. Claus Offe, *Modernity and the State* (Cambridge, Mass.: The MIT Press, 1996), 91.

74. See, for example, John Dryzek, "Green Reason: Communicative Ethics for the Biosphere," *Environmental Ethics* 12 (1990): 195–210; Freya Mathews, ed., *Ecology and Democracy* (London: Frank Cass, 1996); Brian Doherty and Marius de Geus, eds., *Democracy and Green Political Thought: Sustainability, Rights and Citizenship* (London: Routledge, 1996); and Robyn Eckersley, "Deliberative Democracy, Ecological Representation and Risk: Towards a Democracy of the Affected," in *Democratic Innovation: Deliberation, Association and Representation*, ed. Michael Saward (London: Routledge, 2000), 117–32; and Walter F. Baber and Robert Barlett, *Deliberative Environmental Politics: Democracy and Ecological Rationality* (Cambridge, Mass.: The MIT Press, 2005).

75. John S. Dryzek, "Transnational Democracy," *The Journal of Political Philosophy* 7 (1999): 30–51; John S. Dryzek and Simon Niemeyer, "Discursive

Representation," *The American Political Science Review* 102, no. 4 (2008): 481–93.

76. Tim Hayward, "Constitutional Environmental Rights: A Case for Political Analysis," *Political Studies* 48, no. 3 (2000): 558–72, 568.

77. Hayward, "Constitutional Environmental Rights," 558; and Tim Hayward, *Constitutional Environmental Rights* (Oxford: Oxford University Press, 2005). However, Ecuador has taken this one step further by rewriting its Constitution to recognize "Nature, or Pachamama" as having "the right to exist, persist, maintain and regenerate its vital cycles, structure, functions and evolutionary processes. Every person, people, community or nationality, will be able to demand the recognition of rights for nature before public institutions." These amendments were ratified by referendum by the people of Ecuador in September 2008. Ecuador Constitution, Article 71, therightsofnature.org/ecuador-rights.

78. See Peter Roderick, *Taking the Longer View: UK Governance Options for a Finite Planet*, Report for the Foundation for Democracy and Sustainable Development and WWF UK, December 2010, London, 23. At www.fdsd .org/2010/12/taking-thelonger-view.

79. See also Voß et al., *Reflexive Governance for Sustainable Development*, 7.

80. See also Arild Underdal, "Complexity and Challenges of Long-Term Environmental Governance," *Global Environmental Change* 20 (2010): 386–93.

81. Frank Biermann et al., "Navigating the Anthropocene: Improving Earth System Governance," *Science* 335, no. 6074 (2012): 1306–7.

82. The Copenhagen climate conference set a new record in attracting around 40,000 delegates and officially accredited observers, including 192 nations and 115 heads of state/government (at unfccc.int/meetings/ copenhagen_dec_2009/meeting/6295.php), which was surpassed by Rio+20. See, for example, IISD, "Rio+20 Adopts 'The Future We Want' Outcome Document, Voluntary Pledges Reported to Reach US$513 Billion," *Climate Change Policy and Practice*. At climate-l.iisd.org/news/rio20-adopts-the-future-we-want-outcome-document-voluntary-pledges-reported-to-reach-us513 -billion/#more-142422.

83. The United Nations, "The Future We Want—Outcome Document," 19 June 2012, paragraph 248. A/CONF.216/L.1. At www.uncsd2012.org/ Paragraph 248.

84. ICTSD, "Critical Voices Drown Out Official Outcome in Rio," *Bridges Weekly Trade News Digest* 16, no. 25 (27 June 2012). At ictsd.org/i/news/ bridgesweekly/136975.

85. "The Future We Want," paragraphs 56–74, especially paragraphs 56, 59, and 63.

86. "The Future We Want," paragraph 281.

87. "The Future We Want," paragraph 38.

88. The EU has linked its strategy of emissions reductions, energy security, and new green jobs based on technological innovation to its larger growth strategy in its "green growth roadmap." Europa, "Climate Change: Commission Sets Out Roadmap for Building a Competitive Low-Carbon Europe by 2050." At europa.eu/rapid/pressReleasesAction.do?reference=IP/11/272&form at=HTML&aged=0&language=EN&guiLanguage=en.

89. For a full survey of proposals, see Emlyn W. Cruickshank, Kirsty Schneeberger, and Nadine Smith, eds., *A Pocket Guide to Sustainable Development Governance*, 2nd ed., Commonwealth Secretariat, Stakeholder Forum, February 2012. At www.earthsummit2012.org/projects. In the wake of the 1992 Earth Summit, the Commission on Global Governance report, *Our Global Neighbourhood*, recommended reviving the United Nations Trusteeship Council and making it responsible, on behalf of all states, for overseeing the protection of the global commons and serving as the chief forum on environmental and related matters. However, this required amendment of the United Nations Charter to reform the purpose, composition, and functions of the Council, and the proposal lapsed. The Commission on Global Governance, *Our Global Neighbourhood: The Report of the Commission on Global Governance* (Oxford: Oxford University Press, 1995), 251–53. See also see Catherine Redgwell, "Reforming the United Nations Trusteeship Council," in *Reforming International Environmental Governance: From Institutional Limits to Innovative Reforms*, ed. W. Bradnee Chambers and Jessica F. Green (Tokyo: United Nations University, 2005), 178–203.

90. See, for example, Dan Esty, "The Case for a Global Environmental Organization," in *Managing the World Economy: Fifty Years After Bretton Woods*, ed. Peter B. Kenen (Washington, D.C.: Institute for International Economics, 1994), 287–309; and Frank Biermann and Steffen Bauer, eds., *A World Environment Organization: Solution or Threat for Effective Environmental Governance* (Aldershot, UK: Ashgate, 2005).

91. See, for example, Adil Najam, *The Case Against GEO, WEO or Whatever-else-EO* (2000). At www.reformwatch.net/fitxers/142.pdf; and Konrad von Moltke, "The Organisation of the Impossible," *Global Environmental Politics* 1, no. 2 (2001): 23–28.

92. "The Future We Want," paragraph 88.

93. "The Future We Want," paragraphs 84.

94. "The Future We Want," paragraphs 91, 281, and 282.

95. Maria Ivanova, "Global Governance in the 21st Century: Rethinking the Environmental Pillar" SDG 2012, Stakeholder Forum, 15. At www.uncsd2012.org/rio20/index.php?page=view&type=400&nr=220&menu=45.

96. Ian Bremmer and Nouriel Roubini, "A G-Zero World: The New Economic Club Will Produce Conflict, Not Cooperation," *Foreign Affairs* 90, no. 2 (2011): 2–7.

97. World Bank, *Inclusive Green Growth*, 29.

98. Andrew Hurrell and Sandeep Sengupta, "Emerging Powers, North-South Relations and Global Climate Politics," *International Affairs* 88, no. 3: 461–84, 464.

99. Hurrell and Sengupta, "Emerging Powers, North-South Relations and Global Climate Politics," 469.

100. This argument is developed at length in Mlada Bukovansky, Ian Clark, Robyn Eckersley, Richard Price, Christian Reus-Smit, and Nicholas J. Wheeler, *Special Responsibilities: Global Problems and American Power* (Cambridge: Cambridge University Press, 2012).

101. Cam Wing Chan, "Can China's Urbanisation Save the World?" *The Conversation* (1 June 2012). At theconversation.edu.au/can-chinas-urbanisation-save-the-world-7365?utm_medium=email&utm_campaign=Latest+from+The+Conversation+for+1+June+2012&utm_content=Latest+from+The+Conversation+for+1+June+2012+CID_ff6a4e0a6f62590e5739b072c542fb89&utm_source=campaign_monitor&utm_term=Can+Chinas+urbanisation+save+the+world.

102. *Human Development Report 2012—Sustainability and Equity A Better Future for All*. At hdr.undp.org/en/reports/global/hdr2011.

103. Paul Gilding, *The Great Disruption: How the Climate Crisis Will Transform the Global Economy* (New York: Bloomsbury, 2011).

SUGGESTED READING

Biermann, Frank, and Philipp Pattberg, eds. *Global Environmental Governance Reconsidered* (Cambridge, Mass.: MIT Press, 2012).

Clapp, Jennifer, and Peter Dauvergne. *Paths to a Green World: The Political Economy of a Global Environment*, 2nd ed. (Cambridge, Mass.: MIT Press, 2011).

Dryzek, John S., Richard B. Norgaard, and David Schlosberg, eds. *The Oxford Handbook of Climate Change and Society* (Oxford: Oxford University Press, 2011).

Falkner, Robert, ed. *The Handbook of Global Climate and Environment Policy* (London: Wiley-Blackwell, 2013).

Hornborg, Alf, J. R. McNeill, and Joan Martinez-Alier, eds. *Rethinking Environmental History: World-System History and Global Environmental Change* (Lanham, Md.: AltaMira, 2007).

Millennium Ecosystem Assessment. *Ecosystems and Human Well-Being: Synthesis* (Washington, D.C.: Island Press, 2005).

Newell, Peter. *Globalization and the Environment: Capitalism, Ecology and Power* (Cambridge: Polity Press, 2012).

Newell, Peter, and Matthew Paterson. *Climate Capitalism: Global Warming and the Transformation of the Global Economy* (New York: Cambridge University Press, 2010).

Noss, Reed F., and Allen Y. Cooperider. *Saving Nature's Legacy: Protecting and Restoring Biodiversity* (Washington, D.C.: Island Press, 1994).

O'Brien, Karen L., and Robin M. Leichenko. *Environmental Change and Globalization: Double Exposures* (Oxford: Oxford University Press, 2008).

Paehlke, Robert. *Democracy's Dilemma: Environment, Social Equity and the Global Economy* (Cambridge, Mass.: MIT Press, 2003).

Urry, John. *Climate Change and Society* (Cambridge: Polity Press, 2011).

WWF. *Living Planet Report 2010: Biodiversity, Biocapacity and Development* (Gland: WWF International, 2010).

INDEX

center, 51; world's largest national emitter, 108; Zhou Enlai's "Four Modernizations", 144
chlorofluorocarbons (CFCs), 4, 100. *See also* atmospheric commons
citizen-scientists, 97
Climate Action Network (CAN), 97
climate change: 2 Celsius threshold or guardrail, 72–73, 110, 115, 197; 350.org, 167; 4 Celsius global warming, 75, 90, 114; abstract construct, 87; agriculture and land clearing emissions, 86; dangerous climate change, 15, 72; discourses of, 96, 99; early scientific warnings, 93–94; effect of attenuated production/consumption chains, 116; embodied emissions, 116–117; extreme weather, 15, 73, 74, 119; geological timescale, 90; hottest years on record, 74; planetary scale, 89; rise of climate science, 87–96; scientific link between carbon dioxide and fossil fuel use, 90–91; Villach Conference, 1985, 94; weather, relationship to climate change, 88–89. *See also* IPCC (Intergovernmental Panel on Climate Change)
climate change governance: "accountability deficit", 116; "ambition deficit", 114; Bali Action Plan (COP 13), 108; BASIC group, 109, 111, 112, 205; border tax adjustments, 117; "burden sharing deficit", 114; carbon markets, 104, 106–107; Clean Development Mechanism (CDM), 103, 105; Copenhagen Accord, 109, 110; Durban Platform for Enhanced Action, 110; ethical issues (equity, responsibility and burden sharing),

115–116; Joint Implementation mechanism (JI), 105; market-based mechanisms, 104; market failure, 186; marketization as impediment to decarbonization, 117; media, role of, 98; regulatory failure, 186; "top-down" versus "bottom-up" governance, 117; Umbrella Group, 100, 112. *See also* United Nations Framework Convention on Climate Change, Kyoto Protocol
"Climategate Affair", 98–99, 109
climate regime complex, 120
Clinton-Gore administration, 103, 181
Club of Rome, 35, 36, 367, 56
CO2 (carbon dioxide): atmospheric concentrations of (pre-1750 and 2013), 72; consequences of doubling concentrations, 90–93; cumulative, country comparisons, 85; emissions from fossil fuel and cement production (1990–2010), 114; emissions from industrial sources (1750–2010), 86
Coal, the Age of, 78–80
Cold War, 1, 2, 24, 94: and climate science, 94; end of, consequences for production and consumption, 141; geopolitical consequences of end of, 204; and Green Revolution, 143; and oil, 83; and UNFCCC, 111
colonization, European, 42–43
Commission for Sustainable Development (CSD), 167, 202, 203
commodification, 18, 59, 60: of GHG emissions, 105
Commoner, Barry, 39
communicative action, theory of, 8
Conference of the Parties (COP) to the UNFCCC: Bali, COP 13, 108; Cancun, COP 16, 110; Copenhagen, COP 15, 98, 108–109;

About the Authors

Peter Christoff is an associate professor in the Department of Resource Management and Geography at the University of Melbourne. He was formerly a member of the (Victoria) Premier's Climate Change Reference Group, the Vice President of the Australian Conservation Foundation, and the Assistant Commissioner for the Environment (Victoria). He has published extensively in the fields of environmental politics and policy, with a special focus on international and Australian climate policy. His publications include *Climate Law in Australia* (2007, co-editor) and *Four Degrees of Global Warming—Australia in a Hot World* (2013, editor).

Robyn Eckersley is a professor in political science in the School of Social and Political Sciences at the University of Melbourne. She has published widely in the fields of global environmental politics, political theory, and international relations. Her books include *Environmentalism and Political Theory* (1992); *Markets, the State and the Environment* (1995, editor); *The Green State: Rethinking Democracy and Sovereignty* (2004); *The State and the Global Ecological Crisis* (2005, co-editor); *Political Theory and the Ecological Challenge* (2006, co-editor); *Special Responsibilities: Global Problems and American Power* (2012, co-author); and *Why Human Security Matters: Rethinking Australian Foreign Policy* (2012, co-editor).